31st March '90.

Hap... ...B......day......

With...

Craig... & Gavin

xxx.

MORE MACGREGOR'S MIXTURE

MORE MACGREGOR'S MIXTURE

FORBES MACGREGOR

Illustrated by John Mackay

GORDON WRIGHT PUBLISHING
25 MAYFIELD ROAD, EDINBURGH EH9 2NQ
SCOTLAND

The Red Macgregor Tartan on the cover supplied by
The Kilt Shop Ltd., George IV Bridge, Edinburgh

British Library Cataloguing in Publication Data

Macgregor, Forbes
More Macgregor's Mixture.
I. Title
823'91407   PN6153

ISBN 0-903065-42-8

Typeset by Jo Kennedy, Edinburgh
Printed by Clark Constable
Edinburgh   London   Melbourne

Contents

Forbes Macgregor

Introduction

In view of the present state of the world, most people will agree that another large dose of *Macgregor's Mixture* is called for. The last dose has been greatly appreciated by thousands seeking relief from their fears and frustrations in a hearty laugh, a weird tale or a humorous account of unusual events, so here is an entirely new collection of miscellaneous accounts of that strange animal, Man, and also of other forms of life for your entertainment.

The world has not improved in the six years since *Macgregor's Mixture* was published, so perhaps a second and stronger dose of the same medicine will help the patient.

Five hundred years ago a very popular play in Europe was entitled *The World is Sick*. The scene opens on a poor man labelled 'World', seated in an arm-chair, moaning and wailing and wringing his hands. A neighbour rushes in crying 'O World, what ails you? Can I help you?'

'Send for the doctor,' cries the sick man.

Soon the doctor arrives in his cap and robes, examines the patient, and pronounces him to be as mad as a March hare. He asks the troubled man to say what is worrying him.

'Doctor, I have a dreadful fear, a horror that is with me day and night. A terrible deluge of Fire threatens me and all my family and friends. It will descend without warning and consume us all to ashes.'

'World,' says the doctor, 'You are worrying needlessly. You have more need to worry about the sins of the Churches and the states who are carrying out wars of extermination.'

The World, seeing that he can do little about it, dresses in cap and bells as a jester, becomes as light-hearted and ridiculous as any, and is soon cured of his disorder.

The dreadful fear that possessed 'World' five hundred years ago was a religious presentiment of doom. Our present state is much more perilous and we can do nothing about it.

The next best thing is to seek relief from time to time in laughter or perhaps a grim smile at the vagaries of humanity, past and present, particularly at the humours of the Scots, who, as a nation, have a history of threatened annihilation, but have always 'warstled through'.

If the reader is a native Scot he will be struck by these authentic pictures of the diverse characteristics of the race; if he is a reader from outwith the country, this book may well be an eye-opener.

Forbes Macgregor

Babes and Suckers

Barnum, the top showman, said, 'There's a sucker born every minute.' As the birthrate is a lot quicker than one a minute, there must be quite a few million people not so easily taken in. But Barnum found enough gullible people to make a fortune out of them.

Children are supposed to be simple and it's a mean trick to 'take candy from a kid,' or deceive them. But the human mind, even at the outset, is amazingly complex and many an adult has been taken in by a child's apparent innocence. There are, indeed, very rare cases of young children who have shown miraculous mental powers.

Christian Heinecker of Germany, in the 18th century, lived up to his first name. At one year old he knew by heart all the events in the books of Moses; at two he knew the whole of the Bible story; at three he was an expert on history, geography, Latin and French; and at four he could argue and pass judgement on learned matters. Unluckily for all concerned he died at the advanced age of four years and four months, just when he should have normally been reciting his A.B.C.

Quite normal children have a degree of cunning which is deceptive. To get what they want they can devise the most intricate methods, quite original.

A true example was noted of a little girl and boy at a family dinner party. They were forbidden to ask for any dish, but had to take what was served to them, with the exception of salt and sugar. The boy, when he had finished his helping, asked for some salt, which he put on his empty plate. His father was puzzled at first, then he realised that his son had given him a strong hint that he wanted more meat, usually eaten with salt.

The little girl went to work more cunningly. She pointed at dish after dish, saying aloud,

'I've had some of that,' at each one, but very obviously not pointing to a bowl of jelly which she was so keen to have.

Children can usually invent something to suit their purpose. In a Scottish city school the teacher spotted a small boy writing under the cover of his desk.

'Bring that out!'

Sullenly he handed it over. The teacher suspected it was either a *billet doux* or perhaps a ruder note to a male chum. But it was neither. On it were simply the words, 'Sook, sook, blaw, blaw, sook, blaw, sook,' and so for several lines.

'What nonsense is this?' she demanded.

'Please, miss, it's no nonsense. It's the music for my mooth-organ.'

Country bairns know more about biology than many of their teachers. During a Bible lesson on 'The Lost Sheep' the teacher was painting a vivid picture of the ninety-nine sheep snug in the fold, while, out in the wilderness, with the night-storm raging, was the lost sheep, baaing and running hither and thither.

'Now, children, what kind of sheep do you think this would be?'

She wanted someone to say a black sheep, or a lost sheep, or a disobedient sheep. But one little girl's mind was working along more practical lines, for her dad was a shepherd.

'Please, miss, it would likely be the tip oot efter a yowe.'

The modern school teaches the theory of sex, but of course frowns on the practice, which is rather in the spirit of the rhyme of my youth.

Mother, may I go out to swim?
Yes, my darling daughter,
Put your clothes on yonder rock
But don't go near the water.

The biology lecturer invited questions from the primary pupils after his lecture.

'Please, sir, could a girl of twelve have a baby?' asked a boy of eleven plus.

'Not very likely, sonny, but she might.'

The boy persisted. 'Please, sir, could a girl of ten have a baby?'

'Oh, no, certainly not.'

The questioner turned to his neighbour and whispered, 'I tellt ye, Mary, ye were a' richt.'

This other tale is probably apocalyptic. The class, of a pretty dumb level, was asked to write a story of general interest. The recipe for success, said the teacher, was to mention the Royal Family, religion, some mystery and a little sex. This, he felt sure, would keep the essay on a fairly high moral level.

After half-an-hour many pupils had filled a page, so they were asked to finish quickly, and hand in their effort. The teacher began to read them over but saw that the class dunce was still writing laboriously. Thinking to ridicule him, he asked the slowcoach to read his work. It consisted of two lines, very much to the point.

'My God,' said the Queen, 'I'm bairned again and I don't know who done it.'

Here is a well-known schoolroom tale which is certainly not founded on fact, but it was very popular with boys who wanted to get their own back on the kirk disciplinarians.

The Bible inspector, supported by the minister and the kirk session, was putting the top class through its theology. The dominie, or schoolmaster, stood at the back of the room to prevent any inattention. To stir up the lazy lads he held a pin in his hand.

'Who created the heavens and the earth?' thundered the inspector. The dominie pricked the questioned boy in the backside, and he blurted out, 'O, God.'

'Quite correct, boy. Now, the next boy. I want you to use your imagination. What do you think Eve said to Adam when she first saw him?'

The pupil nervously eyed the threatening pin and cried out, 'Don't you stick that thing into me or I'll tell my faither.'

The minister of the Holy Trinity, St. Andrews, was a picturesque character renowned for his dignified mode of dress, as well as his quick wit. On inspecting a primary school he told the headmaster he would award the pupils marks for good answers. The top mark was to be five, the bottom mark one.

Before addressing a young class he laid his silk hat and violet gloves on the desk and smiled benignly on the six-year-olds. Then he asked them, 'I wonder if you know who I am?' A wee girl answered, 'God.' He turned to the headmaster, 'Four marks, Mr. Brown.'

In an upland school the pupils were asked to learn hymn No. 232 off by heart. The first line is, 'O Lamb of God, still keep me.'

To the teacher's satisfaction they all got it word perfect. A year later she announced, 'I shall give a prize of a new hymn-book to anyone who has such a good memory that they can recite hymn No. 232.'

An eager little girl held up her hand.

'Go on then, Peggy.'

Peggy began, 'O, sheep of God, still keep me.'

'You've got it wrong, Peggy, it should be "O Lamb of God".'

'But please, miss, that was last year. It must have grown up by now.'

The minister liked to keep the bairns in the path of righteousness. One Sunday he surprised a small boy fishing in the burn.

'Do you know where little boys go who fish on the Sabbath?' he asked sternly, hinting at a sulphurous punishment hereafter.

'Aye, up at the back o the hill, where the gamey canna see them.'

A Glasgow minister was fishing the Daer Water with dry fly, a very delicate art. Normally he caught a good basket in this fine trouting tributary of the infant Clyde but this morning he drew a blank. As he came round the bend of the stream he discovered the reason. Several local laddies were busy guddling trout and of course alarming them. The minister forgot his gravity and furiously shook his fist at the guddlers who had a string of nice fish, and had cautiously waded to the opposite bank.

'Don't you boys know that you are using a most unsportsmanlike method of catching the poor trout?'

A wee lad bawled back, indignantly, 'It's you that's no a sportsman, cheatin the wee hungry troots wi fause flees.'

Sometimes in school an embarrassing phrase was inadvertently used by the teacher in her effort to speak grammatically.

'Please, miss, I've lost my india-rubber.'

'Use the boy's behind.'

'Why are you late, Nellie? Have you got a note?'

Nellie had dropped it by the wayside and her search was unavailing.

11

'Come away now. Why are you late?'
'Please, miss, I've lost my reason.'

The project method of teaching with all sorts of models and aids to help the imagination is very satisfying, if a bit messy. But it left old-fashioned parents in some confusion to be told by a Sunday-school scholar that 'the teacher gied us Jesus and Jairus's daughter a' mixed up wi plasticine.'

Theology was a strong line in my schooldays. It was far above our heads, in every sense. On our level were such rhymes as:

Matthew, Mark, Luke and John,
Haud the cuddy till I get on.
or
Scottie, Malottie, the King of the Jews,
Sold his wife for a pair of shoes.
When the shoes began to wear
Scottie Malottie began to swear.
or
Ho, Ho, Methusalum,
The Miser o Jerusalem.
or
Solomon MacGundy
Was born on a Monday
Was married on a Tuesday
Took ill on a Wednesday
Saw the doctor on a Thursday
Died on a Friday
Was buried on a Saturday
And rose again on the Sunday
That was the life of poor Solomon MacGundy.

It was all verging on blasphemy, but we lost not a wink of sleep over that. What did worry us rather much was the knowledge that, if we did not commit to memory that weary catechism cant of over a hundred questions and answers, such as the reasons annexed to the seventh commandment, our hands suffered for it.

One boy was asked how far he had proceeded in the learning of the Shorter Westminster Catechism. Quite innocently he replied that he was getting on very well. He was past 'Redemption' and would very soon be in the 'Pains of Hell forever.'

When we got a new book there was a tradition that we had to get to work on it right away with an indelible pencil to prevent it being stolen. A favourite rhyme was:

Black is the raven, black is the rook
But blacker the bugger that steals this book.

Our knowledge of theology at least gave us a choice of our ultimate fate, though it probably escaped the notice of the Recording Angel, to write this on the fly-leaf.

John Macdonald is my name
Scotland is my nation

Kirkintilloch is my hame
And H . . . my destination.

The poet, Alexander Pope, describes his early attempts at rhythm.

As yet a child nor yet a fool to fame
I lisped in numbers, for the numbers came.

But lisping can lead to an embarrassment, as many an inebriated man has known to his cost when asked to prove his sobriety by repeating, 'The Leith Police dismisseth us.' In school the botany teacher was explaining the structure of certain plants.
'Some stems are hollow, but some are filled with pith. Do you know what pith is, Lizzie?'
'O, yeth mith.'

Teachers should always be on guard, for young children are realists, and like to put knowledge to the test. I was told, when at infant school, that the big fat bee was the drone and had no sting. Not being told that this only applied to hive bees, as I went home by a clover field I picked up a large bumble bee to find out. Ever since that painful discovery I have agreed with the little girl who wrote, 'Bees have hot feet.'

The crudities of life occasionally get into the classroom, often to the shock of the teacher. When large families were packed into 'single ends' or one-roomed houses in the rookeries of Glasgow, Edinburgh and Dundee, what chance had a pupil to do homework?
A boy was given a home sum entailing square miles, acres and roods. He came to school the next day with the sum undone. His ironic excuse was, 'There was nae room on the flair.'
Bairns who had never more than a bawbee, or maik or halfpenny, to spend at one time, were tantalised by such sums as, 'What is the total cost of 147 pianos at £257. 18s. 11¼d. each?' And God help them if the answer was a farthing out.

The facts of life were once, it is said, brought home forcibly to a young teacher in a city school. She was asking about the members of each family, in an attempt to make friends with the pupils. But, while most children were communicative, she could make little of one poor wee soul. At last he confided to her in a whisper. 'I'm special. I'm no like them.'
'What makes you special, Tony?'
'I'm ma auntie's bairn by the ludger.'
This, though on a humbler level, is the same relationship which allowed the medieval popes to have innumerable nephews and nieces.

There is an Edinburgh suburban district where the streets are named after characters in national fiction. The newly-entered infants in this area were being enrolled. The Georges, Williams, Johns and Alans presented no problems, but the mistress came to a full stop with a bright five-year-old.
'What did you say his name was, my dear?'
'We cried him efter a famous Scottish warrior, Gooey.'
'Gooey? I'm sorry. I don't seem to have heard of him.'
'O, aye, oor terrace is cried for him. Gooey Mannering.'

Not a stone's throw from King William's statue in Glasgow two ladies got into animated conversation.

13

'Has it come yet then, Bella?'

'O, aye, a week past Tuesday. Did ye no hear?'

'Naw. Whit are ye cryin him?'

'It's no a him. We're cryin her Hazel.'

'Ma Goad, to think there's a holy virgin saint for every letter in the alphabet and ye've got to cry your grand-dauchter efter a bloody nut.'

It wasn't always the scholars who needed correction. Quite a few teachers, in their anxiety to speak posh, made grammatical errors.

Her Majesty's Inspector in a Glasgow school asked a young lady teacher to give a geography lesson on the Clyde estuary.

She started off brightly.

'Now, children. I want you to imagine that the headmaster has arranged to send you and I on a trip to Helensburgh.'

'And me,' corrected the Inspector drily and not too politely.

'O, yes, we'll let this gentleman come too, won't we, children?'

He was perhaps the pedant who was ridiculed in public for his extreme anxiety to inspect the obscurest parts of Bella Houston and Mary Hill. It was a person like this who, arriving at the Golden Gates, was asked by Peter, 'Who's there?' and answered, 'It is I.' To which the bluff ex-fisher replied, 'Another damned teacher. Get the hell out of here!'

Inns were originally intended to provide hospitality for travellers but in many towns and villages the inn was merely a public house. At Christmas time the minister was earnestly questioning some young children about the Nativity.

'Why was Christ born in a manger?'

A bright boy, relying on his local knowledge, supplied the answer.

'Please sir, because it was Christmas time and all the pubs were shut.'

A little boy had early developed the habit of swearing, not unusual in small boys. His mother tried washing his mouth out with water and carbolic soap, but to no effect. Then she threatened to tell the police, which her son did not believe. But she conspired with a friendly bobby to pay a visit to the house.

'I am informed, young man,' said the P.C. sternly, 'that you have been heard swearing.'

'Whae tellt ye?'

'O, a little bird told me.'

'The wee buggers, and I've been feeding them a' winter.'

A perfectly authentic story comes from a mining area in the Lothians.

'How many of you have dogs at home?' asked the schoolmam.

'We've got a greyhound,' replied a sharp lad.

'What's his name?'

'I dinna ken his real name. It depends where he's running.'

'How's that?'

'Ye see, miss, he's got three names, so's to keep the bookies guessin.'

'Does he have a kennel?'

'Nae fear. He micht be pinched. He sleeps in the ben bed wi me.'

In the gym, accidents were sometimes inevitable and parents occasionally came up to complain, though most complaints were rather vague, such as a 'cut lip' or a 'sprained ankle'. But a very scientific mum produced the exact details of her little darling's injuries.

'Ye'll hae tae get the gym flair sortit. It's a mass o spales. D'ye ken Jeanie cam hame at denner-time wi a spale in her bum seven-eighths o an inch long stickin in at an angle o forty-five degrees.'

Fathers seldom visited schools, and if they did, it was only because mother had driven them to it, for she was always reckoned to be more deadly than the male, when it came to a row. But the particular reason for one father's non-appearance was revealed by a chance remark passed to the teacher by an eight-year-old son, when the harassed teacher had threatened to send a letter to his father on his bad work.

'Ye can send it if ye like, miss, but I'm no feart for ma faither. He's that wee he has to dreep ower the side o the bed.

With these few typical tales of bairns we may now proceed to examples drawn from the lives of people today and yesterday whose lives are and were as artless as Adam's and Eve's before the Fall. But with the rapid advance of our sophisticated brand of civilisation the number of naive folk is dropping.

Forty or fifty years ago, when there were corners of the world still untouched by modernity, a missionary in a remote part of Africa stalled his Ford on a jungle road. As he got out to look under the bonnet, he saw to his horror a gang of spearsmen in leopard-skins advancing at a jog-trot towards him. Flight was useless so he prepared for martyrdom. They surrounded him, gesticulating and laughing. He expected an assegai in his ribs at any moment.

But to his infinite relief the leader of the party laid a friendly hand on his shoulder and asked, 'Sumpin wrong wid yo jalopy, boss?'

It turned out that he had worked for several years in Detroit and on amassing a sum of money had come back to his native land. He quickly diagnosed the trouble, put it right, and with his friends, cheered the man of God on his way.

On the other hand there are still primitive tribes in inaccessible jungles whose only tool is an incisor tooth of a jungle rat. But perhaps in a few years these folk will be unhappily employed in computerised units turning out micro-chip T.Vs.

Amusement is always to be had from the sayings and deeds of simple souls.

Ireland is traditionally the home of the bull. With a commendable sense of fun, the Irish have stamped a bull on their shilling piece. A French writer of a book of natural history seriously included 'Irish Bulls' as part of the animal species of Europe. But most countries, including Scotland, perpetrate fully as many blunders as the Irish.

It may be true enough, however, that an old Irishwoman, at a traffic-crossing in Glasgow remarked to the policeman as she watched the lights, 'Sure, it's glad I am to see you don't give these orange boggers much time to cross.'

A crofter on the Atlantic coast of the Highlands decided to do a one-man emigration. As he didn't have the price of a passage but owned a sea-worthy rowing-boat, he got together some water, whisky and food for the journey across the ocean.

That night he set off without telling anyone. He rowed steadily westwards. When it was morning but still darkish, one of his neighbours happened to walk down to the jetty and saw that the emigrant had omitted to slip his moorings. He shouted, 'Hullo, Willie.'

Willie shouted back, 'Hullo, there, who is it that knows me in Americky?'

The celestial objects have always puzzled some folk. A great grand-aunt of mine, otherwise a well-read lady, possessed of a minute memory, had lived for eighty years in a quiet part near the Solway shore. On the death of her sister she was persuaded to finish her days with her niece in Edinburgh. She was met at the Waverley and as the cab jolted down Leith Walk, the full moon was rising over the Forth. She turned to her nephew,

'Is yon the same mune, Willie, as we hae doon at Kirtlebrig?'

At the building of a new kirk in Forfar the steeple was surmounted by large cardinal points above which was a massive weathervane in the form of a griffon or winged dragon.

The architect told the chief magistrate that he feared the effect of a violent gale on the cardinal points would weaken the top masonry.

The provost objected. 'Hoo could a gale affect the airts when the griffon is muckle mair likely to be affected, bein o sic a size?'

The architect replied, 'But the weathervane turns with the wind and therefore only opposes a small surface to it.'

'Weel, then,' retorted the provost triumphantly, 'There's your answer, man. Mak the airts turn wi the gale as weel as the weathervane.'

A Lord Provost of Edinburgh in Edwardian days was a wealthy business man, but of patchy education and culture. Intimating his impending retiral from public life to a hermitage well away from the bustle of the metropolis, he announced, 'Weel, ladies and gentlemen, I'm fair lookin forrit to the day when I can demit this prominent office. I'll tell ye my plans. I'm gaun tae retire to a wee quiet hoose in the country and live the life of a harlot.'

Simple souls don't like to be cheated. An old lady member of the local co-op asked the store butcher if she could have a marrow-bone to put in the stock-pot. The genial head butcher chopped a big bone and wrapped it up.

'Hoo muckle is that, Jimmy?' she asked, opening her purse.

'Naething at a', Bella. It's on the hoose.'

'Na, na, ye're no gettin awa wi that. Chairge me for it and gie me ma check, and dinna try to dae an auld body oot o her dividend.'

An aged lady parishioner had a reputation for great devotion which she was proud of. She continued to read passages from the Good Book in her spare moments. One afternoon she saw the minister approaching her cottage so she hurriedly picked up what she thought was the Bible and opened it at random. She did not realise until it was too late that she had opened the dictionary.

The reverend asked to see the passage she was reading.

'Deary me, Miss Brown, don't tell me you enjoy this book.'

She had to cover her confusion in some way.

'Deed, I canna say I do, for to tell ye the Gospel truth, I never managed yet to get the threid o the story.'

Another old maid who had long been out of the swift current of everyday life was asked to pay a visit to a newly-born infant to bring a hansel, or first gift, and to bless the newcomer. The baby was having a bath preparatory to bed.

On her return a neighbour asked kindly for the new baby.

'Is it a laddie or a lassie, then, Teeny?'

'O, I think it's a laddie, if my memory serves me richt.'

Absence of mind is an affliction which is not much fun for the person concerned, but it is occasionally amusing. Professors are usually the targets for the wits, who tell such tales as these.

The professor went up to his bedroom to change his tie for a dinner-party and failed to turn up because, when he took the first step by loosening his tie, he absent-mindedly carried on undressing and went off to bed for the night. Or coming home from a lecture he hangs his hat on his wife and kisses the hat-stand. These smell of the joke-works, but it is historically recorded that the great La Fontaine the fable-writer attended a friend's funeral and a week later called at his house to see how he was keeping.

Another savant, a lover of old books, became the father of a lovely boy, whom the nurse brought to him and placed in his arms. After a time he absent-mindedly laid the baby on the library shelf and softly covered up one of his precious folios in the cradle.

The new minister of a country parish attended a garden-party at the 'Big Hoose'. There he mingled self-consciously with the elite of the county, for the Duke had a very large circle of friends. The minister wanted to show his interest in all the Duke's affairs, so he walked forward and took up his place in the group centred upon the great man.

It was a warm summer's day, which turned the lagging conversation towards weather. The young padre kindly enquired of his host, 'And how is your Mother the Dowager standing the heat?'

Only when he saw the dismay on the faces of the company did he remember that the Dowager had died six weeks before.

It is refreshing to hear a blunt Anglo-Saxon or Scots phrase when nothing but pithless and prudish language has wearied one's ears and senses. I recall an afternoon in summer nearly sixty years ago when a botany class of teachers in training were doing practical work by the banks of the Esk above Musselburgh. The meadow and wood were rich in many summer flowers, so there were no qualms about picking a few to put into the vasculums.

Mill-girls in bands were going back to work from the dinner-break, down both banks of the river. Those on the far bank, away from the botanists were curious to know what was going on.

'What are they daein?' they yelled.

'Pickin daundelions,' was the ear-splitting chorus.

'We canna hear ye. Tell us again.'

'Pickin daundelions.'

Once again the message did not carry, so a crowd of mill-girls assembled and left nobody in any doubt, within half-a-mile.

'Pickin Pee-the-Beds.'

Another blunt speaker, but in a minor key, was a small farmer in Lochmaben, Dumfriesshire. His farm was known as 'The Bottom' so he was locally known as 'Auld Macgregor o The Bottom,' an ambiguous title. Although an octogenarian he was not unduly worried. He would offer a lift on his 'tumbler-cairt' to anyone going his way but, as he always had a deep bed of straw in the cart-floor, the jolting of the springless vehicle was endurable.

His usual offer, when a nubile female accepted his lift, became a bye-word in the 'Four Touns', as the villages are called. Laying a rough-grained hand lightly upon her thigh he would say, 'I'm no a man like that, ye ken, but I'm aye there if ye need me.'

It was a frosty foggy morning in Glasgow and the grocery store was busy. An inquiring customer, looking out for something tasty for breakfast, approached a worthy citizen standing with his back to a cheery coal-fire, mistaking him for one of the staff.

'Excuse me, sir,' she said, pointing to a shelf. 'But is that your Ayrshire bacon?'

'No, missus, I'm just warmin ma hands.'

17

Foreign names puzzle many folk. When the war of 1939-45 commenced, a Highland wifie was heard to remark, 'That Hitler's no sae bad if it wasna for that bitch o a wumman o his, Miss O'Leanie.' On the other hand the Russians could do no wrong, for many enthusiastic Russophiles spoke of Marshal Timoshenko as Tam o' Shanter.

Electric trams, first introduced into some Scottish areas early this century, were objects of great suspicion, and old-fashioned folk were afraid of stepping on the rails when crossing the street. A timid old lady in Glasgow approached the traffic inspector and asked him, 'If I pit ma fit on the rail, inspector, will it gie me a lectric shock?'

His answer reassured her. 'No, dearie, that's to say, unless you pit your ither fit on the overhead cable and then you'll be wheecht awa up tae Govan terminus.'

Another dear old soul who was a life-long practitioner of domestic economy found that at last her cast-iron antique kettle had an undoubted leak and was past repair. She was shocked when she found out the price of a new kettle.

'Na, I canna afford that. I'll just hae to make dae wi' a pan.'

On leaving the counter she saw bundles of steel wool advertised at bargain prices. She asked the ironmonger for six bundles.

'That's an awfu lot o steel wool. What on earth are ye gaun to dae wi it?'

'Ye may weel ask, mister. Your kettles are that dear I'm just gaun hame to knit yin for masel.'

Away back in the Thirties when the twelve-sided threepenny pieces, with a sea-pink, or thrift, design were newly minted, the bright gleam of the metal caused many mistakes among the gullible.

A young woman entered a branch savings bank and passed four of the new coins over the counter with the request, 'I want to deposit these four new sovereigns in my savings book.'

'But these are not sovereigns. These are the new threepenny pieces.'

'O, the mean bugger,' she exclaimed, 'And I gied him ham and eggs for his breakfast.'

Government departments act on the principle that the general public are 'no a' come,' as they say in Aberdeen. Fishermen are reckoned a simple honest set of men to all appearances, but they are astute enough to see through the tricks of the bureaucrats and politicians.

Two Aberdeen trawlermen were leaning over the harbour wall, idly looking into the slack water where all kinds of flotsam swayed about in the tide.

'Yon's a gweed bit o timmer ower there, Jeemie,' said one, pointing to a plank about six feet long.

'O, aye, yon's a grand board. Fat is it, think ye?'

'I ken this, onywey. It's no the Board o Trade, for it's movin.'

Tickling the Fancy

In Victorian times, and long before and after, sex was a topic which it was impossible even to allude to; that was, in certain levels of society. Such was the abnormal state of affairs which still has its effects today. In most ages and countries, sex has been treated as a natural part of social life.

There is no normal sex pattern, either individually or collectively, anywhere in nature, let alone amongst humans, with their enormous spread of imagination and fantasy. The only generalisation that it is safe to make, regarding homo sapiens, is that attributed to a witty clerical gentleman, the Rev. Sydney Smith; 'There are three sexes, men women and clergymen, as the French say.' That must surely refer to celibate clergymen, for the others are pretty natural, if somewhat reticent.

The ministers of Robert Burns' day were not so lenient. The Burns family belonged to the 'New Lichts', a slightly more broad-minded branch of the Associate Synod, though still tinged in places with fanaticism. On this account poor Robin was often suspected of the crime of Latitudinarianism, and had to sit under a perfect barrage of reproofs for his sexual offences. But he was not one to take it meekly. On a visit, with a fellow-fornicator, to the empty Auld Kirk at Dunfermline, he got up into the pulpit after the manner of 'Daddy Auld,' the Ayr minister, and mockingly took his friend to task for his lust and whoremongering, to his great amusement. Burns recalled one occasion when, to show the prevalence of the public condemnation of illicit sex, he had seven fellow-sinners lined up alongside him on the penitential stools.

The offending ladies were not allowed off either, but their behaviour was often so irregular even when under reproof that the lesson was obviously not going to be taken to heart. In the upland parishes where life was pretty raw, the cutty stool was treated as it deserved. In Heriot, one of the offending lassies, Margaret Montgomery, a clumsy hoyden, actually fell off the stool all her long length on the floor and was henceforth known as 'The Fallen Woman.'

In all the land of the 'Westland Whigs' there was great severity on sex offenders, particularly in Glasgow, where anyone having what is now known as 'a wee shot on the swings' was fined, if found out. In the 17th century Glasgow was a large village built round a cathedral, which had been spared from the fury of the reformers by the citizens themselves, justly proud of the ancient traditions. Green fields and gardens lay for miles around. At first sight it was a paradise, an ideal community, but like most other small places it was subject to tyranny.

There was sex discrimination then, but, strangely, in favour of the ladies. Frail servant lassies were fined only £20 (Scots) for the first offence, while men-servants had to fork out £30 (Scots). The kirk seemed to think that the ladies got only two-thirds of the pleasure that men did. Social injustice was perpetrated also.

The Laird of Minto, who had been a Provost of Glasgow, when caught in the act, was not awarded the D.O.M. though he was a very senior citizen. He was excused because of 'his high standing and venerable age,' which could be interpreted in another sense.

Whores were not spared, however. The manse of Cambuslang was turned into a house of correction for dissolute women, and the Kirk Session ordered the Keeper to 'whip them every day at his pleasure.' Maybe this is where the Marquis de Sade got his idea.

An English visitor to Scotland last century when sex was still anathema, wrote that he was mortally sorry for the Scotch lassies at the hands of the kirk elders, whom he considered a sadistic and hypocritical crew.

No wonder the ladies were often driven to such extremes, sometimes dressing up as men, to escape for a time from this tyranny. One of the most spirited young women in Edinburgh was Anne, the daughter of Lord Royston. She and her maid used to don the silken surtouts, waistcoats and knee-breeches of young bucks, complete with silver-handled rapiers and tricorn hats, and sally forth to walk of a summer evening on the Castle Hill, which belonged to the City by ancient right, based on a charter granted by James VI, but which, for some curious reason, was revoked in favour of the Crown last century. The esplanade was then a rough natural hill-top, chief flirting ground for the belles and beaux of Auld Reekie. Anne's favourite sport was to attract the attention of young ladies known to herself and her companion. Assignations, or dates, were exchanged, which, of course, Anne found it diplomatic not to keep. Such female gallantry shocked the Edinburgh historian who later recorded it. He sourly remarked, 'They showed more wit than discretion.' But, as we say, they did it for the hell of it.

Anyone who thinks the Scots ladies of old were generally lacking in spirit, is greatly mistaken. A Spanish visitor in the reign of James IV reported that the Scottish ladies were absolute mistresses in their own houses, and the so-called Lord and Master soon got to know which partner wore the breeks.

The men, unable to boast adequately of their sexual powers under their own roofs, were often driven to clubs on the lines of the infamous Hellfire Clubs in England. The Ancient and Puissant Society of the Beggar's Benison and Merryland was originally founded in Anstruther, Fife. It was based on an amorous adventure of James V when he rewarded a beggar maid who had given him a pick-a-back over a swollen stream. She repaid him in her own coin, so both went away satisfied.

This club had a branch in Edinburgh, as in several of the Scottish towns. All sorts of ceremonies were performed. Women of loose character were enrolled to excite the depravity of the lairds, merchants and ministers of the kirk, and to encourage them to demonstrate their virility. The President of the Edinburgh branch is said to have worn a wig woven from the pudendal hair of Royal mistresses. How these ewe lambs were shorn is not revealed to history. We might also be amused to know what excuses the ladies of the manses were offered when the reverend came home in the wee sma' oors from such a belated session meeting.

Before we leave the so-called third sex, let us remember how difficult it often was for a young priest to keep aware of his renouncement of the world, the flesh and the devil. In the confessional a young priest was hearing penitents for the first time while the aged parish priest was seated in a shady corner close by, to give advice. A bright young thing confessed her peccadilloes, some of which were of rather hectic love-passages. When she had gone the young priest asked his senior for criticism. 'You did very well for a novice. There's only one wee hint. When you hear a particularly spicy confession it would be more becoming to mutter, 'Tut, tut', instead of emitting a loud whistle.'

The devil is sometimes said to be a woman and on that account priests are more liable to be tempted than laymen. On one occasion the holy father found it easy to refuse a pressing invitation from the most famous of courtesans, Madame de Pompadour. She lay dying. The very aged and infirm confessor performed the last sacrament, and telling her to compose herself for the journey into eternity, said that he had regretfully to leave her.

'Stay just a little longer, father,' she pleaded, looking at his tottering figure, 'then you and I shall elope together.'

A young bachelor minister had received a call to Hawick. The local pronunciation as in Berwick omits to sound the w. This puzzled him somewhat, but he did not wish to betray his ignorance so he kept silent. At last he pulled the beadle aside and whispered in his ear.

'This is highly confidential, John. Can you tell me, being a local man, is there a w in Hawick?'

The beadle pondered for a moment.

'Weel, no exactly, but I've heard on the quiet that the blacksmith's dochter does a bit on the side.'

The word whore, or hure in Scots, is said to be derived from the Persian *houri*, a lady of pleasure in Paradise who provided cheesecake for the faithful Musselmen. In Scotland the word hure is applied contemptuously to all objects, female, male, common or neuter. It is no uncommon thing to hear the weather described as 'a hure of a day', or to see a man kicking a stalled motor-car and calling it by the same loving name. I once heard a Highland shepherd cursing the maggots on his sheep's back and apostrophising them as 'Creeping hures.' It is never a compliment.

This four-letter word should never be heard in the presence of the modern man of God, although it was one of the favourite expressions of John Knox who applied it to his ecclesiastical opponents in such terms as the 'The Hure of Babylon', or 'The Hure that sitteth on the Seven Hills' (Rome), surely a broad-hipped wench. At a village concert the reverend chairman announced, 'Jessie MacIntosh will now sing *The Road to the Isles*.' A pretty girl mounted the stage and a hush fell on the audience, broken unhappily by a gruff male voice in a stage-whisper, muttering 'She is chust a wee hure.' The minister was in no position to contradict this but got over the difficulty by saying soothingly, 'Nevertheless, Miss MacIntosh will now sing *The Road to the Isles*.'

But in former days the word was used in by-laws and acts of parliament in a strictly trade sense, and in the bad old Victorian days, in the dirty rookeries of Glasgow, Dundee and Auld Reekie, when there were infants working in factories and child prostitutes on the streets, the description was universally accepted as a fact of life. An actual incident that happened not a mile from the Trongate concerned the polis seeking witnesses. A girl of thirteen volunteered information and, when asked her name and occupation, stated quite naively that, as to her occupation, she was just a wee hure.

The census officer in a notorious quarter off Leith Street, Edinburgh, was going round the single-ends, or one-roomed houses. The tenant of one of these was a tough young woman. He got the name, age, etc. and asked 'Occupation?'

'Ye ken fine whit I am. I'm a hure.'

'Aye, I ken. But ye canna expect me to pit that doon.'

'What for no?'

'Will I pit ye doon as a horologist?'

'Wise guy. Watch it,' was the witty reply.

'Can ye trim a hat?' he asked next.

'Aye, I have to.'

'Then I'll pit doon a milliner's assistant.'

'A' richt, but it wad be mair like to ca' me a contractor, or a demolisher o temporary erections.'

In a neighbouring room was an even tougher young lady who, when asked the same question, answered bluntly what seemed the same term.

'I canna pit that doon,' he said again.

'And whit for no, then? My brother's a sweep and I shout up the lum at him *Hoo! Hoo!* to keep him to the richt lum. Does that no mak me a hooer?'

As often as not, in former days, the street-walker fell into ill-health. One such frequenter of the Argyll Street beat was finally driven to the doctor, who pronounced her to be in a bad way.

'Can ye no dae something for me, doctor?'

He shook his head, genuinely moved.

'No, my dear, your promenading days are over.'

She made her ultimate plea.

'O, for Goad's sake, doctor. Patch me up and I'll dae for Paisley.'

Some ladies took to the game early, some late. Of the first kind was an unruly young lass who gave her stern father some trouble, for he tried to enforce 'elders' hours' on his household. That is to say, they had to be indoors early. No nighthawks allowed.

One summer evening daft Lizzie came up the tenement stair well after sunset. Father was sitting by the open window overlooking Holyrood Park, reading his evening paper by the long twilight.

'Where hae ye been, ye wee bitch?'

'Me and Maisie was walkin in the park—and look, faither, I was lucky. I found a shillin.'

But Daddy was not deceived.

'D'ye think I'm daft or saft, ye wee leear? Ye come in here wi your back a' gress and your drawers a' torn and tell me ye've found a shillin. Mither, come ben and bring me yin o ma leather slippers.'

At the other end of the scale we have the old lady of pleasure whose frail charms had deserted her. Then came the blackout during Hitler's War and business picked up a bit, or, as she expressed it, 'What wi the blackoot and my auld age pension I'm ay managin tae struggle alang.'

At that time of national danger many desperate remedies were resorted to. A lady who ran a fish-shop found that supplies were hard to get, owing to the naval blockade.

One morning this notice appeared in the fish-shop window.

Owing to Hitler
Supplies getting littler.
A week later this replaced it.
Owing to Hess
Supplies getting less.
And the following week on the closed shutters,
Owing to Goring
I've given up the business
And gone back to whoring.

Edward VII, complimentarily named the 'Peacemaker,' who, because of his libertine life, could also be called the 'Pacemaker,' is reputed like Charles II to have, according to John Dryden, 'scattered his Maker's image through the land.'

When I was a small impressionable boy, shortly after the death of Edward, my grandfather pointed out to me a house of ill-repute, patronised by his majesty in the working class Albert Street, on the Edinburgh-Leith border. Although the bagnio had no sign, 'Conferred by Royal Appointment', I thought at the time that it was a double royal honour to an otherwise obscure locality that an imperial father and son should both choose to notice it. At least two of Edward's male progeny, who closely resembled him, even to the beard (which seems like bragging), occupied positions of profit in the city. One was conspicuous, the other the opposite, quietly slipping into his preferred appointment every weekday at ten, and as little observed (or so he imagined), slipping out again at four. It has been remarked, 'It pays a man, whiles, to be born after his father.'

Robert Louis Stevenson also was accused, on substantial grounds, of leaving his personal image as a memento of one of his Mr. Hyde exploits.

Perhaps the bracing air of Edinburgh was responsible for its reputation as 'good stock country', but I am inclined to think that in olden days the prolific and healthy oyster beds in the Forth, over which the fishers fought battles, were effective aphrodisiacs. Oysters were sold last century in posh restaurants for as little as four shillings (twenty modern pence) per hundred, with all the accompaniments.

For those with less well-lined pockets, who were still keen on provocatives, a skate supper at sixpence was reckoned a good buy. The skate was nicknamed 'the bedroom fish' by the genteel. It served the same purpose as birds' nest soup, rhinoceros or red deer horn and was very much cheaper, more appetising and accessible.

Ladies who had tried time and again, without success, to conceive, were recommended to feed their husbands on some of the products of the Forth estuary, or failing these, to take a trip to Whitekirk in East Lothian, there to pray at the shrine of an alleged promoter of fertility, before going home to have another go.

But there were supposed to be more effective aphrodisiacs at hand in the form of potatoes and tomatoes. Chocolate was reckoned a good love potion, so much so that chocolate shops in London where parties went to drink the new import, were named the Devil's New Universities. Monks in particular were requested to dispense with cocoa-time breaks, an insinuation which they strongly resented.

Although oranges are not included in this salacious list there is reputed to be an instance where they were directly responsible for fertility. When rationing was in force in the 1939-45 war, a lady in a city suburb, passing a fruiterer's shop, spotted a friend coming out with a basket of oranges, a fruit that had been unobtainable for years. She hurried into the shop and asked for some.

'You only get these on a special book. They're only for pregnant women.'

'Put a dozen aside for me. I'll be back in twenty minutes.'

But asparagus was the King-pin of provocatives. In Holland, Father's Day is celebrated at the first cutting of the asparagus, for an obvious reason. A continental hostess who had served asparagus to her guests was, to her embarrassment, solicited an hour or two later by a rather respectable male friend. She refused, though like many women, she was perhaps pleased to have been asked. The following day the gentleman apologised profusely. 'Oh, it's quite understandable,' she replied. 'I don't blame you in the least. It was my fault for serving asparagus.'

Whatever provocatives are consumed, they often prove to be quite useless. Some men, whatever they eat or drink, are essentially virile, often to a great age. Their life-style, subsisting even on the bare necessities, seems to maintain their prowess. The Highlanders have a reputation, perhaps undeserved, for virility. When the Jacobite army was in retreat towards Scotland they occupied Carlisle to the great panic of the douce burghers. A Carlisle old maid is said to have retired to her bedroom overlooking the Botchergate for a whole week, dressed only in her flannel nightie, peering occasionally at the bands of wild clansmen as they passed up and down. At last she ventured downstairs and asked a neighbour when the raping was due to start. To her disappointment she was told that the kilted host had all departed and had crossed the swollen Esk for ever.

Shepherds live a strenuous life and so seem to qualify as good stockmen. A tale is told of a minister in the Garioch district of Aberdeen who ventured far up the glen to visit a shepherd's house, isolated and hard to find. In his conversation he was often interrupted by squads of bairns of different ages running in and out asking for 'pieces'.

'You seem to have a large family, James. Such splendid little olive branches too.'

'Oh, aye, a gweed smittrie o loons and quaens, meenister. Aboot the dizzen, I wad jaloose.'

'How I envy you. My wife and I have no family. She is quite healthy but of a delicate disposition. That must be due to the damp and enclosed position of the manse. I wonder if a spell up here would restore her to robust health and perhaps fecundity?'

'Weel, sir, you could aye bring her up here and try.'

'How long would she need to stay here, James, do you think?'

'Oh, nae that long, meenister. Gin ye were tae bring her up, say, on Setterday efternoon, when I'm deen wi the hirsel, ye could jest leave her here, tak a bit daunder doon the burn and smoke a fill o baccy, then ye could tak her back wi ye.'

Scotsmen are reputed on good evidence to be very phlegmatic and indeed often completely lacking in chivalry, gallantry or romance.

It was a lovely summer evening by Loch Lomondside. Dugald and his lady friend stood gazing at the moonshine reflected across the loch.

'Dugald,' breathed the fond lassie, 'Do ye no think that this is the kind o nicht for you an me to be twined in each other's airms awa up yonder amang the purple heather?'

'Och, Mary, what aboot the midges risin oot o the heather and creepin up ma kilt?'

'But Dugald, once we was deep in a passionate embrace we would forget every earthly trouble.'

Finally Dugald consented and they consummated their passion.

On the way down to the loch Mary stopped.

'D'ye ken, Dugald, if onything should come o this nicht's wark, d'ye ken what I would do?'

'No, Mary.'

'I would go doon to yon crag and throw mysel into the deepest bit o Loch Lomond . . . Now, what d'ye think o that?'

'Wumman, ye've nae idea what a terrible load ye've ta'en aff my mind.'

At a political conference in Edinburgh the discussion turned to the effect of the oil-rigs on the scenic beauty of the North. One of the lady delegates, quite innocently drew a great horse-laugh from the conference with this complaint.

'I live up in Easter Ross, a lovely part of Scotland. I used to have a rare view. Now when I wake up in the morning the first thing I see is this enormous erection.'

There was a round of applause. Presumably for her husband.

Even in prudish Edwardian days there were incitements to salacity and voyeurism. One tailor in Scotland, well-known for his inexpensive, well-cut and expeditious products, rather neglected modesty in his zeal to promote business. His huge sign proclaimed to the public, 'B. Hyams trousers down again. Your personal inspection invited.'

Over the Channel the Briton has never been understood. Both English and Scots whatever their difference here, are all considered alike eccentric from birth. An imperfect knowledge of French does not help to correct this view.

During the Kaiser's War the major commanding an artillery unit wished to protect his large quantity of small armour-piercing shells from the Flanders damp. He had the brilliant idea of covering each one with a condom.

Entering the local chemist's store he asked if they stocked such indelicate articles.

'But, yes, of course. How many?'

'Five thousand, please.'

Madame threw up her hands and shouted through to the back-shop. 'Marie! Celine! Come at once!' When the young ladies rushed through she pointed to the major.

'Now, girls, there's a real man for you!'

Another innocent got confused between the word for a condom and a waterproof coat. Entering a rubber store in a provincial town he said he wished to buy a waterproof. The assistant, mistaking his need asked what colour he preferred.

'Black, if you please. My wife died recently.'

She gazed at him with admiration.

'O, monsieur, what delicacy.'

As we are in France we may recall a miracle which took place in the retreat from Mons in 1914. But it only concerns angels indirectly.

A wounded man of the Argyll and Sutherland Highlanders was taken to a base-hospital, with a deep flesh wound across both his thighs. The doctors were puzzled that his *membrum virile* was intact. They asked him to explain this phenomenon.

'Weel, doctor, it was like this. Just as the Jerry sniper potted me, by the Grace of God, I was thinking of the wife's young sister at the time.'

Many years ago the madam in charge of a famous Edinburgh brothel recruited Diana, a simple lass from up the country, whose sexual experiences had been minimal. She was given an apartment and conducted a very popular séance for her first evening, enthusiastic clients coming and going like bees about a hive.

In the small hours of the morning when the shutters went up Madam called her girls to account. When Diana came to the office she laid out £9 10s 6d.

Madam remarked, 'No' bad for a first night, but who was the mean bugger that gave you sixpence?'

The innocent looked slightly surprised. 'They all gave me sixpence. That's the usual in our parish.'

After waiting twenty years till the chosen minister grew up and went through the divinity course, Seumas and Morag decided to tie the hymeneal knot. They announced their decision to Morag's aged parents who were over the moon with delight.

'Ach, I always knew that you were made for each other,' said Mrs. MacSporran. 'There's nothing like being sure, so what does twenty years matter?'

Old Donald McSporran burst out, 'We'll be having the grandest wedding this side of the Minch. We'll engage Ian Campbell's band and hire the village hall. Go through to the kitchen and make a list of all the friends and relatives you want to invite.'

The happy pair came back two hours later with four hundred and forty-one names.

'Well, now,' said old Donald, 'The hall has only accommodation for four hundred. You'll have to cut it down by forty-one. A pity, but it can't be helped.'

Seumas and Morag returned to the kitchen and after much head-scratching hit on a simple plan.

'Take this pin, Morag,' said Seumas, 'Shut your eyes and make forty-one stabs at the list. These'll be the unlucky ones.' Morag did this and they took the perforated list through to the old folks.

'Here you are, father,' said Morag, 'We're no inviting the ones with the wee pricks.'

'Och now, isn't that a terrible pity, whatever,' sighed old Mrs. MacSporran, 'for some of them are grand tenor singers in the Gaelic.'

Old age is even more deadly sure than the sniper's bullet: and although it has been sententiously remarked many a time that 'it's a gey auld horse that winna nicker when he sees corn', old age, though not always unpleasant, takes away a man's freshness.

Three elderly men were sitting on a hill above the village grave-yard.

'Aye, I'd like fine to be lying doon thonder aside Alison McTavish, my dear departed,' sighed one.

'And me as weel,' said his friend. 'I'd lie until eternity at peace there wi Peggy Broon.'

The third added, 'And for me naething wad please me more than to be lying doon there the nicht wi Maisie Robertson.'

The other two exclaimed, 'But Maisie Robertson's no deid yet.'

'I ken no, and neither am I.'

Old Donald MacTavish was called to the funeral of a clansman. When he arrived at the clachan he found a great gathering of mourners with the whisky birling merrily round. They held the wake in great style, renewing the drink and the candles until the dawn. By the time of the funeral not a soul knew his arse from his elbow, but they got the corpse interred. Donald staggered down to the road to get a lift home, but fell fast asleep by the bankside.

Two touring ladies with knapsacks came along but failed to awake him to tell them the way. Now was their chance to satisfy their curiosity so they lifted his kilt to have a look, and tied a red ribbon round his manhood. He came to his senses at last and sat up quite unaware that anyone had seen him. On arriving at his wee but and ben, he undressed for bed and was mystified at the red ribbon. Scratching his beard he muttered, 'Weel, Donal, I don't know where we was, or what company we was in, but it looks like we was awarded the first prize, whatever.'

Old wives have often good grounds for complaint. We have this recorded for us in song in the ancient version of *John Anderson, my Jo,* which Burns cleaned up for the parlour, but which was well-known in England long before his time, as well as in Scotland.
One verse is of regret for lost youth and virility.

John Anderson, my jo, John,
When first that ye began,
Ye had as good a tail-tree
As ony ither man;
But now it's waxen wan, John,
And wrinkles to and fro;
I've twae gae-ups for ae gae-doon,
John Anderson, my jo.

John does not seem to have any say in the argument, but now and then the wife does not get the last word.

Another but a less irate complaint, came from an old wife of a patient nature.
'When we were first marriet, Willie, ye didna gie me time to tak aff my stockings.'
A long pause.
'Noo, I could knit a pair.'

A family party, wife, husband and three bairns, were up for the day at Calder Park Zoo, Glasgow. They were very anxious to see the chimpanzees, but to their disappointment they were not to be seen. Paw approached an attendant.
'Hey, mister, where are the chimps the day?'
'Oh, they're in their cave, they're matin.'
'Will they come oot for a biscuit?'
'A biscuit! Wad you?'

The various circumlocutions used to describe mating, such as coitus, marital consummation, sexual intercourse, oval fertilisation, intra-vaginal insemination, etc., have often bewildered simple minds.
A Buchan farmer attended a meeting on cattle-breeding, hoping to pick up a few tips, but he was lost in a forest of 'lang-nebbit' words. At the end of the meeting he approached the lecturer.
'Tell us maister, tell us this. D'ye ken this sextual intercoorse ye're ay on aboot? Has it onything to dae wi the bullin?'

This recalls a true incident when a ferry steamer carrying a young bull with other stock drew up to a pier in Islay. Lining the pier was a crowd of young lassies, as was the custom when the ferry came in. The West Highland captain, quite innocently, it is thought, yelled out in fog-horn tones, 'Iss there anyone there among you for the bull?' At which there were shrieks of girlish laughter.

Artificial insemination has its friends and its foes. Those who favour it are usually in the business for the money. Those against it are thinking of the loss of pleasure suffered by the participants.

At an agricultural conference the arguments were hot and long on the use of stored semen from prize bulls. Some plain speaking came from the old-fashioned stockmen. One of them was reminded of the financial benefits of artificial insemination. He could put twenty heifers in calf without any trouble, for a moderate cost, by injecting them in this way. But he had a ready answer, which, if it did not entirely convince the conference, at least convulsed it.

'Gentlemen, nae doot there's a guid argument for daein the bull oot o his business, but there's a better yin agin it. When I gang oot and look ower the herd at bullin time, naethin in the warld gies me mair pleasure than to cast my een ower the queys and see a score o contentit faces.'

Bulls are so famed for procreative powers that their sexual prowess is taken for granted. Judge then the frustration of a stock-breeder of limited capital when a prize young bull of high pedigree, for which he had paid £5000, refused to co-operate when led into a field of heifers. After a futile fortnight the farmer decided to reimburse himself to some small extent by showing his bull to his neighbours at fifty pence a time. Many paid willingly but one family man objected strongly.

'Na, na, I canna afford that. I've a wife and twelve bairns to keep.'

'Twelve bairns! Here's a fiver, Willie, awa hame and I'll bring the bull ower tae see you!'

In Scotland, marriage by repute, or in common-law, was widely known. A curious way of obtaining documentary proof of marriage, without going through all the formalities of a church wedding, was for long a practice in Rutherglen. Couples who co-habited saw to it that the sheriff got to hear of their breach of the law. He issued a summons, and on appearing at court they were fined a small nominal sum, about five shillings, and given a receipt for it. This document was accepted as a proof of marriage. These alliances were known as 'Ru'glen weddings.'

But our ancestors were fairly lax in sexual matters and it was a very rare family that did not have quite a few skeletons in its cupboards, which is a pretty good excuse for not following out family trees.

Human Form

Pig-faced ladies, elephant-headed men, fat ladies, Irish giants, Siamese twins, poison dwarfs and other monsters are a never-failing attraction even today, when we would have thought that deformity was a haunting evil. Perhaps, luckily for us, we have not the strong stomachs of our ancestors who could look unmoved upon more sensational spectacles, that are denied us now in actual life, but which the cinema, T.V. and other media increasingly supplies.

At London's Bartholomew's Fair these were exhibited in the reign of George I. 'A prodigious monster with one head and two bodies; an admirable work of nature, a woman with three breasts; a child alive, a year and a half old, with three legs.'

In addition to these monstrous human forms there were also 'learned pigs who could do sums in arithmetic; a ram with six legs, a large fish which had in her belly 1700 mackerel; a mermaid (manufactured from a monkey and a fish-tail) and a mare with seven feet.'

Probably most of these exhibits were catch-penny fakes, but there have been all sorts of strange human forms through the ages which still fascinate, even in the telling.

Dwarfs abound in fairy tales, but real dwarfs are also quite numerous. From these we must exempt the pigmies of equatorial Africa, who were known to the Pharaohs. Pepi, one of the early Pharaohs, had a dancing pigmy brought to him from the jungle, who became his friend and adviser. But pigmies hardly count as abnormalities, being a distinct race development.

The smallest dwarf of antiquity was Philetus, a native of the Greek island of Cos. His mind, however, was not dwarfed. He was an ingenious poet and grammarian. Not only was he short of stature, he was so light that he had to wear lead-soled shoes to prevent his twenty-inch body being blown away.

To come nearer home, 'Bloody' Mary, daughter of Henry VIII, had a two-foot dwarf named Tom Jarvis. This person perhaps gave Henry Fielding the idea for his burlesque play *Tom Thumb, the Great*, though the tale of Tom Thumb, who lived in Arthur's court and who died of the bite of a poisonous spider, was a tale known all over Britain.

Attached also to a royal court was a very dangerous dwarf named Jeffrey Hudson. He was the favourite of the queen of Charles I. He was first brought to the queen's notice when he came to the royal table 'baked in a pie'. Being nine years old and still only eighteen inches high he could easily be accommodated under a large crust. But when he grew older, but not much taller, he betrayed his origin by becoming very crusty. He was knighted, and appointed a captain of the cavalry in the Royal Army during the Civil War. He could hardly be seen behind his horse's head, for he never exceeded two feet, and must have been likened by the Englishmen of that age to the proverbial 'tom-tit perched on a side of beef'.

Nevertheless he killed his man, though not, as far as is known, on the field of battle. At court he provided comic relief by fighting a duel with a turkey-cock, which towered and bubbled with rage far above him. Eventually he got the better of it.

A courtier named Crofts annoyed him, so the fiery particle challenged him to a duel in public. Crofts arrived armed with a water-squirt, but he had little time to repent of his impudence, for Hudson shot him dead with a pistol. A poison dwarf indeed.

Dwarfs seem to be worth steering clear of. At the same court of Charles and Henrietta Maria, the miniature painter, in both senses, was the dwarf Richard Gibson. He was encouraged to marry a lady dwarf. Their wedded life was long and happy, but for one sad incident. One of Gibson's paintings, which was much prized by Charles, was mislaid by the Keeper of the Royal Gallery, who was so upset by his carelessness that he emulated his pictures and hanged himself. The missing picture was found soon after, not far off.

Another little fellow, not to be trifled with, was the French dwarf Richebourg who, though he lived to be ninety, failed by an inch to reach two feet. He was an ardent supporter of the Royal Family and during the French Revolution he carried secret messages for the Bourbons in and out of Paris, under the noses of the Republican Guards. He was easily disguised as an infant in arms.

Willie Merrilees of Edinburgh, famous for his spy-catching exploits during the last war, tells of a similar disguise he adopted to catch a rascal who had been attacking young women in a quiet lane near Leith Links. Though by no means qualifying as a dwarf, Merrilees dressed his head up in a baby's cap and crushed himself into a baby's pram, which a young woman pushed along the lane. As he says himself, 'No man ever looked so surprised as the assaulter did when the baby leapt out of the pram and grabbed him by the scruff of the neck.'

Every Scottish town seems to have had at least one dwarf. Many of these, in addition, were very eccentric characters. Perhaps the most formidable was Davie Ritchie who was the original of Walter Scott's *Black Dwarf,* a title he gained from his hair and grim features. His house was a mile or two out of Peebles. To suit the owner, who built it alone and unaided, it had low doors and windows. The large stones for the lintels were lifted into place with ease by Ritchie's powerful arms. Scott admits to being awe-struck when Ritchie gripped him by the arms and asked him the strange question, 'Hae ye the pooer?' That is, supernatural force.

Ritchie's legs were very short and deformed, and he had to draw himself along by leaning on a stout cudgel. He was not, properly, a dwarf. His malformation was perhaps caused by rickets or some infantile disease, which arrested the growth of his legs.

The present Draconian cuts in University grants are not a new phenomenon. When the state of the nation was decadent in the late 18th century, the splendid classical building which had been earlier envisaged to replace the Old College of Edinburgh, was left unfinished. Neither parliament nor the city gave it financial aid. At the beginning of last century, crows, hawks and owls were building their nests in the unfinished structure and in the shrubs growing on it, overlooking the South Bridge. But a stranger bird than these had his nest at the very entrance to the quadrangle. He was Geordie More, a dwarf. Perhaps this was a humorous ironic nick-name for him, bestowed on him by the Gaelic-speaking City Guard, for in Gaelic it means 'Big George.'

Without interference from the lethargic authorities, Geordie built a sort of bothy of sticks, stones and tiles among the masonry, and made of himself a kind of gate-keeper to the house of learning, though it is unlikely that he himself had any of the three Rs.

Such was the state of a famous Scottish educational foundation when it boasted that it sustained learning on a little oatmeal.

When dwarfs die, they do it with as much trepidation as giants, but their graves are less demanding. In Kilsyth Kirkyard is the grave of a notable Scottish dwarf. Suitably his epitaph is as neat and short as the subject of it.

Beneath this stone there lies a man
Whose body was not full three span
A bon companion day and night
Sir Thomas Henderson of Haystoun, Knight.

Another gifted dwarf, perhaps malformed like Ritchie, was 'Bowed Geordie' Cranstoun who lived in Shoemaker's Close, Canongate, Edinburgh. Though awkwardly shaped for athletic prowess on land, like the penguin, he was so expert in water that he advertised that he would teach swimming, back or forward, to any gentleman who paid the modest fee.

Scotland can beat every other land, in every age, for giants, or rather giantesses, though this one was probably not a native. The *Chronica Scotorum,* Chronicle of the Scots, records that in the year 900 A.D. in the reign of Donald III, a 'Ben Mor', not a hill but a mountain of a woman, was washed up on the Scottish shore. 'She was 192ft. long. Her hair was 17ft. long, her breasts 6ft. apart, her fingers 6ft. long, and her nose 7ft. long. She was as white as sea-foam.' An unbeliever of my acquaintance, a fisherman, thought she would be a whale, which has to suckle its young, but the records state emphatically that she had human form.

Before leaving this question of great and small stature, we should consider briefly the incompatible mating of giant and dwarf. The question is of course ludicrous, as Swift indicated in *Gulliver's Travels*, where Gulliver is accused by the Lilliputians of creating a scandal by having an affair with a court lady of that kingdom who was six inches tall.

In nature there are great differences in size between the sexes. For example, a cock-sparrowhawk is only half the size of the hen. A certain sea-shrimp carries the difference to excess, for the male spends all his life in the left kidney of the female.

It recalls the story of the worried fiancé who is said to have written to the agony column for help. 'I am only three feet seven inches and my fiancée is seven feet three. How do you think I'll get on?'

The Auntie replied, 'You'll get on all right, I have no doubt, but you'll have nobody to speak to.'

The country tale is told of a tough wee chap who was courting a willing lass; she was not endowed with much charm, but made up for her ill-formed appearance by her readiness to co-operate. Her chief handicap was her stature which was a bit over a fathom. Her keen wee lover had an opposite handicap for he was also out of reach, being just under four and a half feet.

One enchanted evening in the village smiddy their incompatibility was adjusted by Wee John making successful love to Big Aggie by standing on the anvil.

It was a dark night as they strolled the half-mile to Aggie's cottage. John wanted to kiss his lofty love goodnight and renew their liaison, but Aggie was not in the humour and refused his entreaties.

'Ye micht hae tellt me that at the smiddy, Aggie,' he grumbled, 'Ye wad hae spared me cairryin the bloody anvil alang the loanin.'

Some people have pined away for love but this cannot be said of a young man in Aberdeen, named Henry Scougal. He was attracted by a 'bonnie Jean in the streets of Aberdeen,' but being of a pious disposition he decided to make himself inaccessible to her charms. He locked himself up in the steeple of St. Nicholas church and devoted himself to study. But he did not forget the 'mercies' as they were called. He ate and drank to excess, and as his only exercise was opening and shutting books and his mouth, he soon got very fat. He died aged twenty-eight. As his corpse could not be taken down the narrow stairs it was lowered from one of the windows.

A true tale that gripped me when I was a mere infant, and has been recalled every time I pass along Princes Street, concerns my grand-uncle Tom Bell, a prosperous farmer, well-known and respected throughout the Southwest of Scotland. He was a large stout man, fully twenty stone. On a visit to Edinburgh with his cousins, of whom my grandfather was one, he wished to climb the Scott Monument.

With cousins Charlie in front and Willie behind, he slowly made his way up the 287 steps. It was a warm summer day, so many halts were made. The top flight is narrow, and Tom, half-way up, got wedged between the walls. He could not advance, retreat he dared not. Willie had visions of the fire-brigade being called with an escape ladder, or the top of the monument having to be demolished. He was on a sticky wicket, being immediately below two and a half hundredweights, but at last with much manoeuvring, Tom got down, turned about, and vowed to stick to street-level ever after.

To Captain Francis Grose all Burns enthusiasts owe a great deal, for he was a close crony of the poet, and it is to Grose, who was an antiquarian, that we owe *Tam o Shanter*. He suggested to Burns the writing of a poem on the Auld Kirk of Alloway, little anticipating the brilliant form it would take.

Grose was very fat when Burns first met him; it seems that when employed as a paymaster in the Surrey militia he was rather lax and self-indulgent; consequently his belly increased at the expense of his purse.

During a social gathering in 1789 in Auld Reekie, Grose, for a joke, asked Burns to compose an epitaph for him, knowing that the bard was keen on supplying these grim verses for his friends—and enemies. In a few moments Burns brought the table to a roar with this.

The Devil got notice that Grose was a-dying
So whip, at the summons, old Satan came flying
But when he approached where poor Francis lay moaning
And saw each bed-post with its burden a-groaning,
Astonished! Confounded! Cry'd Satan, 'By God,
I'll want 'im, ere I take such a damnable load.'

Grose died of an apoplexy in Dublin, two years later, but the above famous, if irreverent epitaph, was not put over him.

George IV was also a round man. When he paid a royal visit to Edinburgh in 1822 to grace the hysterical 'Celtic Revival', he brought in his train an even fatter man than himself, Curtis, Lord Mayor of London. King George was dressed in Highland costume of Stewart tartan, but the Lord Mayor got himself rigged out ludicrously also in a Stewart tartan kilt, the last costume to suit a tun-belly. William Dunbar's description of the giant Finn MacCoul would almost have fitted this magisterial figure of fun:

Five thousand yards went to his coat
Of Highland plaid of hair.

So far we have kept off the ladies of embonpoint, though there have been notable Two Ton Tessies through the ages. A well-known character, whom I have often seen myself, going on her fish-hawking rounds in Edinburgh and Leith sixty years ago, was Jean Lindsay. A certain line in the old ballad *The Battle of Otterburn* would not have suited her, for it speaks of 'The Lindsays light, the Gordons gay'.

Jean was so ponderous that she had to be drawn on a float by a pony. She sold her fish without descending to earth. Edward Albert, English master in George Watson's Boys' College, wrote a novel around her entitled *Herring Jenny,* but he did not include an apocryphal tale which went the rounds during her life.

Jenny fell off the float on to the tramway lines near the terminus on the shore road near Newhaven, her native place. A number of folk ran to her assistance but could not budge her. At last two hefty Leith policemen appeared and tried to hoist her up between them, with no better success, for the heels of her shoes were tightly wedged in the tram-rails. By this time a line of electric trams was held up, so someone cycled along to summon the sergeant of police, suggesting a lifting gear from the docks. With this Jenny was finally hoisted back on to the float. Her parting remarks were directed at the sergeant and the constables.

'Sergeant, thank Goad the force has a man like you, o some rumgumption, for to guide them. Thae gomerils o polis hadnae the brains to ken whit to dae when ma heels stuck in the rails. Could they no hae slid me alang to the terminus and gotten them oot?'

Of the Seven Deadly Sins, Gluttony is perhaps the best advertised on T.V., with Lechery and Ire running it close. It is hard to believe some of the feats of gluttons in ages past, yet they are well-authenticated and would put into the shade all our champion pie-eaters.

I know from eye-witness accounts that the winner of a fish-and-chip supper eating contest in Portobello consumed nineteen suppers before giving up and throwing up. It has been said that a man may sustain life on an olive a day, and this seems preferable to winning the above contest.

John, Duke of Lauderdale, that persecutor of the Covenanters, was such a gormandiser that, when he had sent invitations to a dinner-party in Thirlestane Castle, near Lauder, he devoured a whole leg of mutton beforehand so that, as he called it, 'he could start fair,' in the gluttony stakes.

An Englishman of Kent named Wood probably holds the record. He was said to eat as much as would have satiated thirty. 'Two loins of mutton and a loin of veal were merely as three sprats to him.' When dining with a knight his motto seems to have been, 'The proof of the pudding's in the eating of it.' He got so full on free food that a servant man had to lead him to the fireside before a log-fire, and anoint his paunch with grease and butter to make it stretch. We are pleased to hear that his host, who had generously provided for him, was so disgusted that he ordered him into the village stocks for a long stretch, with the Shakespearean advice, 'If the call of Nature is strong, thy bum sitteth close enough to thy breeches.'

Rob Roy is supposed to have said that if a roast of beef were placed on the far side of the pit of Hell an Englishman 'wad mak a spang at it.' The Scots were of the opinion that the English were a nation of gluttons, though when the Scots got a chance they were not backward.

The story of the Glasgow glutton and Dr. James Gregory in *Macgregor's Mixture* is founded on fact. The Italians, at any rate, thought the English worshipped the Belly God. A well-known Italian proverb says, 'As busy as the ovens of London at Christmas.'

But great gluttons, approaching cannibalism, were to be found in Europe, and still are, among the northern nations. When Gustavus Adolphus was besieging Prague, a Bohemian peasant with a terrifying array of teeth and a large belly was led into his tent. He offered, for a fee, to eat a whole hog, raw, before their very eyes. A hardened old campaigner, General Konigsmark, who had seen, unmoved, many gruesome sights on the battlefields, felt his stomach turn at the proposed orgy, and told Gustavus to burn the boor as a wizard. At this, the glutton suggested that, if the old general were stripped of his sword and spurs, he would use him as an hors d'oeuvre before he began his dinner in earnest on the pig. That tough old war-dog turned pale and fled from the tent to escape from his would-be devourer.

Gluttons there will always be, even today, when a third of the world is on short commons. At a hiring fair the farmer noticed a fine strong young man.

'Hoo wad ye like to labour for me up at Burnheid Mains?'

'What's the wages?'

'I'll no stint on the cash. Wad £40 a week suit ye?'

'Fine, but I warn ye, I'm gey fond o ma meat.'

'We'll no sterve ye at Burnheid, never fear.'

'Weel, I'd better tell ye I like a guid breakfast. A big bowl or twa o parritch, six rashers o bacon, three eggs, breid, scones, marmalade and a pot o tea. Then I'll need my elevenses ootby in the field. Currant scones, sandwiches and a quart o tea. I'll hae worked up a gran appetite by denner-time so I'll be needin a guid bowl o broth for starters. Then tatties, meat and plenty o fresh biled carrots or cabbage wi lashins o buttermilk. And I'm gey fond o clootie dumpling, and tea tae wash it doon. And then there's the three o'clock snack in the field and by six I'll be in fine fettle for ma tea. Jist the usual ham and eggs or maybe a wee bittie o biled ham twice the size o ma steiket neive. And then at supper time a slice or twa o toasted cheese, or a couple o fried herrin and a big waucht o porter.'

The farmer listened with ever-growing apprehension and at last remarked;

'I'll strike the bargain then. £40 a week. The grub just as you say. And we'll settle for that if I can hae your muck at five bob a ton.'

Drinking to excess is usually accompanied by gluttony. The Scots proverb expresses this. 'Eat-weel is drink-weel's brother.' But we shall tackle that in another chapter.

A brief account of cannibalism seems suitable here. Most people abhor the very idea, and when, as has happened recently, the survivors of an air-crash or other accident have subsisted on the flesh of less fortunate victims, we read of it with fascination but with revulsion. Even cannibal fish, which form the major part of the finny tribes, often having no other food than their own progeny, are viewed with distaste.

Christopher Columbus has enough to answer for already, so we are sorry to add that he is also guilty of presenting us with the word cannibal. He said in his journal, recording his arrival near the West Indies, that many of the natives were terrified of the Canibals, that is, the inhabitants of Cariba, from which the Caribbean Sea is named. But the people of Cariba were not unique in their behaviour; it was general throughout Central and South America as well as in Polynesia. The Maori were cannibals in early times.

However, as Montaigne explains at length in an essay based on information received from a traveller in the Americas, the practice of eating one's enemies, and occasionally, one's own dear departed daddy, was not from any love of human flesh, but was a religious act. One wonders how the Christian missionaries, who followed in the wake of Columbus, managed to reconcile their condemnation of ritual cannibalism and their insistence on the transubstantiation of bread and wine into flesh and blood in the sacrament. The warriors of the tribes who fought with iron-wood swords were brought up never to show cowardice. When taken prisoner and threatened with death and providing their own funeral feast, they kept a stiff upper lip. Any sign of a nervous breakdown delighted their captors.

Robinson Crusoe's cannibal descriptions, of the bones left around after the feast, used to fascinate me as a boy. I later learned that Scotland has a record of man-eating much less moral than the untutored savages.

The Attacoti were a British tribe inhabiting what is now part of Strathclyde, formerly Dunbartonshire. Reliable historians describe them as cannibals, who preferred the taste of the shepherd and his wife and family to the best spring lamb.

The Northumbrian King Ethelfrith encouraged cannibalism at his court, if indeed he did not practise it. He was the conqueror of Lothian, so the Edinburgh area knew cannibal chiefs in the 7th century, as well as the Glasgow area had done, earlier. Ethelfrith had a renegade Welshman at his court who ate two of his own people, male or female, daily. So nice was this bloody hypocrite that he slew two men and two women on the Saturday, to avoid breaking the Sabbath.

Centuries later, when the Golden Age of Alexander was fled, and Bannockburn was wiped out by English victories, and when Edward III had reduced Scotland to a wilderness, famine drove a monster nicknamed Christie Cleek to live on human flesh. Not far from Perth he had his munching-ground. He lay in wait for stray passers-by and drew them down with a large cleek or catchpole before devouring them.

Lindsay of Pitscottie, a quaint old chronicler, writes about a family gang in the reign of James II of Scotland. In the county of Angus they had their den where they lived on the flesh of children and young men and women. They were finally all captured and burnt at the stake, except a one-year-old baby girl. But such mercy was ill-repaid, for when she grew up, she was back at her old practices. Caught red-toothed she was condemned immediately. Amid the curses of the Dundonians, she was dragged to the place of execution. She died, not only unrepentant, but doing a commercial for her favourite food as the flames licked round her. Her final speech to the mob was to the effect that 'gin they had but aince gotten the taste o a man's meat intae their gabs they'd ne'er hae eaten ony ither flesh, either o kine or sheep.'

In Kirkcudbrightshire, in the parish of Minnigaff, far up country, lived the dreaded 'Sawney' or Alexander Bean, whose name was used for generations after his death to frighten 'waukrife' bairns to sleep. He and his numerous progeny lived in a cave in the Kells range, and preyed on the solitary travellers who traversed the sequestered valleys of the area.

So, with these home examples before us, we should not be too hard on the Caribs.

The largest mammal is the whale. We have mentioned how a woman of such proportions was stranded long ago. We should not like to forget the largest land mammal, the elephant, and claim for Scotland the distinction of having many of these in human form. Oliphant is a good Scottish name and has included notable persons. It is an old spelling of elephant, from Old French, olifant. Mrs. Margaret Oliphant, Laurence Oliphant and Caroline Oliphant were famous literary people of last century. But Oliphants go back for centuries. How the name arose is rather peculiar. In the Middle Ages a large horn made out of an elephant's tusk, and named an oliphant, or olifant, was carried in battle by a knight of high rank. The horn was ornamented with carvings and inlaid precious metal. The loss of it was even more disgraceful than the loss of a standard. The bearer of such an object took his family name from it.

Most people have to be content with one body. Only rarely do we meet with 'prodigious monsters with one head and two bodies' though there are creatures in nature, like the terrapins shown on T.V. with two heads and one body. Perhaps pedestrians who wish to survive in an age increasingly accelerated will arrange to be born with two heads like the cartoon figures in the old advertisement 'That's Shell—that was!'

The Russian anatomists have recently been debunking the saintly relics of the Orthodox Church and found them distinctly Heterodox. The skeletons of 'Christian' martyrs are found to have been the framework of Mongolian heathens in life, and St. George, who is a Russian as well as an English patron, has about half-a-dozen skeletons and innumerable spare parts from Nishni-novgorod to Leningrad.

However, in Lothian, we have almost as remarkable an example of multiple human forms. St. Baldred was a hermit of old whose refuge was on the Bass Rock. When he died his body was claimed by three parishes which disputed the possession of the Bass. Relics of saints were valuable assets. Battles could be won, sterility avoided, plagues prevented by the possessors. The parishioners of Auldhame, Whittinghame and Preston gathered their forces to wrestle for the corpse of St. Baldred. However, they were advised by the churchmen to be patient and to let it lie overnight, and pray for a miracle. Sure enough, in the dawn, there were three bodies in three coffins, so alike that it was not possible to tell them apart. Thus the matter was settled and each parish had a St. Baldred to carry away. Nobody came forward to assist the local police with their enquiries as to the disappearance of two venerable persons.

Professional strong men abound in the annals of the Scots. David Webster, in *Scottish Highland Games,* details the feats of these heroes. They are of several nationalities, Scots, Europeans, Americans, but the best all-rounder of his day was Donald Dinnie, 'a loon frae Aboyne', Aberdeenshire.

Dinnie was very clever, especially at Latin. His copperplate handwriting did not seem to have come from the same hand that could putt a 16lb. stone nearly 50ft. I think the Dinnies as a race must be intelligent, for I well remember that the dux of my primary class at school for four years was an Oliver Dinnie.

Donald Dinnie was invincible when at the height of his powers in the athletic field; but not so in business, where after trying and failing in many businesses he even set up as an undertaker. Unluckily he chose one of the healthiest parishes in Scotland. That was bad enough for trade, but Dinnie insisted on providing a horse-drawn hearse, whereas the people most concerned insisted upon a shoulder or 'carried' funeral.

A.A. Cameron was also a natural strong man, who had a spell as a 'polis' in Glasgow where he found his 6ft. 1in. and his 17st. were quite helpful in gaining a respect for law and order. He took his strength from his maternal side, the MacMillans.

The story is told by David Webster that when one of the MacMillan ancestors was digging peats the horse and cart got stuck in the bog. MacMillan loosed the harness and heaved the frightened beast on to terra firma then, with a superlative effort, he dragged out the cart and consoled the poor horse with a pat on the neck and the remark, 'I dinna wonder ye couldna pu it oot, cuddie. I had a gey job masel.'

It would be unchivalrous, as well as dishonest, not to mention in some detail the strong women of Scotland, most of whom unfortunately are anonymous.

The fishwives of Newhaven used to supply Edinburgh with their wares, carrying their wicker baskets or creels, surmounted by a shallow creel or skull. The load of fish, herrings, haddock or shellfish was frequently two hundredweight, or a hundred kilos. Many of the fishwives were active young women but not a few were elderly, yet they climbed the steep gradient from sea-level to the High Street, a distance of two miles and an ascent of three hundred feet, with these loads. The Fisherrow women had a longer if less steep journey to Auld Reekie, but they daily trudged the six miles each way with loads that the average man could not even lift.

No wonder these women were totally independent and cared little for the criticism of the sober-sided citizens. Once their fish was disposed of, usually by midday, they treated themselves to a dram and a bite, and linked arms, their baskets now light, to sing their way back to the sea-shore. Woe betide the poor male who was bold enough to encounter them as they swung down the broad avenue of Leith Walk, or by the narrow Fishwives' Causeway to Musselburgh.

There is a quaint record of a competition held in the year 1661, shortly after the Merry Monarch had returned from exile and the sour-faced Puritans were themselves under a cloud.

The *Caledonian Mercury* newspaper of that time gives an account of a footrace for Fisherrow fishwives. They had to trot from Musselburgh to the Cross in the Canongate. Sixteen of these amazons entered for the six mile race, for which there were twelve prizes. Each prize consisted of 'a pair of lamb's harrigals,' that is, the heart, lungs and liver, of a lamb. It seems a pretty tough ordeal to trot six miles for a load of offal.

But this was only a consolation race. The big prizes had been competed for the previous day. Twelve browster-wives, or brewers of ale, 'all of them in a condition which makes violent exercise unsuitable to the female form,' were to have a footrace from the Figgate Burn (where Portobello now stands, but which was then a barren moor), to the summit of Arthur's Seat. The distance is two miles and the summit in 822ft. above sea-level. But the prizes were really worth the effort for these pregnant pedestrian ale-wives. The first arrival at the peak got a hundred-weight of cheese, which no doubt she could easily carry home, but the second prize was so much more attractive that it makes us wonder if there was not a temptation to fix the race. Second home won a budgell of Dunkeld aquavitae and a rumpkin of Brunswick rum, both provided by the Dutch midwife, who no doubt expected a rush of customers after this mountaineering feat.

What a handicap it is to have short arms, or worse still, to suffer from 'Duck's Disease', having a bottom too close to the ground.

A wee Glasgow wifie, a couple of centimetres over four feet, went to consult her doctor about a very private complaint.

'Ye see, doacter, I cannae understand it. Every time it rains the insides o ma thighs get terrible hawkit. They're reid raw and sair frae moarnin to nicht. I've tried Vaseline, but it's nae guid.'

'Stand up on that stool,' said the doctor, 'and let me have a look.'

She lifted her skirts and the doctor examined her.

'No doubt about the abrasions, my dear. But I think we can effect a cure with a simple operation.'

'O, my Goad, an operation! Will Ah need to hae an anaesthetic?'

'No, it won't be necessary. You won't feel a thing. Just stand still and close your eyes.'

The doctor produced a large scalpel and after a few minutes work stood back.

'There now, step down and walk up and down the surgery once or twice and tell me if the irritation has gone.'

'O doacter, it's a modern miracle. The pain's away. What on earth did ye dae?'

'Not very much, really,' said the medic, 'I just sliced three inches off the tops of each of your wellies.'

The little African boy felt compelled to ask his Daddy some pressing questions which were puzzling him.

'Daddy, why is my skin so black?'

'God has given you a black skin to protect you from the ultra-violet rays of the sun.'

'Why are my arms so long and my fingers so strong?'

'God has given you long arms and strong hands so that you can climb trees and throw spears at wild beasts.'

'Why is my hair so short, black and curly?'

'God does not want your hair to be caught up in the thorns and creepers of the jungle. Now are you satisfied?'

'Yes, Daddy, but why are we living in Auchenshuggle?'

Some dear old ladies who have no desire to hurt a fly, have little hesitation about having their tom-cats 'treated', to render them more domesticated. So, in hopes of bringing home to them the gravity of their behaviour in human terms, we round off this topic with a moral fairy tale.

Once upon a time in a top flat in Morningside there lived a homely old lady with her sandy tom-cat. One dreary winter afternoon the dear old maid put on the kettle to make a fly cup and poured the top of the bottle into Peter's saucer.

Until the kettle boiled, she idly rubbed the antique silver family tea-pot to make it shine. As she did so there was a smoky flash and a genie dressed in tartan appeared. The old lady was astounded and Peter left off lapping.

'I am the genie of the clan. Effie MacPherson, I grant you three wishes, no more. So think hard before you speak.' He melted into the gloom.

Effie sat pondering, incredulous. At last, not heeding the whistling kettle, she spoke in a determined tone, 'I wish I lived in a lovely palace!' In a trice she was surrounded by splendid furniture, a scented log-fire in an Adam fireplace. 'I wish I were a lovely young princess!' She was instantly sweet-and-twenty in frills. On looking at Peter's wistful expression, she did not hesitate to expend her last wish.

'I wish Peter were a handsome young prince!' There he stood in the prime of elegant manhood.

They exchanged loving glances for a few moments, then Peter broke the silence.

'And now, Effie my dear, don't you regret taking me to the vet?'

Strong Waters

Drunkenness has been universally condemned but never drink. Try to imagine Scotland without whisky, France without wine, England without ale. Like all God's mercies, strong drink can be abused, but in Scotland, the ancient invention of the Highlanders was the foundation of a cult with ceremonies and customs fully as well established as the forms of any religion. No Polynesian taboos were as carefully observed as the laws of the whisky fraternity.

Every man's character was decided by the acid test of *usqueba*. Whisky was the first thing the infant smelt, and sometimes tasted, on entering this vale of woe. It was the last flavour enjoyed by fleeting mortality.

Burns has penned the completest pictures of Scotch drink and the place that drink occupied in the imbiber's life. Perhaps the most spontaneous inspiration is his 'epitaph' on John Dow, innkeeper of Mauchline, written for entertainment while Dow was still able to enjoy it. A dow, or a doo, is Scots for a dove or pigeon.

Here lies Johnny Pigeon
What was his religion
Whae'er desires to ken
To some ither warl'
Maun follow this carl
For here Johnny Pigeon had nane.

Strong ale was ablution
Small beer persecution
A dram was memento mori
But a full flowing bowl
Was the saving of his soul
And port was celestial glory.

The Romans had two gods to represent the celestial glory of drinking. Bacchus was a young golden-haired man full of wit and vivacity, who enjoyed the juice of the grape in merry company; Silenus was a swinish lecherous drunkard, a parody of humanity. By these two opposing gods the effects of drink may still be understood.

The various stages of drink-taking used to be represented by eight animals. 'The first stage is ape-drunk, and he leaps, sings, halloos and capers to the heavens. The second is lion-drunk and he flings the pots about the house, calls the hostess whore, breaks the glass windows with his dagger, and is apt to quarrel with any man who speaks to him. The third is the swine-drunk, heavy, lumpish and sleepy, and cries for a little more drink and a few more clothes. The fifth is sheep-drunk, wise in his own conceit when he cannot pronounce a single word.

The fifth is maudlin-drunk, when he weeps over his drink and kisses you and says, "Captain, I love you," then puts his finger in his eye and cries. The sixth is martin-drunk when a man drinks himself sober again.

The seventh is goat-drunk, when he thinks of nothing but sex. The eighth is fox-drunk when he turns crafty, like some Dutchmen who will never drive a bargain until they are fully drunk.'

Laws have been made throughout the ages to prevent men and women from passing through these stages, but in vain.

Edgar, who handed over Lothian to the King of Scots on condition that the Anglian inhabitants kept their own customs, laws and language, was one of the first to try to control drinking. He was a thorough-going fellow, who did not confine himself to ale, wine and spirits, but included water. He ordered iron cups to be attached by iron chains to all the wells and fountains in England, including Lothian. A pin was inserted near the mouth of the cup to mark the limit of each drink. The same thing was done in the inns, with wooden drinking-vessels. Anyone filling the cup over the pin and drinking it out was fined a penny, a considerable sum then.

When I was a boy, Edinburgh was very much better provided with drinking-places in the shape of street-wells (and horse-troughs) than it is now. There were also many public urinals, built of iron pierced by star-shaped holes, on the sides of the streets.

The stand-wells were supplied with an iron handle. When you turned it the water poured out from an iron lion's head into a semi-circular basin. Each well had two half-pint iron cups attached by iron chains. Each well had also a dog's drinking-trough near the ground. There were also numerous iron horse-troughs which provided us with amusement when the great Clydesdales sucked up huge draughts of water and sometimes threw their heads and snorted with pleasure after drinking. These troughs had an irregular use too. Obstreperous drunks were now and then immersed in them by the police in the tougher quarters of the town.

I am sorry to say that drunk men were also a source of amusement to us small boys and at that remote age there seemed to be more of them about than now.

When a man is in drink he often has 'Dutch courage', another insulting phrase made by the English to fit their naval rivals. He shows bravado quite alien to his character. A story of my schooldays concerns a practical joker in a tenement building in Edinburgh who had got hold of a skeleton, not a difficult thing to acquire in a world-famous medical centre. He thought he would scare the life out of the coalman, so he propped the skeleton against the coal-cellar door, to fall forward when the door was opened. But the coalman had had a few drams to help him carry his customary two-hundred-weight bag up four flights. The practical joke fell flat, for, as the skeleton threw its arms over the coalman's shoulders, all he said was, 'Tak your bloody airms aff me, ye baney bugger'.

A habitual boozer, a hefty ploughman, turned up with his wife at the christening of their baby. The minister suspected that the father was not quite sober, but decided not to make a fuss. However when the ploughman took the child in his arms he began to sway, so the clergyman whispered to him, 'John, my good man, I do not think you are fit to hold up the child, in the state you are in.' John did not see the spiritual side of the remark, but thought it a reflection on his physique.

'Fit to haud him up, meenister. By Goad, I'm fit to haud up a twa-year auld stirk,' he bellowed to the shocked pews.

The parish of Whittinghame was for long haunted by the ghost of an unchristened child. Few people cared to pass along the quiet lane by the kirkyard after the gloaming had set in. It was commonly believed that ghosts walked because of some injustice done to them in life, but nobody could imagine what injustice could have been suffered by an innocent babe.

A local farmer who had spent the winter evening in the pub, came into the night with no fear of spectral figures, so he staggered stoutly along by the churchyard wall. The ghost of the child, clad in baby clothes, and footless stockings that were customary in that district, suddenly popped up from behind the wall. No whit afraid, the farmer, pointing to the footless stockings, known as 'short hoggers', cried out 'Houts, Short Hoggers, ye're oot late the nicht. Time ye were beddit.' At that, crowing with delight, the ghost vanished over the wall chanting, 'Hoorah, at last I've gotten a name. They ca' me Short Hoggers o Whittinghame.' It never haunted anyone again, drunk or sober.

A midnight reveller on the other side of the Forth was not so lucky. He was rolling along near the Calliards (or Old Hags) Knowe between St. Monans and Elie when he was seized by a coven of witches and carried three miles through the middle heavens to Kilconquhar or Kinneuchar Loch. The carlins flew with him seven times round the loch and finally dropped him where they had picked him up. That was his story.

There are many similar tales from all over Scotland, the best known one, of course, being what befell Thomas Reid of Shanter, when he got roaring fu before setting off for home by Kirk Alloway. The real reason for Tam's mare losing her tail is more prosaic. Tam was in his favourite howff drinking the hours away and forgetting that poor Maggie was tethered outside. The local urchins seized their chance to get fishing tackle for nothing. So they crept up, taking care to avoid Maggie's flying hoofs, and tugged out the tail-hairs, strand by strand, leaving poor Maggie scarce a stump. When Tam emerged at last he was astounded at Maggie's bare behind, and put it down to the account of witches. Burns got to hear of this incident, for it was the laugh of the season, and put it to good use.

There used to be comical recitations of ridiculous events such as 'The Fire at the Ice-works,' describing how firemen at great personal risk, carried blazing blocks of ice out of the building. Another favourite was 'The Man that swallowed the Soapworks and died with a dirty neck.' But a true tale, equally ludicrous, is of a drunkard who swallowed a large sandhill and died of thirst.

On the west side of Leith Walk, halfway between the capital and the port, stands

Shrubhill, though there are no longer shrubs or a hill. But in olden times, before the 1745 Rising, this was one of the most gruesome spots in Britain. The Tyburn of Scotland. A gibbet stood permanently at Shrubhill on the Gallows Lee, reserved for witches and the more atrocious criminals, although five innocent young men of the Covenanters were cruelly murdered there at the height of the Killing Times. I shall return to this blood-chilling spot in a later chapter. The manner of the Shrubhill's disappearance is curious.

The proprietor of this piece of poor ground discovered to his joy that his hill was composed entirely of sea-sand, part of the 'fifty-foot beach' that formerly marked a much higher shore of the Forth. The city was beginning to expand beyond its old walls and speculative builders were looking for sand near at hand. Incorporated in this sand were the ashes of many poor old women burnt for witchcraft, but no qualms on that account worried the owner of the hill.

He began to sell his heritage by the cartload to builders for making mortar. All he had to do was sit by the hill as the cart rolled up and, whether his fee was a groat, a sixpence or a shilling, he hastened with it to the tavern over the road and immediately converted it into drink. An enterprising publican built a bar on the spot, being certain of the steady custom of an unsteady customer as long as the Shrubhill lasted. Eventually, where a large hill had stood, there remained only a hollow, and the ghost of the man who swallowed the sandhill probably haunts it to this day. I cannot prove that shrubs ever grew on the hill although the old Botanical Garden was only a stone's-throw away. Recalling that shrub was the name given to a beguiling concoction of lemon or orange juice, sugar and rum, I think that may well be the origin of the name.

Just across the street from Shrubhill is the Boundary Bar. It was so named early this century because the boundary line between the separate burghs of Edinburgh and Leith ran through the centre of the bar. There was nothing unusual in this but for the fact that closing-time in Edinburgh was 9 pm while in Leith it was 10 pm.
'Time, gentlemen, please,' has been described as the most unwelcome phrase in any language.

But in the Old Boundary Bar the harshness of the 'Time' call was softened by the situation. At 9 pm the drinkers on the metropolitan side lifted their glasses and crossed unconcernedly to the port side.

Many of the pillars of the Scottish police force in Victorian days were men from the North and many also had the Highlander's love of *usqueba*, a hereditary liking. One of the first police-boxes to be installed with a telephone to headquarters was situated not far from the Boundary Bar, at the west end of a long street of tenement houses named Albert Street. At the east end of the same street is a short street leading into the Eastern Cemetery, the long home of countless thousands of local citizens.

A police sergeant, reputedly of bibulous habits, had been warned that delirium tremens, or DTs was on the cards, but he pooh-poohed the idea and continued the treatment as before. His career ended suddenly one day, soon after the head office got an urgent phone call to send a strong posse of constabulary to Shrubhill.

'Who is calling?' asked the telephonist.

'Sergeant MacRahanish. I can see them a' marching in line of eight across the hale breadth o Albert Street, and there's only me to stop them. For God's sake send the Mounted and the Black Marias.'

'Who are they then, the rioters?'

'They're the deid frae the Eastern. It's the Resurrection. Can ye no hear Gabriel's Trump up there in the High Street?'

The P.C. hero of the following story related it to me over forty years ago. His beat took him round the whisky bonded stores in the Leith Dock area, where there was temptation he could never resist, or even try to. One forenoon he had had a few drams of overproof spirit with the friendly warehouseman, when an apprentice hurried in to say that the police superintendent was approaching. There seemed no way of escape. Luckily the warehouseman saw an empty hogshead, got the constable crammed in, and knocking the top on, proceeded to roll him out to a nearby lane under the super's nose. But, what with the drink, the topsy-turvy rolling of the barrel over the cobbles and the fear of dismissal, he was from that hour a reformed man and drank only in permitted times and places.

The modern tests for sobriety are the breathaliser and the micturationiser, to use two clumsy barbarisms. The puff and the pee would be better English and much more euphonious. In the days before science, suspected drunks walked on chalk lines, or were tested for thickness of speech or misplaced syllables. The smell of their breath was often an inspiration as well as a respiration. From the lips of those under the affluence of incohol 'Truly rural' would emerge as 'Tooralooral', an affectionate farewell. 'The Leith Police dismisseth us' often ended in the very reverse; while the tongue-twister 'Whether would you raither, or raither would you whether, a soo's snoot stewed, or a stewed soo's snoot?' was decidedly below the belt. 'The British Constitution' often tailed off like an exhausted soda-siphon. It was all good clean democratic fun compared with the present Big Brother business, and of course traction was mostly by teetotal quadrupeds.

It was often hard to get home after a night out. A roystering old toper was veering and tacking along the moonlit highway, before the days of motors, when all good horses hit the hay at sundown. He stood for some time and addressed the full moon, 'O, aye, I ken why you're makin sic a puir mooth, John Heezlum-Peezlum. Ye're just jealous o me, ye puir auld crater. You can only get fu yince a month, and I can get fu ilka nicht.'

A crony drew up to him. 'Aye, John, are ye gettin' hame, then?'

John staggers about. 'No a' the time, Tam. Just whiles.'

Another bibulous Scottish elder unhappily met the Free Kirk minister, who showed the whites of his eyes in disapproval.

'William, it grieves me to the inmost soul to meet you in this condition.'

'Nae need to excuse yoursel, meenister, for to tell ye the God's truth, I'm no that sober masel.'

'No, no, William, you misunderstand me. I mean I am sorry to see that you have left the straight and narrow path of righteousness and are now on the broad road that leadeth to destruction.'

'Broad road, did ye say? Guid faith, I could dae wi ilka inch o't.'

Another tippler came home in the wee sma' oors with a great grievance. 'I was gettin hame fine withoot ony help frae onybody, when a big muckle stot o a Glesca polis strampit on ma fingers.'

Drinkers with two legs are more able to maintain their equilibrium than the handicapped, so a group of bipeds helped their wooden-legged pal home. His wife opened the door and gave them the edge of her tongue for bringing her man home in such a state. She finished with the nasty threat, 'Next time I hear o him gaun oot wi youse lot, I'll lock his wooden leg up in the cupboard.'

Crestfallen, the party crept away, only to find at the foot of the close, that the wooden leg had become unstrapped, and was lying in the street. The bravest of the band was sent back to meet the storm. He rapped on the door and when it was flung open, without awaiting an answer, he threw in the leg and shouted, 'Hey, missus, here's the rest o your man,' and fled.

To stot is to bounce like a rubber ball. A common bit of repartee in West Edinburgh in the area of the long-established North British Rubber Mill, was as follows:
'Hello Jessie, is your man ay workin in the rubber-mill?'
'Aye, Teenie.'
'I thocht as muckle, I saw him stottin hame last nicht.'

An aged man on his death-bed was being comforted by the minister.
'Is there anything troubling your mind, Alec?' asked the reverend.
'Aye, there is. I was wonderin to masel gin there wad be ony whisky in heeven.'
'O, that's a sinfu thocht for a man in your condition.'
'Surely no, for I wouldna hae ye think that I wad be drinkin it, ye ken, but ye maun admit yoursel that a bottle o the Auld Kirk looks gey weel on the table.'

Some pious folk, when a bottle of whisky was spotted in the press by a visitor, excused its presence by saying that it was kept for medicinal purposes. To this the invariable answer was, as the visitor passed his tongue over his dry lips, 'Why not drink it when you can enjoy it and not wait till you're past it?'

In Galloway, away up in the wilderness at the source of the Black Water of Dee, or at Back Hill o the Bush, which I used to frequent, there was little chance of getting medical aid. A panacea which never failed, well, hardly ever, was:
Whisky for the folks
Sulphur and treacle for the sheep
And them that dees just dees.

The techniques of whisky-making are comparatively simple to learn. For generations, after the licensing of distilleries was enforced, the Celts were turning out illicit liquor. The chief difficulty was not in making it, for there are many inaccessible spots in the Highlands; delivery was the trouble, for excise officers watched the access roads to the markets.
An old Rannoch woman died in Glasgow. Her final request was to be buried in the ancestral clan graveyard above the loch. Her son got her 'kisted' in a braw coffin and, hiring a cart, set off for the north. About a week later an acquaintance met him coming down Lochlomondside, driving the cart with the coffin still in it.
'Did ye not get the auld leddy buried then efter a'? Or did ye bury her in her sark and brocht back the kist to sell it?'
'Och, aye, she's lying yonder content at last at Kinloch Rannoch.'
'What's in the kist then, Iain?'
'No a word to a leevin' saul and I'll gie ye a gude waucht oot o ma bottle. There's eicht gallon o the cratur in it weel screwed doon. Ye see I thocht it was vera proper to tak awa the body to her native place and bring back the speerit to Glesca, that she was ay sae fond o.'

An old clansman had a model still, pot, copper worm and all, displayed on his mantel-piece. One day an excise officer happened to call on other business and very officiously asked the veteran if he had a licence for the model still. He was told, no, as it was only an exhibit. He was reported for committing an offence, and had to appear before the sheriff on a charge. His explanation was not accepted and he was fined £5. He objected strongly to this injustice and sarcastically asked the sheriff if he was also being charged with rape. He was told that he was being in contempt of court, by his ridiculous comment. To this he replied, 'It is no more ridiculous than what you have just done. Old as I am, I have all the equipment, the technique and the ability to rape, just as I had with the model still.'

Rob Roy had four sons by his wife, Mary Helen MacGregor of Comar. He adopted a relative, Duncan, who, to comply with the law prohibiting the use of the name MacGregor, called himself Duncan McPharic. He was out with his clan in the Forty-Five and for many years was notorious in the Lake of Menteith region as a 'drouth' always ready to turn his hand to any scheme, however dishonest, for the price of a dram. He was highly connected, by a sheer accident. His comely cousin, when on ship-board in the Mediterranean, had called at Tripoli and had taken the fancy of the Emperor of Morocco, becoming his favourite wife. Duncan, already boasting as a MacGregor, that his race was royal, now traded on his connection with the Empress and persuaded the ale-wife at Port of Menteith to marry him. There is a kirk at the Port as well as a pub. The hypocrite was heard more than once to say that he had taken up his domicile there, 'to be near ta Wort,' which could mean either the Word of God, or the wort from which the ale was brewed.

When we read of children drinking ale we should remember that water was generally undrinkable, and milk-drinking was a certain way to contract tuberculosis. Browsters or brewers of ale were usually women who not only prepared it but sold it in their own homes. At one time the burgh of Anstruther in East Fife was so populous and prosperous that it had eighty women browsters and was in consequence the merriest town on the coast.

A tax on ale was imposed during the reign of James VI and by sheer coincidence, we assume, a most destructive storm swept over Scotland only a day or two later. Many meal and salt mills were destroyed. This was put down by many ministers, in their prayers, and sermons, to God's displeasure at the iniquitous levy on ale. With a threat from a displeased God hanging over his head the Chancellor of the Exchequer might be less disposed to slap increases on our simple pleasures.

Porter is a word used more south of the border than north, to describe a dark-brown bitter ale, much drunk of old by porters and labourers. In Edinburgh, in Walter Scott's time, an English lady asked if she could have a little porter, as she felt she needed one. The maid-servant was sent off in search of one and was away for such a long time that it was thought some mishap had occurred. However she at last entered the room dragging a protesting little man by the arm.

'I've been a' through the toon, ma'am, and this is the sma'est porter I could find.'

It was an old honoured custom to conclude a bargain with a dram, or to give a dram to a stranger entering a house for the first time. Sometimes foreigners from beyond the Cheviots started off on the wrong foot through ignorance of this ancient formality.

An affluent Englishman bought a farm in Stirlingshire and knowing very little about the running of it very wisely agreed to retain the manager. He arranged to see old MacPherson at a certain time and the Scot duly appeared and was led by the gentleman's wife into the parlour to wait for her husband. To pass the time she engaged him in conversation.

'I have been very puzzled, Mr. MacPherson. We have a lady pig who has just given birth and I notice she has got only twelve nipples, but she has a family of thirteen. How will the odd fellow manage when all the places have been taken up?

'Och, just like masel, Mistress,' said MacPherson. 'Sit down on his dowp until he's offered a drink.'

Alcoholics Anonymous claim to have the answers to some drink problems and have proved that bad cases may be cured, but our ancestors had an absolute cure that was drastic but was never known to fail for both drunkards and gluttons. They were arrested and commanded to eat or drink their fill and were then taken and drowned in a fresh water river. Something a little less excessive would have served, as this true tale shows.

In 1771, in the month of November, excessive rains had so swollen the Solway Moss, a huge peat bog, that the banks gave way, and the thousands of tons of black liquid poured across several neighbouring farms and swallowed them up. Many cattle and horses were drowned in the peaty liquid, but one cow was miraculously discovered still alive in her byre, though only her head showed above the black mush. She took such a horror at liquid that she could never again be persuaded to drink. There is a good idea here. On the other hand people must drink something even if it is only water. But there is danger too, in water-drinking, and avoidance of alcohol, or such drinks as tea, cocoa, and coffee, which all contain the drug caffein. A fearful tale is told of a French man-of-law, a fanatical hater of wine, tea, coffee and spirits, who drank almost to excess of Adam's wine. He had forty-five lawful children.

A Lauderdale farmer told me half-a-century ago of an unusual way in which he and his cronies had cured an inveterate drunkard. The River Leader is a good trouting stream, and it also has large numbers of eels. A common sport with the Oxton lads was to get a sack, a torch or two and a few pairs of blacksmith's tongs. After dark they 'burned' the river. The eels, attracted by the light, left the clay bank or perhaps were out foraging in the dark. They were gripped by the long tongs and popped into the sack.

When the sack was full of wriggling eels, the lads, one night, were at a loss what to do with them, as there was an ancient prejudice against eating them. For a prank, they went up the tributary burn to a lonely cottage where a boozy old bachelor lived alone. They climbed on to the roof and tipped the sack of eels down the lum. Old Davie was in bed. The strange noise in the lum made him jump barefooted on to the floor, where, slithering about among the eels, he was certain he had a bad attack of 'deeleeritness'. Vowing to heaven to sign the pledge, he dashed out of the house and sought refuge with a neighbour, while the lads collected the eels and released them in a nearby burn.

Burns wrote the initial lines in a poem, *Inspiring bold John Barleycorn*, but not all poets have got inspiration from strong drink. Lord Byron found that his best prelude to writing glorious verse was a large dose of Epsom salts. But one man's drink is another man's poison and it cannot be denied that Burns wrote many a brilliant piece of verse or prose when well on in the drink. Two letters of his may yet be read, in which he excels in description, and confesses his intoxication.

The first, to which I shall later refer, describing the caprice of Jenny Geddes, was addressed from Carlisle in June 1787, to Nicol. At the end of a comic letter, in Braid Scots, which Walter Scott said would break the teeth of most Scotsmen of 1830, Burns excuses the brevity of his note in this enlightening paragraph.

'I was gaun to write you a lang pystle, but, God forgie me, I gat mysel sae noutouriously bitchify'd the day afore kail-time that I can hardly stoiter but and ben.'

The second letter, eight years later, was when Burns was very much depressed for various reasons which are well known. As he wrote at the time to Mrs. Dunlop, 'I write to you from the regions of Hell, amid the horrors of the damned.' The letter is to Thomson, whom Burns supplied gratuitously with all his lyrics. It is sent from Ecclefechan, a village later made famous as the birthplace of Thomas Carlyle; by a strange coincidence, that rugged genius was conceived only a month after Burns' letter was written in 1795.

This passage shows the temper the bard was in.

'I came yesternight to this unfortunate wicked little village . . . snows of ten feet deep have impeded my progress . . . a scraper (fiddler) has been torturing catgut in sounds that would have insulted the dying agonies of a sow under the hands of a butcher . . . I have been in a dilemma, either to get drunk or hang myself . . . of the two evils I have chosen the least and am . . . very drunk at your service.'

To be snowed up in a remote village or county town did not appeal to Burns, nor to any man of intellectual bent. My grandfather told me that he was once snowed up in Duns for three days until the railway lines could be cleared of enormous drifts. I asked him how he spent the time in the White Swan Hotel, but all I got was a discouraging look. I believe there was at that time a total abstinence society in the town which indicates that there was a reason for it.

Ministers of the gospel have sometimes copied Noah and King David and got themselves immersed in the juice of the grape, or of the barleycorn. One such venerable preacher was fond of a dram and made no attempt to hide his liking. A deputation of pussyfoot parishioners, headed by a vinegar-faced elder, came up to the manse to remonstrate with their pastor. He patiently heard all that they had to say, then quietly turned to them and replied, 'Nae doot there's some grounds for your complaint against my personal habits but remember this. It's no the lamp ye follow. It's the licht. I'm only the unworthy bearer o the message. Go hame noo, and praise the Lord this nicht that ye dinna dae as I dae but that ye're to dae as I tell ye. Guid nicht.'

Unconscious irony on the speaker's part has often ruined a temperance meeting. The preacher, fond of alliteration, thundered, 'Drink is Damnation. It is the Curse of Clydebank. The Destruction of Dumbarton. The Ruination of Ru'glen. I say without hesitation, Down with Drink. The audience cheered and cried 'Hear, hear.' and 'Hallelujah.' He then ended his exhortation, 'Would that all the whisky, gin and vodka were poured into the Clyde. We should conclude by singing Hymn No. 594, *Shall we gather at the river?*'

'When the drink is in, the truth is out,' and the value of whisky as an ice-breaker has been long established. Sir Richard Steele of the *Spectator* on a visit to Auld Reekie wanted to get some inspiration for his essays on the humours of low life, so he invited all the beggars of the town to a supper. There were no empty seats. As the night wore on and the 'maut got aboon the meal', these wry and droll Scots gave Sir Richard a very fair return for his money in the shape of songs, stories and antics. Edinburgh at that time was famed for its oyster suppers far into the night, when even titled ladies, like the gay witty Duchess of Gordon, enjoyed, and added to, the very free exchange of pleasantries.

There is said to be some connection between religion and drink. Whisky has many aliases, one of them being 'The Auld Kirk.' Guinness has a papal disqualification which denies it to the Proddies. A 'Bloody Mary' sounds a bit political as well as religious. Perhaps if we round this chapter off with an ecumenical fable we shall avoid the charge of partisanship.

The parish priest was jogging along in his jaunting car when he overtook a parishioner to whom he gave a lift. Some way on, he obliged another pedestrian, a stranger who walked a bit unsteadily. After half-a-mile the stranger had to alight to stand behind a tree. The same kind of halt was made twice in the next mile, then the incontinent stranger thanked the father and departed.

'Now, Mick, who on earth would that be? I've not seen him in chapel.'

The staunch parishioner replied, 'Sure, father, saving your rivirence, judging by his observances he must be either an Episcopalian or one of those Urinitarians.'

The Northern nations, Germans, Dutch, Danes and English were reputed to be mighty drinkers. They carried the ceremony of drinking to a most elaborate extent. It took on the appearance of a religious rite.

One of the acknowledged essentials was the award of a trophy to the victor of a swilling contest, that is, he who was last to remain conscious, and could prove it by blowing a whistle. He kept the whistle until he was defeated.

In the reign of James VI a mighty Dane came over in the train of James' bride, Anne of Denmark. He had defeated all the topers of Sweden, Poland, Russia, Denmark and the German and Dutch states, and naturally his boasting irritated the Scottish drinkers. But the Dane over-reached himself. He challenged the Scots to acknowledge their inferiority and incurred the wrath of Sir Robert Lawrie of Maxwelltown, a Galloway gentleman. A contest was arranged and the Dane put his ebony whistle on the table.

For three days and nights the swilling went on, bottle for bottle, with no sign of either sliding under the table. At last the Dane became 'paralytic' and disappeared. Sir Robert seized the whistle and blew it to the glory of Scottish Bacchanalians.

The Scots, especially the Highlanders, had long been accustomed at funerals to drowning their sorrows in whisky.

A very amusing account was given by one of the mourners after he had regained consciousness following a Hielandman's burial.

'I was bidden to the laird's burial the Tuesday after he deid. The first service o drink was strang Ferintosh, famous peat-reek, and there was nae grief amang us. I found the bees bizzin in ma heid in a wee while. At last we lifted the laird and were tellt, 'whaever wished a bottle for their pooch could tak it.'

'We set aff, leaving Will drunk at the outset. Bob landed in a briar-bush. Whaup-nebbit Sam fell into a peat-bog. We cam to a dyke and laid the laird on top to rest a while till we feenished half o the bottles. Then we wrestled and played at quoits but I dinna ken whae won. When we got to the kirkyaird the sun was gaun doon. We put the coffin twice in the grave the wrong way roond. We got it to fit at last, and in wi the soil. We made a beast o the gravedigger. Sic a grand funeral I was never at afore.'

Bedfellows

'Misfortune makes strange bedfellows,' is an ancient saying in many languages. But this does not mean that it is only bad luck that forces people to go to bed together. Sometimes it is sexual attraction, sometimes for profit, for warmth, for curiosity, for fear, or a hundred other reasons.

In the great Roman epic, the *Aeneid*, the gods sent a sudden storm of rain and hail, which drove Aeneas and Dido into a cave. There they 'bedded', and as Cotton, the burlesque poet put it,

And in that very place and season
'Tis thought Aeneas did her reason.

That is, in modern phrase, he completely satisfied her. But, from this trivial and haphazard bedding, sprang an enormous personal and racial conflict and tragedy. So it shows the danger inherent in a careless relationship.

Luckily for humanity few beddings have such consequences, but are usually considered as short jolly romps, with less fear of consequences than formerly, when there was a good deal of point in the Wellerism, 'As one strawberry said to another, if we hadn't been in the same bed together we wouldn't have found ourselves in this jam.'

'To sleep with' is in legal circles usually taken to mean having sexual intercourse. This is presumption, as the following tale shows.

The accused was being cross-examined.

'Have you ever slept with a dark-haired woman?'

'Yes, m'lud.'
'Have you ever slept with a fair-haired woman?'
'Yes, m'lud.'
'Have you ever slept with a red-haired woman?'
'Not a blessed wink, your honour.'

Bernard Shaw, not very wittily, said that marriage was popular because it combined the maximum of temptation with the maximum of opportunity. But most people anticipating marriage realise that such a combination has a very short duration, traditionally a month of honeymooning. A much more down-to-earth, if rather cynical view was expressed over a century ago by a rustic rhymster known as Berwickshire Sandie.

Love wishes ay his darling to be seen
In public or in private neat and clean,
Thinks in her absence ilka hour a week,
Attends wi transport if she deign to speak;
But Marriage, ah, how rude and how ill-bred
Can kick his once-loved object out of bed,
Turn frae her charms that he did once adore
Then put his night-cap o'er his een and snore.

Despite the obvious dangers attached to the marriage state, many girls are keen to try it. A Scots lassie came rushing in one night and informed her parents that she had had a good offer and intended to accept. She hoped that they would agree. After hearing who the intended was, and half-inclined to see few faults in him, her father very cannily advised her to think it over for a week or two.
'It's a very serious thing to be married,' he remarked gravely.
She replied with some heat.
'It may be as you say, faither, but let me tell you this from my point o view. It's a muckle mair serious thing no to be mairret.'

Willing or not, girls expect to be wooed. The Laird of Cockpen, who set off to get a wife, thinking that his money and status would prove irresistible, was a blunderer. Had he gone down on his knees before Mistress Jean MacLeish, in her humble cottage at Newbattle, he would perhaps have won her hand. Had he attempted to force a kiss he might have won her heart. But she showed no sign at all of melting when he blurted out his proposal as if he were buying a hen in the market.

When the lady says no, she often means it, despite the old proverb that 'Nineteen nay-says is half a yea-say.' But some men won't take no for an answer and that usually leads to trouble, but not always. Sometimes an anxious lover resorts to tricks to win his lady, and on the other hand, ladies have been known to stuff cushions up front to force simple suitors into a fatuous union.
The Earl of Stair, a Campbell, one of the leading statesmen of the eighteenth century in Scotland, resorted to a dirty trick to secure in wedlock the young and beautiful Eleanor, widow of a weed, inappropriately named Viscount Primrose. Eleanor had been so cruelly treated by Primrose that, on his death, she saw an unexpected release from misery, and made a solemn vow never to re-marry.
But the Earl of Stair resorted to bribery and cunning in his anxiety to win her from her vow. He tipped her servants to admit him to her house, which overlooked the High Street of

Edinburgh. Once inside, and knowing that she was in the habit of retiring to a small bedroom to say her morning prayers, he hid himself in the bedroom until she entered. The window of the room opened on to the High Street, a busy thoroughfare. Stair then showed himself openly at the window, clad only in his shirt. Such was the scandal in the city, on the assumption that there had been misconduct, that Eleanor was forced to revoke her vow.

Apart from habitual drunkenness, he proved quite a pleasant bed-fellow, despite the nasty manner of his courting. Once only did the marriage show signs of breaking up. In a drunken fit he struck Eleanor on the face and drew blood, but when she showed him the bruise in the sober light of the morning, he foreswore drink for the rest of his life, such was his remorse.

Another lady of the same place and period was not so lucky as Eleanor. She was Rachel, Lady Grange. Like Lady Stair, she was an uncommonly beautiful woman. She had only one flaw. She had a hell of a temper, which she inherited from her father, the notorious Chiesly of Dalry, who had murdered the Lord President of the Court of Session by shooting him in the back as he entered his own home. Chiesly was not wholly sane, but being caught red-handed, he was summarily executed with the usual barbarism. Perhaps the terrible fate of her father affected his child.

Her courtship is quite the opposite of Lady Stair's. She had been seduced by Lord Grange, a leading Jacobite, and perhaps he expected to get away with his misdemeanour. But he had picked upon a virago. She turned up at one of his meetings with his friends and threatened to pistol him if he did not lead her to the altar, reminding him that she was her father's daughter, and was fully as determined to get revenge as he had been, regardless of consequences. He quickly acted on this gentle hint.

After love and peace and bed-sharing for twenty years, the fruits of the marriage being several fine children, Grange fell out with his wife. He offered her £100 per annum, quite a handsome sum at that time, if she would set up on her own and leave him. But she was not willing to suffer this indignity, and unfortunately for him, she knew many of the schemes in which he was involved, to upset the Government and raise a Jacobite rebellion.

Once at least she scolded him and assaulted him in public. He was, however, forced to take desperate measures when she threatened to betray his political plots to the authorities. He bribed a Highland chief to help him get rid of Rachel for good.

One moonlight night in 1730, a party of West Highland caterans violently abducted her from her lodging in the High Street. Nobody had the courage to go to her rescue. She was taken to Loch Hourn, the horrific Loch of Hell, on the Atlantic Coast, imprisoned for a time, and eventually carried to St. Kilda, the remotest Hebridean islet. All efforts, by law, to free her, were frustrated by her husband. She turned insane from anger and despair and ill-treatment and died miserably in a wretched black house in the wilderness. Her once loving bed-fellow expressed neither interest nor regret.

Sexual desire, as we showed in another chapter, is such a fugitive quality that it cannot be relied on. Young bridegrooms, who to all appearances could have satisfied such nymphomaniacs as the Queen of Aragon, have been found wanting, for no apparent reason. Witches were frequently blamed for rendering a young man impotent and, in such a case, burning was much too good for them. At the other extreme, were the very uxorious husbands against whom there were not so many complaints.

Two young wives were discussing their husbands.
'Has your man any hobbies, Jessie?'
'What kind o hobbies?'
'Is he interested in politics? Is he keen on UNO?'
'Aye, he never thinks aboot onything else.'

Procreation is the most valid excuse for intercourse, if it needs an excuse. Two very famous Scottish families have demonstrated this beyond doubt. The most ancient of these were the Haigs of Bemersyde from whom Douglas Haig, the British army commander, so much criticised, was descended. A prophecy, supposed to have been made by Thomas Learmonth, or Thomas the Rhymer, in the thirteenth century says,

Tide, tide, whate'er betide
Haig shall be Haig of Bemersyde.

But of course this could only be fulfilled if there was a male heir. In the eighteenth century the line of Haig of Bemersyde looked like coming to a terminus, for the laird's wife produced daughter after daughter in an unbroken line of a dozen. In desperation, for old age was creeping on, the Laird had another go; what technique or spells or aphrodisiacs he used is a secret, but in due course a son was born. Thirteen was lucky for once.

The Duke of Eglinton, holding one of the noblest Scottish titles, was married three times, but varying bed-fellows did not bring any changes of sex in the end-product. Each wife bore him daughters, the last of the trio yielding seven, who all grew up to form the handsomest procession in Scotland, when following the Duchess to church from the ducal home in Edinburgh. Finally, when all hope had seemed gone, and *anno domini*, with its concomitants of illness, ineptitude and impotence, drew nigh, a son and heir was born. He was the pride and joy of his twelve sisters.

Alas, thirteen in his case proved egregiously unlucky. The handsome Eglinton heir, tenth Duke, was shot in a poaching affray by Mungo Campbell, whose deserved fate will be fully described in all its gruesome details in another chapter.

While it was quite common for old men to become fathers, with women, only a tiny minority conceived after sixty. I remember the amusement I caused as a small boy when I asked my reverend granny, just over sixty, when she was going to have another baby. I then informed her that she still had plenty of time, for Sarah had a baby to Abraham when she was ninety-one, and Abraham was a hundred.

A son was conceived when all hope seemed lost, and was named Isaac from the Hebrew verb to laugh. In Genesis is the only joke in the Bible, and it is a sex joke, for Sarah laughed to scorn the news that she was pregnant, while Abraham fell all his length on the earth, convulsed with mirth. It seemed just as amusing in 1914 as in 1898 BC.

Burns did not usually miss the chance to put such tales into satiric verse, and he may have written a poem on this funny situation and, as was his habit, burned it if dis-satisfied with it. But he certainly left us, what he, with his tongue in cheek, called a 'bawdy, abominable and wicked song or ballad' on Abraham's grandson Jacob, which he mockingly recommended 'to be burnt at the Cross of Ayr.' The first verse read:

As honest Jacob on a night
Wi his beloved beauty
Was duly laid in wedlock's bed
And noddin' at his duty.

How lang, she says, ye fumblin wretch
Will ye be f. . . .g at it?
My eldest wean might die of age
Before that ye could get it.

It is a great loss that Rab did not do the same for Jacob's grandparents.

Scriptural ages seem exaggerated. Adam begat Seth when he was a mere lad of 130, and Methuselah begat Lamech when only 169, eight centuries before he expired. Still, it may have happened, for we have non-Biblical accounts of men in quite recent times who have become fathers when they could reasonably have been great-grandfathers.

William Horrocks, by his second marriage, had a son in 1744, when he was 87. The son lived to be a centenarian, so there can be little cause for assuming that the baby would be feeble. When he died in 1844 he could say that he had a brother born in the reign of Charles II.

In the *Edinburgh Courant* of 3 May 1766, is this notice.

'The wife of Sir William Nicholson of Glenbervy was delivered of a daughter. Sir William is 92 and has another daughter of 66. He married his present wife when he was 82 and now has six children of her.'

A more fabulous tale is of an aged man who was impertinently asked by an acquaintance if he was still co-habiting, to which he replied that he had not done so for three weeks.

'So the old enemy has at last caught up with you?'

'Naething o the kind. The fella that lifts me on is awa to Troon for his summer holidays.'

The wife was usually happy to have an adequate husband. A social club went off on a day-trip by bus, naturally calling at one or two pubs. The return journey was over a long stretch of moorland, which put a strain on the capacity of the male drinkers. At last the bus came to a rather sparse wayside hedge, but, bearing in mind the old proverb, 'Better a wee bush than nae bield', the driver drew up, and the husbands stood in line, using the hedge as an inadequate screen. They got back into the bus, much relieved.

One decent body remonstrated with her man.

'Whit a place to choose. The hedge was that thin we could see a' ye had.'

A long pause.

'But, o John, I was prood o oors.'

'Decent bodies' do not like to be affronted by immodest conduct. Rarely did a husband and wife in Scotland kiss in public. Think then how very upset a Glasgow woman was, when her plan to stimulate her husband proved too successful.

She had asked the doctor if she could have some hormone pills for her rather 'wabbit' man. He gave her a bottle of them and told her to pop a few into her husband's tea to disguise them. She went away beaming. Next week, so the story goes, she met the doctor, who asked her how the experiment had gone. 'Did it really work?' 'Work?' she exclaimed, 'I thocht it would stir Willie up a bit in bed. I didnae bargain for the strength o the mixture.'

'Was it successful then?'

'Successful? I dinna mind things in moderation, but no on tap o a table in Cranston's Tea-room on a Ferr Setturday.'

It must be galling to mismanage an amorous situation. Three young Scots were on a cycling tour in France. They were benighted on a lonely road in Normandy near a small farm. They asked in their best French if they could be accommodated.

'But yes, there is a double-bed in the attic, for two of you. For the other monsieur there is unhappily a poor choice. To sleep in the straw in the cowshed, or to share a bed with baby.'

The odd man out plumped for the cowshed, for he had visions of an incontinent infant. At breakfast the three cyclists met the family, which consisted of Pere, Mere and a pretty daughter of about twenty. They exchanged names. The two bedfellows, Charlie and

Robert, Pere was Andre, Mere was Cecile and the daughter was Bebe. The man who had slept with the cow was asked his name. 'O, I'm just the silly bugger who wouldn't sleep with Bebe.'

Some ladies like romantic lovers, others are more down to earth. A promiscuous dame, who liked 'a proper young man' had made a date with a handsome young fellow, unaware that he was a poet. She lived in good style with a maid-servant, in a high-class house. The prospective lover was welcomed and ushered by the maid into the bedroom. He was enraptured to find the lady in her bed in negligee. He fell on his knees by the bedside, and began a romantic address.

'How I have longed for this meeting. I cannot sleep at nights for thinking of you. I imagine us in the depths of the forest, the flowers perfuming the air, and the birds carolling their love-songs, and not a solitary intruder for miles . . .' His rhapsody was cut short.

'Deep in the forest. Alone. Do you want to make love to me, or cut my throat and rob me? Get to hell out of here at once, you imbecile.' She pulled the bell-rope and had the poor poet chucked out.

A lovely lady in bed is thought to be a very desirable piece of property, put at its lowest terms, but some few men in history have been caddish enough to disdain such a partner.

Louis VIII of France was seriously ill, and the doctors of that time, who had the quaintest ideas of cures, prescribed what they rarely do now, that a beautiful girl should be slipped into bed beside him; nature, they supposed, would do the rest. But they reckoned without their host. Louis was a devout Christian and refused to commit a deadly sin, lest it should debar his soul from Paradise. He breathed his last not many hours later.

I have long tried to find a moral in this improbable but true tale, but the only thing I can think of is rather immoral. It is the Dutch proverb, 'A bird in the hand is worth ten in the sky.'

Jane Welsh was one of the most attractive and vivacious little flirts of her time. She rather amazingly married Thomas Carlyle when she could have had her pick of the country. He was humorous too, but in a pedantic and wry manner.

On the wedding night Jane got into bed in a fever of pleasurable excitement, as was only to be expected from such a spirited girl. Thomas entered in his long nightgown with a lighted candle in his hand, like a criminal in his shroud, going penitentially to the drop. This was too much for Jane. She began to giggle and titter.

He was furious, growled out 'Hm, women.' and went out slamming the door and leaving Jane to lay the foundations of a life-long neurosis.

A titled Border lady, visiting her tenants, called at a but-and-ben where she found Bella sitting weeping by the fireside, while half-a-dozen bairns tumbled about the house.

'Dear me, Bella, what's wrong with you? This isn't like you.'

'I ken, but the day I'm fair bamboozled wonderin whit to dae wi a' thae bairns. And to croon a', I'm in the family way again.'

'Well, Bella, he's a good man and sober, and in a short time the bairns will be working and a comfort to you. So don't give up the struggle, Don't turn your face to the wall, Bella.'

'I've tried that as weel, your leddyship, but Geordie's just as gleg the tae way as the tither.'

Some ladies have got themselves an undeserved reputation for loose living. When many Polish troops were stationed in Scotland during Hitler's war, a few misunderstandings arose over the name Pole.

A respectable wife in Gorgie, Edinburgh, was shopping in the forenoon. 'Weel, I'll hae to be hurryin alang, May,' she confided to her neighbour, 'I'm expectin a couple o poles about eleven o'clock, then I'll be able to get my claes up.'

Only when the clothes-poles arrived was her character cleared.

Servant lassies were liable to be the prey of unscrupulous employers. A new kitchen lass from the Highlands felt pretty safe, for she had been hired into the home of a very religious family. Every wall in the house had a framed text on it.

On the first night in her new job she was undressing, to earn a well-deserved rest, when her eye lighted upon the text over the head of her bed. It read, 'Watch, therefore, for ye know not the day nor the hour when the master cometh.' She immediately dressed, packed her bag, and did a moonlight flitting.

Death is solemn enough to most mortals, but it was nothing but an irritation to a Dundee woman who had seen five husbands off to the 'Howff', the graveyard up on the hill. The minister called on her fifth bereavement, to console her, little expecting her remark. 'Meenister, it's awfu guid o ye to offer up prayers and sympathy for a puir auld weedow body. As shair as ye're staunin there, ne'er a decent wumman was plagued wi sic a set o deein men.'

When a young woman married an old man the proverbial saying was often quoted, 'There's mony a new pair o breeks will draw doon an auld doublet,' meaning that the demands of a new wife would soon kill him.

An old hypocrite said that he had married a lusty young wife 'to close his een,' but soon afterwards had to confess, 'By Goad, she's opened them.'

Many a woman has seen off a procession of bedfellows in her time. Such a one was Jean Lyon, an ancestress of the Queen Mother. She married first, Douglas of Lochleven; second, the Earl of Angus; last, Alexander Lindsay, a young noble of James VI's court. Her marriage to such a young man was a current joke. King James' letter on the subject, to Lindsay, is still to be seen.

'Dear Sandie,

We are going on here in the auld way and verrie merrie. I'll not forget you when I come home; you sall be a lord. But mynd Jean Lyon, for her auld tout will mak you a new horn.'

The rude pun at the end shows James in character. He had to change his tune when he went to reside in London, but, earlier in his reign, as King of the Scots, he had shown a very decided bias against English women, for in his Parliament was passed a law forbidding Scotsmen to marry Englishwomen without specific permission. He seems to have forgotten for the moment that his great-grandfather married a hot-blooded thirteen year-old English princess, Margaret Tudor.

Some Scots are as insensitive about their bed-fellows of many years close acquaintance, as the callous Lord Grange was towards Rachel Chiesly.

A golfer was putting-out on a green near a public highway at Gullane. As his friends waited anxiously to see whether he would get his birdie, he stopped in the act of addressing the ball and, laying his putter down, took off his cap and bowed his head. The three others looked puzzled at these gimmicks and asked him to explain himself. He pointed to a passing funeral cortège.

'Is that what all the fuss is about? You're not usually so respectful.'

'No, I admit I dinna aye observe the conventions, but, in this case I think it's only richt. Efter a', for the last thirty-two years she was a guid wife to me.'

Husbands have often gone to great lengths to please their bed-fellows, and vice versa. Sometimes the trouble taken has been worth while; now and then it was not appreciated. Here is the complaint of a loving spouse in Berwickshire at a time when tea was such a novelty that few were sure how to use it.

I coft my wife a pund o tea
And boilt it weel as weel can be
And choppt it up wi butter fine
And made it sweet as saps o wine
But still she gloomed as black's a craw
And wisna pleased wi't efter a'.

In mediaeval times in Britain many people wore no night-clothes. Many have reverted to this custom, sanctioned by Adam and Eve. It is really nobody's business what one wears in bed, but everybody makes it their business when ladies appear in public in their night-attire, as they frequently did in the days of the Merry Monarch. One of the delights of going to bed lies in casting off the day-time wear, boots, socks and all.

A young Lothian lass who had had to make love under the hedgerows was at last married to her young man. She was tongue-tied by nature and upbringing, so she expressed the supreme delight of her life in these few telling words. 'Ye've nae idea hoo nice it is in bed wi your boots aff.'

One of the Covenanting ministers was named David Williamson. Being pursued by the dragoons he took shelter in the house of Cherrytrees, or Kirroughtrees. To hide him from the search he was hastily put to bed with the daughter of the house, still wearing his riding-boots. This proximity, despite the danger he was in, led to the daughter becoming pregnant. She became the first of Williamson's seven wives.

Burns wrote his own version of this incident and entitled it *Dainty Davie*. Having his boots on did not detract from his pleasure and added to the ludicrous side of the true tale.

Twin beds are a fairly modern device. When they first came into vogue an old family friend, a bit of a wag, visited the newly-married couple. On being shown the bedroom he was told that the object of the twin beds was to promote hygiene.

After he had gone the couple noticed that a little mantelpiece clock had disappeared, so after a long search, they wrote and asked him if he had inadvertently put it in his baggage.

The reply was a telegram, 'Hygiene be damned. Look in other bed.'

Ill-matched partners are common and it is by no means unusual for old men to marry young girls and for striplings to be united in holy deadlock to well-heeled old crones. But suits of patrimony are not often brought by mature women against schoolboys. This happened in Dumfries, however, last century, when a boy, barely fifteen, was accused by a woman in her thirties. The boy's mother was shocked and indignant and said it was not possible, but the homely old magistrate clinched the case with a parable.

'Wumman, there's mony a wee laddie can put his heid in at the door and spit in the fireplace.'

Earth-born Companions

The chapter title is from Burns' universally known *Address to a Mouse*, where the ploughman apologises to a field mouse and sympathises with his 'earth-born companion' and fellow-mortal.' Humane people have made common cause with animals ever since the world of man began; and although the theory of man's close relationship with the 'higher' animals was first scientifically advanced by Charles Darwin, it had been in many minds for ages before.

Lord Monboddo, an eccentric law-lord of Burns' time, was ridiculed for his writings suggesting that humans originally had tails, but had lost them because of their habit of sitting on them. He is said to have peeped through the keyhole when midwives were bringing babies into the world. He suspected them of conspiring to cut off all babies' natal tails. But long before Monboddo, philosophers pointed out that animals are not just turned out like robots, but each one has as much individuality as humans, and that, when necessary, they can count and reason.

William Cowper, Burns' English contemporary poet, had three pet brown hares. He closely studied their behaviour and verified that each had its own likes and dislikes. They had distinct personalities and were as capable (apart from the power of speech) of expressing love, hate, fear, curiosity, suspicion and so on.

Burns too knew the personalities of his animal friends; Jenny Geddes his mare, his dogs, pet ewes, and even the twenty different characters of the wild birds that come into his songs. One of the most humorous pieces in Scots literature is Burns' letter from Carlisle on Jenny Geddes (pronounced Gedds in Ayrshire). We quote only a part, on the mincing behaviour of Jenny, not at all like her bold name-sake who threw her creepie-stool at the preacher's head.

'She's as poor's a sangmaker and as hard's a kirk, and tipper-taipers when she taks the gate, first like a lady's gentlewoman in a minuet or a hen on a het griddle.'

Many other horses have become famous for various reasons, and as Jonathan Swift chose horses as the superior animal, fit to rule man, he would have approved of placing them first on our list.

Black Agnes, the palfrey of Mary, Queen of Scots, was named after Countess Agnes of Dunbar who defied the English invaders in defence of her castle. Black Agnes carried Queen Mary on many of her dangerous exploits. Her other pony was Rosabelle, probably named in memory of the unfortunate member of the Sinclair noble family drowned when sailing to see her lover.

In the courtyard of the City Chambers in Edinburgh is the statue of Bucephalus, the ox-headed horse of Alexander the Great which was trained to kneel when his master mounted him. Not far off in Parliament Square is the horse of Charles II cast in lead, and thereby being so heavy that in recent times his legs have had to be strengthened to prevent his kneeling permanently. In 1767 the Edinburgh magistrates had the bad taste to paint both horse and rider snow-white. A wit of the time printed a satire on the blunder, of which the last four lines are the most biting, for Charles II was noted for his very dark countenance.

The milk-white steed is well enough;
But why thus daub the man all over,
And to the swarthy Stuart give
The cream complexion of Hanover?

Wellington's charger may also be seen in a city which seems to specialise in equestrian statuary. At one time it was a strict convention that only royalty should be sculpted mounted, but that distinction has long been ignored. Wellington, who had defeated an emperor, was never questioned on this point of etiquette. His horse was named Copenhagen after the famous naval victory there, which gained Britain the hatred of the Danes. At Waterloo the Iron Duke rode Copenhagen from four in the morning until midnight, during which time 60,000 men were killed or severely wounded, but Copenhagen and his rider were unscathed. Copenhagen went blind from old age and was buried with full military honours.

Some humbler horses have achieved immortality. When the notorious Bell-Rock or Inchcape Rock (which had caused many shipwrecks off the East Coast of Scotland) was provided with a lighthouse, the stones for the base had to be cut and fitted beforehand in Arbroath. The Inch Cape Rock was tidal and work had to be done between high tides. A solitary horse, belonging to an Arbroath labourer, James Craw, did all the stone-carrying, over the years occupied in the building. When the work was completed the Lighthouse Commissioners looked upon the horse as an OAP and put him to graze on Inchkeith, an island which they owned in the Firth of Forth. There Brassey enjoyed the rich pasturage and drank from the clear spring until he died of old age in 1813. His bones were collected by an admirer and wired together. The skeleton was presented to the museum of the College of Surgeons in Edinburgh. A few years later the museum was broken up and the faithful horse's skeleton went north, perhaps to the land of his labours.

As may be realised, the chief diseases of horses were hoof and wind ailments. Camp Meg was a strange character who lived a solitary gipsy life on Camp Hill above Dalkeith. She was a horse-doctor of quite considerable skills, and her first job, when an ailing horse was brought to her, was to put a broad canvas under the poor beast's belly and with help from several hands, hoist it off the ground with a pulley attached to a stout limb of an oak-tree. This was done to take the weight off the beast's hoofs and allow Meg to attend to them. She was usually successful in her treatment.

It is imagined that the historical 'King' Arthur, who was really only a war-leader, led a cohort of horsemen, about six hundred strong, drilled in Roman manoeuvres. This very mobile force covered great distances in Arthur's wars with his enemies. But who these enemies were, where he fought them, or any details of weapons or armour, are always matters for guesswork. We know for sure that the British warriors of that age set off from Edinburgh in a band of three hundred or more on horseback and were practically wiped out in an attack on the Angles at Catraeth, supposed to be Catterick.

There have been killers among horses, for the stallion is by nature ferocious, and uses his teeth and hoofs with murderous results on his own kind as well as on other animals. A story, perfectly true, is told of a Peebles doctor who was offered a handsome black 'baggit' horse, or stallion, at the market at a very low price. Only after he had hesitantly bought it was he told over the grape-vine that his new mount had already two homicides to his credit. However, although very wary, he began to ride it on his rounds. One Sabbath as he rode up a hill on the road by the Kirk, to an urgent call, the horse stopped in his tracks and refused to budge. The kirkgoers laughed to see the doctor standing like a statue on the road. But despite his embarrassment he made no attempt to touch the beast. He had been waiting for months for something unusual to happen and he realised that the moment had arrived. When the kirk 'skailed' over an hour later the stallion of its own accord moved on as if nothing had happened, and carried the doctor to his patient. He had this fine beast for very many years and it never repeated the performance nor showed any sign of aggression. It turned out, that when it was a foal, some stable-boy had ill-used it and caused it to seek revenge on anyone showing signs of attacking it. Had the doctor used spur or whip when it stopped, he would undoubtedly have been beaten to death by its fore hoofs.

In a collection of comic tales by Dugald Graham entitled *The Sayings of Wise Willie and Witty Eppie*, which pokes unwarranted fun at the people of Old Buckhaven, in Fife, there is a story of an ass which began its hideous braying on the moor behind the village. A crowd of the simple inhabitants went up from the shore. They had never before seen a donkey, and on account of its large ears, thought it must be a hare of enormous size. To them hares were associated with Satan and on the very mention of a hare they would refuse to put to sea that day.

'It maun be Beelzebub himsel, the faither o a' hares and sic like witchin craturs.' As they said this the donkey laid back its ears and brayed with all its might. The entire population fled in a panic, helter-skelter, locked themselves each in their own houses and clutched any iron articles that came to hand, to protect them from the Evil One.

Elephants are the horses of the less temperate zones. As an Indian elephant has a life-span approximating to a man's, putting out money for a young elephant is a popular form of family insurance. The chief expense is in the feeding, especially, of course, if they happen to have been born white and must, by ancient law, be fed upon the dearest commodities. The only analogy to these expensive beasts is with an ancient Rolls or Daimler in town use, consuming petrol at seven or eight miles per gallon. But the strict economy of elephant keeping (which I am not likely to put into practice) has a parallel in canny Fife. In that seat of Scottish kings, the royal burgh of Falkland, there was a large colony of 'scrappies' or travelling tinkers, who went around the country with light carts drawn by ponies. They were never known to purchase fodder for their beasts. They helped themselves to fodder from farmers' fields in passing, or grazed their ponies by the wayside. On that system an elephant's keep is a mere trifle.

The late Sir Henry Wood, the famous conductor, attended a middling performance where, at the end of the show, a troup of performing elephants filled the stage. As they shuffled off to applause two of the troup halted momentarily to deposit their excrement on the stage. As is well-known, jumbo-jets are the size of quartern-loaves. I have cause to know of this, for long ago, as I cycled carefree along the Dunbar highway, not aware that a troup of circus animals had recently passed, I was thrown over the handlebars as my front wheel struck one of these obstacles. At any rate the concert audience gave renewed cheers at the elephants' encore. But these were nothing to the cheers and laughter when Sir Henry gave his vote of thanks. He referred very briefly to the musical part but his final remarks were more pointed. 'Elephants, ladies and gentlemen, may have something to learn as performers, but O, what critics!'

Like humans, and all our animal companions, dogs react strongly to treatment. A dog story most universally known is that of Greyfriars Bobby. Unfortunately, as I became aware when I started research into the actual circumstances, the story that the dog was owned by an old Pentland shepherd is quite untrue. Bobby's owner, who was so kind to the wee Skye terrier that after his death Bobby frequented his grave for fourteen years, was a police constable named John Gray.

John Gray lived in the Tron parish of Edinburgh, a squalid area named Hall's Court, with his wife and son, who was also called John. Dying of consumption, aged 45 years, whilst on sick-pay from the police, he was buried in the High Yard of Greyfriars. Only residency in the St. Giles district qualified any person for burial in that place.

I have a copy of John Gray's Death Certificate with all the details and, as far as I know, I am the first and only person to have applied for it since 1858, though it was available to anyone.

Bobby, having accompanied his master as a police watch-dog, on his beat, which included the Greyfriars Churchyard, looked upon that area as his own territory and, knowing his master to be there, refused to leave him. It is a moving story, the more so since it is now properly authenticated.

Dogs do not usually adopt half-measures. If they take a liking or a disliking, the object soon gets to know. A certain devil-may-care fellow had annoyed a dog of a fierce nature, called a 'rough' dog in that olden time. It went for him so he killed it with a halbert, a form of pole-axe. He was taken before a magistrate and charged with malicious killing.

'Why did you not strike it with the shaft of the halbert?' asked the magistrate. 'There was no need to use the point.'

'So I would have done if the dog had attacked me with his tail, but he wouldn't oblige.'

Naming dogs is not difficult, for, unlike children, the dogs do not object and wish they had been christened differently. In Scotland many shepherds name their dogs after rivers, such as Tweed or Jed. There are also traditional names like Luath, one of the 'Twa Dogs' in Burns' poem. Luath was a dog in Ossian's poetry. Bran was the name of Fingal's dog in the same poem. Diamond was Sir Isaac Newton's favourite which, being locked in a room, upset a lighted candle. Newton's notes, of years of work, were burnt, but all he said to Diamond was, 'Thou little knowest the mischief thou hast done.'

Toby is Punch's dog. Barry was the Great St. Bernard mastiff who saved forty lives from snowdrifts. His stuffed skin is in the museum in Berne.

Humorous names have been given also. A former Chancellor of the Exchequer's dog was 'Budget', not funny for tax-payers, however. In the old Pantomime, the comedian's dog was called 'Sausage', because, as he punned, 'He never saw-such a dog', at which the many-headed gods screamed with mirth.

A dog's world is different from ours, as an old maiden lady found out to her great annoyance. She had a pedigree Pekinese bitch named Tu-Tu, her pride and joy. A friend suggested that she could earn an honest guinea or two by breeding puppies.

'How would I go about that?'

'You have to take Tu-Tu to someone who owns a pedigree Peke dog and have her served.'

'Served? What on earth is that?'

'She has to have sex with the male dog.'

Having got over her initial shock she took Tu-Tu along and called back the following day. The owner of the male dog said the operation has been successful. He added:

'And the fee, madam, is ten guineas.'

She held out her hand.

'You misunderstand me, madam. You have to pay *me* ten guineas.'

'Good heavens. Don't tell me that Tu-Tu has to pay for it. I never heard such a preposterous thing in my life!'

Puppies are a delight, but like all young things they are incontinent. A young boy with a covered baker's basket got into a suburban train and put the basket on the overhead rack. At the next station a minister got in and sat under the basket. Shortly afterwards he wiped his hand across his coat shoulder and said to the boy, 'My boy, do you know that your pies are leaking?' The answer did not make him any happier. 'It's no pies, mister. It's the pup.'

The best puppy in the litter was often hard to choose, though the bitch always knew which one it was. Dog-fanciers in olden times had one or two tricks to find out what was in the bitch's mind. A favourite scheme was to burn straw in the shed where the kennel was. The mother, thinking the place was on fire, picked up the puppies one by one and carried them to safety. She always picked first the apple of her eye, and he invariably proved an excellent dog when he grew up.

It is said that dogs were domesticated from wolves in primordial times. However this may be, wolves have been very much maligned for ages. A prominent Scottish naturalist, David Stephen, defends their character and has even re-written the story *Little Red Riding-hood* to put the wolf in a better role. But the saying 'Give a dog a bad name, then hang him,' still holds good.

Scotland and England used to abound in wolves and there are several contradictory accounts of the 'killing of the last wolf in Scotland.' The truth is that wolves lingered on in the wilder districts, though the last wolf in the North-East was killed in Kirkmichael, Banffshire in 1644, and the last in Perthshire by Cameron of Lochiel at Killiecrankie in 1680. As late as 1743, according to James Ritchie's *Animal Life in Scotland*, a persistent tradition records that a Highland hunter Macqueen, slew a wolf that had killed two children on the hills near the River Findhorn.

It was the burning of the forests that got rid of the wolves, as well as caterans and robbers and outlaws. Incidentally it was not the building of the *Great Michael* warship that alone spoiled the woods of Fife. They were certainly reduced by the felling of great oaks, but it was to destroy the harbourage of robbers and wolves that most forests were felled and burned. Iron-smelting also made great destruction of natural forest.

There is a very strong tradition that a wolf did the killing of the young wife of the tenant of Gamielshiel in the upland valley of Faseny Water in the Lammermoor Hills. The record says that she was 'worried', that is, bitten to death. Her husband never recovered from this tragedy.

January was named wolf-month by the Anglo-Saxons because folk were more liable to be attacked then by hungry packs. So despite undoubted exaggeration there is some truth in tales of people eaten by wolves.

Foxes or tods still abound and come right into the suburbs of Glasgow and Edinburgh. I have repeatedly seen dog-foxes not far from a bus-stop. The fox, a dedicated wanton killer, was long believed in Scotland to be a grimly humorous, if coarse, fellow. A rude old Scots proverb says, 'That will be a guid fire when it burns,' quo the tod as he keiched on the ice, 'The reek o't's risin a'ready.'

As a T.V. star Miss Piggy is much more popular than Miss Universe. That is not to be wondered at, for pigs have always had a fascination for some folk. In Ireland he was always referred to as 'the gentleman who pays the rent.' The Irish nightingale is another title for pigs, as they can 'smell the wind' and squeal in chorus when a gale is approaching. The Irish goddess of poetry is pig-headed on this account, as the wind is said to inspire poets, a true saying however you look at it.

Pigs were originally kept as scavengers. The Old Town of Edinburgh was one of their stamping-grounds. They roamed the High Street and other garbage dumps, providing sport for young hoydens who rode them barebacked to the horror of the strait-laced citizens.

Lord Gardenstone, an eccentric law-lord, had a passion for pigs. He adopted a piglet which followed him around like a dog, through the streets to the Court of Session, and around his own house. It even slept on his bed. As his lordship, like most of his circle, was in the regular habit of drinking all night (and yet being clear-headed on the bench next morning), perhaps the pig had the bed to himself quite often. When it grew to full swinehood it was too large to be accommodated with his lordship in the bed so it was allowed to sleep on the floor on top of Gardenstone's clothes. We hope the creases were properly folded.

Sows, when served by the boar, were said to be 'brannt', a brann or brawn being a male pig. An improbable tale concerns a sow that was to be driven to the boar in a trailer. The first attempt at branning was a fiasco. Like pandas, pigs have to be in the mood. A second time the trailer was pulled in to the yard and with some trouble the sow was persuaded to climb into it. Once again the mating was a misfire.

In desperation the farmer drew out the trailer a week later and, to keep up his strength for the encounter, went in for breakfast. To his surprise when he came out the sow was lying in the trailer wearing on its face the nearest look a sow can screw up to show pleasant anticipation.

A gentleman cattle-breeder was engaged in cross-breeding certain strains to build up a new herd. On the night when he had arranged with his stockman to introduce his prize bull to two pedigree heifers, a brown and a white, he was also giving a dinner-party to his county friends. Nevertheless he told Bob the stockman to bring him the details of the bulling, even in the midst of the dinner.

At the second course the door bursts open and Bob announces:

'Maister John, the black bull has f . . .it the white coo!'

The ladies and gentlemen pretend to discuss the sirloin.

'Bob,' said the host, 'I appreciate your keenness. But it would perhaps be better to announce the event by saying "The black bull has surprised the white cow".'

I'll mind on,' said Bob.

An hour later, coffee being served, Bob bursts in again and exclaims:

'Maister John, the black bull has surprised the broon coo!'

'Very good, Bob, very good.'

'Aye,' cried Bob, 'It's f . . .it the white yin again!'

Apes are uncomfortably close to humans in the biological tree, and don't they know it. The chimpanzees not only smoke cigarettes. They inhale and blow the smoke through their nostrils. Often they chew them, rolling the quid about like old sailors. It has long been said that they could talk if they cared to, but they know that by doing so they would be forced to work.

A smart young city man, travelling through the Highlands, amused himself by asking silly questions of the cottagers and laughing openly at their puzzled or astonished looks. But he got the worst of it, once. A dear old granny sat knitting at her 'black house' door.

'Good morning, my dear,' says the smart Alec, 'Can you help me please?'

'Maybe I could be doing that, young man.'

'Well, have you seen a lorry-load of monkeys going by, on their way up the glen?'

'No, my dear, I don't think I have. Did you fall off?'

Perhaps the best short story of Scottish diablerie is Walter Scott's *Wandering Willie's Tale*, which introduced 'Major Weir', the tame monkey of *Redgauntlet*, in real life Grierson of Lag, one of the bitterest persecutors of the Covenanters. This ape was named after the Edinburgh wizard burnt at the stake for his lewd practices with witches in Satanical meetings. It was dressed in a full costume, tail-coat, tricorn hat, walking cane and breeches with a hole to accommodate his tail.

James IV had expensive hobbies which he indulged at other folk's expense. His favourite was witch-hunting. High on his list was head-hunting. So much, in pieces of silver, being paid for each head of outlawed Highlanders, chiefly Macgregors. A less inhumane hobby was collecting foreign animals for the 'royal menagerie' in London. His assortment, maintained at high cost, included flying squirrels from Virginia, live sables from Russia, white falcons from Iceland. Accounts may yet be seen for the keep of the elephant, a gift of the Spanish King. 'Feeding for the elephant at 10*s*. per diem is per annum £180.'

But the elephant's drink bill was much more, for he had to have six bottles of wine each day. In addition there were five camels, also from Spain's monarch, but they grazed cheaply in the park.

A few years later a great attraction came to Edinburgh. The advertisement reads quaintly.

Ane heigh great beast, callit ane dummodary, whilk being keepit clos in the Canongate, none had a sight of it, without three pence per person. It was very big and of great height, Cloven futted like unto a kow and on the back ane saitt as it were a sadill to sit on. Thair was brocht with it ane lytill baboun, faced like unto an aip.

Three pence Scots was equal to a farthing, for admission.

We come now to some curious tales about 'rats and mice and such small deer.'

Rats are said to have a sixth sense which warns them when a building is about to fall. They anticipate the disaster by migrating *en masse* to some securer building. I find it hard to believe this story, for I have seen hundreds of them killed at the demolition of a corn-stack which they had not the sense to leave in time. On the other hand, when I was a youth, I shared a terrifying experience with a chum when we were returning across the fields near Temple in Midlothian on a winter moonlight night. We were about to leave a clump of trees when we heard a weird noise like a chorus of rusty bed-springs. Coming across the stubble field, towards the small wood where we were standing, was a large gray shapeless mass like a moving puddle of mud. It was an army of rats, hundreds strong, tumbling and leaping in confusion. We froze against a tree-trunk. Luckily the schiltron of rodents passed us by on their way to some stacks of oats at the end of the field. No doubt the tawny owls would be floating down to pick up the stragglers. We did not linger to find out.

Charms were used to get rid of rats and mice, though a 'harmless necessary cat' was more effective. One such rhyming charm was pinned up where the vermin, unless illiterate, could read it.

Rattan and moose
Lea this puir woman's hoose;
Gang awa ower to the mill
And there ane and a' ye'll get your fill.

A gruesome tale concerns a mouse with a rich appetite.

During the 'Killing Times' a gentleman sought by the dragoons took refuge in his family mausoleum, where he had to endure the sight and musty odour of the bones of his forebears peeping above the soil. One night a moonbeam from the tiny iron-barred window moved across the earthen floor. To his disquiet it eventually lit up the bleaching skull of a relative protruding from the mould. As he watched, fascinated, the empty eye-holes began to wink at him. His hair stood on end. He doubted his sanity, after weeks in this abode of death. The skull continued to wink grotesquely at intervals. He could stand it no longer. He walked forward and kicked the loathsome object, and to his infinite relief a mouse ran out between the fallen jawbones. It had been banquetting on the brains.

I had a similar experience though not of such a morbid kind. I was half-snoozing in an arm-chair by a glowing log-fire in my old cottage on Heriot Water one November night. For refreshment I had a paper-bag of liquorice all-sorts on a small table beside the fire. There was a slight movement on the table and I could scarcely credit my eyes when a brown, pink and black all-sort popped out of the open top of the bag and rolled on to the table, as if to say, 'Come, eat me.' A fieldmouse had crept inside and this was going to provide his supper. As a reward for his enterprise I threw it down to him in a shady corner after he had fled from the bag.

As a comic relief let me tell a merrier tale out of school, about a strange mythological animal. The teacher in a Leith school of my acquaintance asked her class to give definitions of five words each day during the English lesson (to most of the bairns a foreign language). For the first lesson she took the initial 'a'. The words she chose were ancient, armadillo, aspidistra, attic, average.

They managed most of them but wee Willie wasn't very happy. However he struggled on and, with his neighbour's help, got all but the last.

'Come on, Willie,' encouraged the teacher, 'What's an average?'

'Please, Miss, I think it's an animal.'

'You're thinking of an armadillo, or an antelope, aren't you?'

'No, miss. An average is an animal, I'm sure, for I heard my auntie tell my mum that she gets a ride on an average four times a week.'

Extraordinary events concerning smaller animals have happened in Scotland. On several occasions is has rained showers of creatures from the skies. Tadpoles and small frogs, apparently lifted out of the ponds by the suction of whirlwinds, have been carried for miles and then dropped on roads and fields. I have twice seen whirlwinds lifting small branches and wisps of hay to a great height on hot summer's days, so I suppose light animals could also be swept up.

Showers of small herring, in hundreds, are recorded from Islay and Dingwall; and during a severe southerly gale many herrings were carried from the Firth of Forth for eight or ten miles and dropped around Loch Leven. When a herring-shower landed on Wick early last century nobody would lift this fishy manna which lay invitingly all round the town. It was common belief that Satan was up to one of his old tricks to tempt the faithful. But the Wick folk did not credit Auld Nick with much intelligence, for sending herrings to Wick was like sending coals to Newcastle. Now, a few cases of Highland Park whisky drifting down by Satanic parachute from Orkney, might well have lured even the stern elders into sin.

When in Caithness we should tell of a brave attempt by Sir John Sinclair, the statistician, to bring the amenities of Southern England two centuries ago to his almost treeless native country. In London he advertised that he would pay a shilling each for nightingales' eggs. Soon he had all the nest-harriers from Oxford to Gloucester at their nasty work.

When Sir John got the eggs safely to Wick by special express carrier, he engaged men and boys to insinuate them into the nest of unsuspecting foster-parents, robins, hedge-sparrows and other warblers. The young nightingales were duly fledged and migrated south in autumn. They were expected to return to their birth-places the following spring, but never returned, being seduced on the way by the warm insect-filled thickets of the southern English valleys.

It would be as easy to memorise a whole chapter on *Nightingales in Caithness* as Dr. Johnson found with Chapter LXXII, *Concerning Snakes in Iceland*. 'There are no nightingales to be met with throughout the whole country.' In any case there were, and are, many Scots who do not rate the jug-jug of the nightingale very highly. One patriot said, 'I wad raither hear the wheeple o a whaup than the best nightingales that ever sang.'

Somewhat similar tales of trickery concern life on the Bass Rock, off the East Lothian coast. It houses an immense colony of solan geese on the cliff-faces; on the turf of the less steep slopes on the southern side was a limited flock of sheep.

Bellenden, a historian with a good imagination, recorded that the keepers of the castle on the Bass kept themselves in firewood throughout the year by gathering in spring the nests of solan geese which, he said, were built of small twigs and branches brought by the geese from the East Lothian woods and shores. Now the remarkable fact about solan geese is that, apart from dried seaweed or the stems of flowering plants, they have never built nests of sticks and branches. Their nests, if they make any at all, are of their own dung, but more often on a bare rock shelf. One egg only is laid, its pear-shape preventing it from rolling into the sea. The birds are as tame as penguins and this led to their immense slaughter in past centuries. They were sold in the Edinburgh poultry market described as 'excellent provocatives'; of what, it is easy to guess—booze and wenching.

A small flock of thirty sheep was fed on the Bass within a walled rich pasturage. As this included lambs it is easy to calculate that, to keep the stock up, only ten or twelve of these animals could go to the meat market each summer. Yet such was the honesty of the Edinburgh butcher who dealt in this delicacy that he boasted of selling a hundred Bass lambs each year.

Brown hares are timid beasts and only 'get their dander up' in the breeding season when it is not uncommon to see half-a-dozen bucks chasing an attractive doe across roads and fields, mad with spring-fever. They are not as prolific as mice or rabbits, but, with five pairs of leverets at intervals through the summer, they can multiply amazingly if left undisturbed. In the seventeenth century, owing to the civil wars and the terrible plagues of 1645 and 1650, much of the Lothians, Borders and Fife was depopulated. The hares bred unhindered in the neglected fields, and the climax came one autumn day in 1654 when the town of Edinburgh was invaded by a vast army of hares from the east country, which filled the Canongate, High Street and all the adjacent wynds and closes to the superstitious horror of the godly, who thought them to be the legionaries of Beelzebub.

I should include a short paragraph on barnyard fowls. There are few better passages in descriptive literature than Chaucer's vivid lines on the barnyard cock and his harem stepping forth on a summer morning.

The cock is an emblem of virility, though his morality is non-existent.

The morality of some of the German courts, especially in the provinces of Hanover, Saxe-Coburg and Hesse was likened to that of a barnyard, though few Royal menages were much better.

But we must be fair to the barnyard. There is a well-known case of a cock that was far from promiscuous. This was in the village of Auchencraw, or Edincraw, in Berwickshire where this celibate cock had a rhyme composed and recited on his strange behaviour.

Fy, shoo! Fy, shoo!
Robbie Bogue's cock.
Feint a hen he'll treid ava,
The laziest cock in Edincraw.

An impatient farmer knocked at the door of a neighbouring farmhouse. The daughter of the house answered.

'Is your faither in?'

'Na, he's at Lanark merket. If it's the services o the reid Ayrshire bull ye want, the chairge is £50.'

'Na, it's no that . . .'

'Weel, the Gallowa' beltie bull is £40.'

'Na, that's no what . . .'

'The wee Hieland bull is only £30.'

The visitor rudely interrupted her.

'That's no what I've come aboot at a'. Your brother Airchie has bairned ma dochter Meg and I want to ken what your faither proposes to dae aboot it.'

'Oh weel, ye'll hae to see him yoursel. I dinna ken what he chairges for Airchie.'

I feel I should end this long chapter on a religious note, and as the early Christian sign, scrawled on all the walls, was a fish, this will be a fishy story.

St. Mungo, or Kentigern, was once able to perform a miracle to help a lady out of a scrape. The queen of the Strathclyde Britons had fallen in love with a handsome soldier of the court and had given him a ring which had been her husband's betrothal gift. The king was informed of this affair and finding his wife's lover asleep, he slipped the ring off his finger and threw it into the Clyde. He then demanded that the queen return his ring.

In a panic, for kings at that time had nasty habits, she went to Kentigern and asked for his saintly help. He knew what canoodling had been going on, but saying nothing, he got out his fishing-rod and sat hopefully by the banks of the Clyde. Using a special fly, or perhaps salmon roe, he caught the very salmon that had swallowed the queen's ring. He gave it back to her and told her to be a good girl in future.

This is a fishy tale probably known to every Glaswegian, so I claim no credit for anything except the remarks I now make. There is an old proverb that only those who have been in the oven themselves know what it is like to be in it. Kentigern, having been born on the wrong side of the blanket, was not too severe on the sins of the flesh. I only hope that this tale of old Glasgow will not send too many anglers down to catch sparklers. Salmon nowadays come up the Clyde in tins.

Tit-for-Tat

'Presence of mind is a wonderful thing when one is in a difficult situation,' observed the English philosopher, 'What could be more useful?' 'Absence of body,' cracked the Irishman with great presence of mind.

As the Scots proverb says, 'Want o wit is waur than want o gear.' Repartee, riposte, or apt retort requires ready wit and that is a quality that cannot be purchased or learned. It is innate.

Where wit is wanting there are hundreds of ready-made retorts available to the person with a good memory. Proverbs used to be freely exchanged in battles of words. A good example comes to mind.

The Duke of Lauderdale was giving a dinner-party in London when one of his guests very impudently remarked 'Fools mak feasts and wise men eat them,' to which the Duke, despite his anxiety to appear polite, could not refrain from replying, 'Aye, and wise men mak proverbs and fools repeat them.'

But proverbs have fallen out of favour and have been replaced but such stock answers as, 'We had one but it died,' when an unusual name is mentioned, or mere rude replies like 'Sod off!' or 'You're so sharp you'll cut yourself' or countless others which constitute most of the humour on T.V.—none of these make up for ready wit.

Women like to have the last word, but few have had it with such tremendous effect as the lady in this true tale. When the Bible was being translated into the vernacular tongues a German lady got a glorious chance to stand up for Women's Lib. Her husband had bossed her for years and to some extent had also neglected her, in favour of his translation of the Old Testament. After his life's work went to the press, his wife was allowed to visit the printer's workshop whenever she liked to see how the work went on.

She went secretly one night and abstracted the type for a line in Genesis, third chapter, which was being set up. The verse to which she took exception was the sixteenth in which God is alleged to have made man the everlasting overlord of women. The German word for lord is Herr, but Narr, meaning a fool, a buffoon, or a clown, fitted beautifully into the black-letter type-face where the substitution could not easily be detected. The Bible was completely printed and copies distributed all over the German states before anyone noticed the error. The culprit was found out and punished for blasphemy but she secretly gloated over her success at getting her own back. The Narr Bibles went like hot cakes at high prices on the black-letter market. Indomitable dames all over Germany read and re-read, chuckling, 'Man shall be thy fool.'

A little blasphemy was once very useful in bringing the minister back to earth and making him realise that his sermons should not exhaust Time and encroach upon Eternity. A parish preacher had wearied the patience of his pews with his discourse on the beatitudes. 'Blessed are the poor' would have been enough for one sermon but he exhausted the list. After the two-hour sermon a bold woman approached him.

'Why did you miss out one of the beatitudes?'

'I was not aware that I had missed any, my dear lady.'

'O, yes, you missed out a very important one, 'Blessed are those that were not present at your sermon for theirs was not the boredom of it.'

The man of God got his own back with a little interest.

Two young lads out for a bit of fun accosted the parish minister.

'D'ye ken the latest news, meenister?'

'No, tell me please.'

'It's vera guid news, sir. It'll mak your job easier.'

'What is it then?'

'Nane ither than that Auld Nick's deid.'

'Indeed, is that so? Then I maun pray for twa faitherless bairns.'

The parish priest was hearing confession in the Highlands. The young woman penitent had opened her heart and disclosed quite a number of indiscretions. For the life of him the priest could not recall her name but was curious to know it.

'What is your name, young lady?'

With ready wit she replied, 'My name's no a sin, father,' and departed anonymous.

A young married woman of attractive appearance made a full confession of her infidelities to a cleric whom she assumed to be her parish priest. When she had ended he remained silent.

'Are you not going to give me absolution, father?'

'I cannot. I am not a confessor.'

She was embarrassed and angry and threatened to report him to the bishop.

'Please yourself, madam, but if you do I shall feel it my duty to report what you have told me to your husband.'

A drawn game.

To go back for a moment to long-winded preachers, a story is told of a wee kirk in the Highlands where the congregation, sorely reduced by the Clearances, consisted of about two dozen hillfolk. One autumn day the afternoon sermon went on and on through all of the 'heads'. One by one those nearest the door slipped quietly away. At the tenth 'head' the preacher announced that he would go through the whole twenty-two parts that day. At this one of the shepherds rose. 'Where are you going, William?' demanded the minister. 'To get my night-cap for I see you are not going to be finishing until after dark.' Still he did not take the very broad hint and the numbers diminished as the gloom descended. At the eighteenth 'head' the caretaker woman cried out 'I'll leave the key in the vestibule, sir. I have to go home to the milking. When you leave will you lock the door and leave the key at the back of Seumas MacNab's tombstone?'

Rude replies are often very effective, but rude actions speak louder. The great Duke of Argyll had given offence to a small landlord on the borders of his extensive estates. The offended one was a pretty short-tempered member of the 'gey' Gordon clan, that is to say, the unpredictables. Gordon wondered how he could be avenged on MacCallein Mor, for force was out of the question. At last he had a brain-wave.

He went down to the pottery works near Paisley and took with him a highly-coloured painting of the Duke, resplendent in full wig. Regardless of expense he ordered several hundred chamber-pots with the Duke's portrait ornamenting the bottoms. These he gave away as presents to as many of the Argyll's tenants as he could visit, so that, whenever they felt the urge to show their affection for the Duke, they could do so with little trouble.

A lusty young shepherd in a border village was a favourite with the girls. This incurrred the jealous spite of a maiden lady, one of the great army of the unenjoyed. She made it her business to spread rumours and innuendos about his conquests. This at last came to his ears, so he thought he would teach her a lesson. He left his bicycle leaning against her cottage wall all of a summer's night, where it was seen by many passers-by. In the morning he wheeled it away, leaving the gossip, like Lord Byron, 'to awake and find herself famous.'

Canary breeding has been a hobby from time immemorial in the border towns. A lot of skill is needed in choosing the best birds for breeding, and even then some of the serins or linnets, when mated, do not produce good offspring. These are then said 'to hev fauts' of various kinds, which sometimes reduces their market value to nil. As in every other market, so in canary breeding, 'wise men buy and sell and fools are bought and sold.'

A beginner in the bird trade came to Hawick from Jedburgh one Saturday to buy a cross-bred canary. He was recommended to go to a well-known stockist of 'Border Fancies' who showed him a wide selection of birds, and soon suspected, rightly, that he had an ignoramus on his hands. He thought he was safe to sell him a poor specimen.

Next Saturday the purchaser came back with a small brown paper bag in his hand. 'Div ee mind thon bird ee sellt mie, Will?' he began.

'Aye, Geordie, I mind it fine. Ye paid me half-a-crown for't. What o't?'

'Div ee mind ee said it had nae fauts?'

'Aye.'

'Weel, it's deid,' and he tipped it out of the poke on to the table.

The breeder regarded it sadly and scratched his head.

'Man, Geordie, I canna understand it. It never did the likes o that wi mie.'

The baillie, or magistrate, of an East Coast town in Angus was a baker to trade, but when he was in the seat of judgement he was very much on his high horse and let everyone know it.

A female householder was up before him for beating her carpets outside the permitted hours, which seemed to her such a petty infringement that she felt very ill-treated.

'Mrs. Robertson,' said the bailie sternly, 'You do not deny that you were beating your carpets in the public thoroughfare after 8 a.m. Have you anything to say before I pass sentence?'

'Onything to say? Aye ye can stop ma rolls for a start.'

A doctor's first business has little to do with the Materia Medica. It is to gain the confidence of the district, no easy task among the canny Scots. The old doctor of a Fife parish had retired and his successor moved in. He bore the very estimable name of Yuill and his academic qualifications were first rate. But he was to learn unexpectedly that the coincidence of his name and his comparative youth was a barrier.

One of the elders of the community greeted him early in his stay.

'Guid day to ye, doctor. Are ye settled in yet?'

'Yes, thank you. I think I'll like this place.'

'I hope sae, doctor, but I doot ye'll hae a struggle.'

'How's that?'

'Weel, it's an auld proverb on this side o the country that 'A green Yule maks a fat kirkyaird.'

There is a shocking poverty of language which is fairly common. Hazlitt said, 'The English (it must be owned) are rather a foul-mouthed nation.' So are many neighbouring nations, including the Scots. But there was once a certain art, now lost, in swearing, which lifted it to almost poetic heights.

Here is how a notorious swearer was paid off by his friends in Ayr in Robert Burns' time. He could swear for a quarter of an hour and never repeat himself. His favourite phrase was 'The Devil Almighty', so he got that for a nick-name. He was an elderly little fellow who looked harmless, but when his passions were aroused he broke out into a storm of blasphemy which made the listeners stop their ears. As an invariable prelude to this performance he shut his eyes tight and kept them shut until he had exhausted his store of oaths.

The frequenters of the howff, or pub, where this usually took place, conspired to teach 'The Devil Almighty' a lesson. One winter evening, when a storm raged outside the snuggery, and the candles burned brightly among the glasses of liquor, he was egged on and taunted to give a swearing performance. After he was fairly launched, his eyes tight closed, as usual, his cronies snuffed out all the candles. The inn was pit-mirk, as black as the pit. At the end of his screed 'The Devil Almighty' opened his eyes.

'In the devil's name,' he cried, 'I can see nothing. Am I blind?'

'What makes you think that?' asked one. 'I can see well enough. Let me give you a toast. Here's confusion to all cursers.'

At that 'The Devil Almighty' thought that God, for his blasphemy, had stricken him with sudden blindness. He began to pray, to sob, to cry for forgiveness. His cronies were ready to burst with laughter. They opened the door and admitted the light from a neighbouring room. The swearer was cured from that hour and never referred to the trick played on him.

It was a common habit of many scholars to publish their works in the Latin tongue when the subject was too frank to be printed in what was inaptly called the vulgar tongue. Latin also ensured that the writing reached a wider audience, as it was the second language of most countries. A Polish gentleman named Sterkowski, or Stercovius in Latin, visited Edinburgh in the good old *Gardezloo* days. His Polish dress was ridiculed by the Scots and he was mobbed in the streets. To be avenged of them he widely published a treatise in Latin, in Warsaw, on the Dungy Capital of Scotland. Although his report was too circumstantial to he denied, it angered King James VI, who hired an assassin, Patrick Gordon, for the enormous sum of £600, to go to Poland and silence Sterkowski for good. Edinburgh, in common with most British cities, remained a dunghill for centuries.

Malice aforethought is always with us. In Edinburgh in the eighteenth century, if you wanted to get your knife into somebody, figuratively, and had not the ability to do it yourself, you could hire a professional satirist to do a good job every time. His *nom de plume* was Claudero, his baptised name was James Wilson. He was a native of Cumbernauld but he had left that parish with a deep grudge, for the minister had beaten him so severely with a stick that he was lamed for life. But he got sweet revenge by officiating at irregular marriages, called half-merk weddings, thus depriving the priests of their customers, and pocketing sixpence ha'penny for his marital services. He had no lack of subjects for his sharp pen, because the magistrates of Auld Reekie at that time were vandals and destroyed many historic buildings in the name of progress. But even Claudero's sharp bolts of wit failed to penetrate their rhinoceros hides and the vandalism continued, unrestrained by shame or remorse.

Nobody anywhere loved the hangman or the inventor of lethal machinery. Myths were invented and believed by the populace to the effect that the hated men died by their own machinery. But this was only wishful thinking in an anxiety to get revenge. In Scotland, the Earl of Morton, who was beheaded by the Scottish forerunner of the guillotine, named the 'Maiden', was erroneously said to have invented it. Deacon Brodie, who was hanged by the 'improved' trap-door and drop, was credited with being the inventor, but this is untrue. Dr. Guillotin is said to have tasted his own sharp medicine, but he died in Paris in bed many years after the Reign of Terror.

Nevertheless three Edinburgh hangmen were to suffer a tit-for-tat. The first in time was Alexander Cockburn who had executed more than a hundred innocent persons in Covenanting times in the Grassmarket. In the end justice caught up with him. He murdered a King's Bluegown, an old privileged almsman, and was executed for this atrocious crime on his own gallows amidst the hoots and curses of the Edinburgh mob.

In 1754, Rob Roy's youngest son, Robin Oig MacGregor, was executed in the Grassmarket for the abduction of Jean Kay of Edinbellie, a wealthy widow of nineteen. When the hangman, after the execution, tried to appropriate Robin's clothes, as was the custom, he was stopped by Malie MacGregor, a grand-daughter of Rob Roy. She set about the hangman in a style that Rob would have approved of. She 'swung him off', to use a trade term; and the mob cheered as the villain slid on his back across the causeway, covered with the usual filth of an Edinburgh February day. The body of Robin Oig, still clothed in his Sunday best, was piped home to Balquhidder by a formidable band of his clan, to lie beside his father and older brother.

A gentleman who had come down in the world was forced to take up the obnoxious job of hangman in Edinburgh. He wore a mask when on duty, to preserve his identity. But one evening when golfing on Bruntsfield Links his secret was betrayed. The hue and cry pursued him out of the city to Holyrood Park. Here, in despair, he flung himself off a crag into Duddingston Loch. The fatal rock which saw justice done to him is still named the Hangman's Crag.

Robert Burns was noted for his rapidity of wit. He was not one to take an injury lying down. On coming to Edinburgh in 1786 he sought out the grave of Robert Fergusson, to acknowledge, at least in token, his gratitude to that unlucky poet who had in many ways been his inspiration and model. Finding the grave unmarked, twelve years after Fergusson's death, Burns went to a monumental sculptor in Abbeyhill, half-a-mile off, and ordered a plain stone on which was to be inscribed a four-lined verse of Burns' own composition, beneath a notice of Fergusson's name and dates. Burns was frequently in

Edinburgh during the next few years and with growing irritation saw no sign of the stone he had ordered from Gowans the sculptor. Three years passed before the stone was erected, but the account was sent promptly to the bard for £5. But he put it aside, and in a characteristic letter to a friend, mentioned that Gowans would be paid in the same time as he took to do the job, and should be lucky to get the money at all from such an unaccountable and penurious profession as a poet's. The bill was paid in 1792.

The stone did not endure the weather for long, becoming illegible owing to flaking. The Aesculapian Society of Scotland (medical men) replaced it, adding an inscription crediting them with the erection. In turn this stone was also replaced and some years ago the third stone was painted with a preservative of dull grey colour, unbelievably inappropriate for such a bright spirit's memorial, but symbolic of Edinburgh's attitude to her brilliant son.

A dashing young Englishman named Burton asked Burns to write his epitaph, a pretty fool-hardy request. Burton was much given to swearing, like many of the bucks who considered this accomplishment added to their reputation as men of 'good tone.' Burns, like all writers of top rank, made use of blunt expressions when he felt they fitted the case, but this unnecessary use of oaths he condemned, as Burton knew to his cost.

On Mr. Burton

Here cursing, swearing Burton lies,
A buck, a beau, or Dem my eyes.
Who in his life did little good,
And whose last words were, Dem my blood.

In drinking rounds, the general rule is turn about. If a large party is having a convivial evening the drink bill should be shared *per capita*.

A famous drinking story, entailing the above principle, was so well known to all clergymen in Scotland, at one time, that it was openly discussed by Doctors of Divinity before classes of students.

James VI, as is well known, habitually travelled incognito through his kingdom so that he could enter into the common pleasures of his subjects. On coming to Markinch in the centre of Fife he called for refreshments at the solitary inn. The landlady told him that the public room was occupied by the minister and the school-master, who had been drinking for some time. These worthies agreed to allow James to join them, though they were unaware of his identity. For several hours the trio caroused, the stranger being very acceptable on account of his jolly jests and singing.

At last, as midnight passed, the reckoning had to be met. James drew his well-lined purse and offered to pay his third share. The dominie demurred, saying that he had joined the party late and moreover was their guest and entitled to be treated. But the minister broke out, 'Na, na, there's nae reason in that. Ye ken the law in Markinch. The birkie maun pay his share. Higglety-pigglety's the law here.'

King James, irritated by the argument as well as by the niggardly attitude of the minister, at such a late hour, cried out in disgust.

'Weel, weel, higglety-pigglety be it,' and threw down his siller. But, revealing his true self the following morning, he arranged with the authorities that henceforth the dominie, who had been poorly paid compared with the minister, should now be paid an equal stipend, or salary.

In 1826, when Robert Chambers told this tale of tit-for-tat, Markinch was still the only place in Scotland where the schoolmaster and the minister had nearly equal pay. But as I found in the records of 1860, the minister's stipend was £284 and the schoolmaster's was

£35. Nowadays the position is reversed.

A Scottish king, perhaps the above, could not endure long-winded people.
Travelling on horseback one day he met a man, also mounted, trotting along. The king cried in passing,
'Whaur dae ye come frae? Whaur are ye gaun? What dae ye seek?'
'Frae Dunfermline. To St. Andrews. A kirk.'
'Ye'll hae it,' replied the king over his shoulder, and was as good as his word.

A Scottish judge, known to be very stern against the law-breakers, and of the opinion that 'Nane o them would by ony the waur o a hangin,' was also renowned for this confirmed sociality. One of his boon companions used to engage his lordship in chess, over the claret, and many a hard-fought battle they enjoyed over the dambrod, or chessboard.
Unluckily the judge's friend fell foul of the law. He was brought for trial on a serious charge before his chess opponent, who, although embarrassed by the situation, nevertheless put on the black cap and pronounced doom on the prisoner.
As the poor soul was led from the dock the judge could not refrain from leaning towards him with a grim smile and muttering 'Checkmate'.

Religious men can get their own back just as effectively, if not always as readily, as their lay brothers and sisters. The Franciscan friars in the old days were strictly bound by their vows. A Franciscan met with a Protestant minister as they travelled through a wild country district. They came to a river. There was no bridge or boat, so they drew lots as to who should carry the other across. The friar lost, so he gave the minister a pick-a-back and began to wade across, not very pleased at the pain which the double burden caused his feet, for the river was full of sharp stones. When they reached midstream the burden became unbearable.
He asked the minister, 'Have you any money on you?' 'Why do you want to know that at such a time? queried the other. 'It's very important.' 'Well, I have quite a sum in my purse.'
At that the friar pitched him without warning into the middle of the current, explaining his rudeness in this way. 'I'm really in despair at the inconvenience this causes you, my dear friend, but our father St. Francis made a strict rule for all our order. We are absolutely forbidden at any time or in any circumstances to carry money.'

Boasters are fair game for those who can stand their bragging no longer. A military man was spinning a yarn about the prodigious alligator he had bagged in his early days in the Amazon valley.
'It was no less than fifty-one feet and two inches.'
The entire company was browned off. A naval officer took up the challenge.
'A pretty big beast, major, but a pigmy compared with the halibut we landed off Bear Island in 1919. When we'd drawn it on to an ice-floe with the donkey-engine it measured one acre, two roods, twelve square poles and a few square yards.'
The major seemed to think he was being demickified. His face took on the colour of old port. He demanded an apology but all the satisfaction he got was this offer of a compromise. 'One square rod, pole or perch off the halibut, for every inch off the alligator.'

Fortune treats us like shuttle-cocks, dealing out good or bad luck indiscriminately, and a wise man makes the best of it, as this tale of ups and downs shows.
Two friends met after many years.

'How's the world using you?' asked one.

'Not too well. I got myself spliced soon after I last saw you.'

'Belated congrats. old man.'

'Far from it. I married a proper bitch.'

'That's too bad.'

'O, not so bad after all. She inherited ten thousand from her uncle.'

'That would help to soothe your feelings.'

'Did it hell. I bought a flock of pedigree sheep, who were all chased into a lake by a dog and drowned.'

'Hard luck indeed.'

'No, not too deadly. I sold the fleeces for as much as I paid for the sheep.'

'You made up your losses then?'

'Quite the reverse. My house with all my money and goods was burnt to the ground.'

'That was a dreadful catastrophe.'

'Not so bad after all. My wife went up with it.'

A white-haired Highlander walking down a glen one October day, met a band of sportive young women. They thought they would tease him about his venerable appearance. They giggled and pointed to his white locks.

'Hullo, bodach. Winter's come early. The snow has fallen on the hill-tops.'

'It's well seen that's true,' said he, 'when a herd of cows are coming down into the glen.'

In Roslin Churchyard in Lothian is a humble gravestone to a lady named Burns who died obscurely and prematurely in 1792. But she had had her 'crowded hour of glorious life', three years before her death, when she was the focus of nationwide attention.

Her father, a merchant in Durham, had lost his fortune. His daughter, a beautiful girl, decided to come to Edinburgh, perhaps to win a husband among the social celebrities there. She had scant means, so she rented a lodging in Rose Street, a haunt of the demi-monde, or ladies of shady reputation, in 1768. She dressed so gaudily and so extravagantly that she rapidly gained a reputation which her behaviour scarcely deserved. She was of a devil-may-care nature, but she had had a good education and could carry herself well in any assembly.

As it chanced her back windows looked across to the back windows of Lord Swinton, a Law Lord, in George Street. What he saw when his blinds were drawn back we can only guess at, but at his request Miss Burns was brought before the magistrates on a charge of indecent and scandalous behaviour. One of the chief magistrates was Bailie William Creech, the bookseller friend of Robert Burns. Miss Burns was ordered to leave the city, and threatened that, should she return, six months in the 'House of Correction for Dissolute Women' would be her fate.

But she found this judgement to be tyrannical. She fought the expulsion order and won her case. By this time, so great was the publicity, the London papers got a hold of the story. A leading journal *The Courier*, I think, announced for a laugh, that Bailie Creech, the literary celebrity, was about to lead Miss Burns to the hymeneal altar.

Creech was furious. He threatened the editor with litigation, but he should have kept silent, for the editor contradicted the rumour in terms which made the affair ten times worse.

'We have now the authority of that gentleman to say that the proposed marriage is not to take place, matters having been otherwise arranged to the mutual satisfaction of both parties.'

Robert Burns naturally came to the aid of his fair namesake, and contributed his bit of repartee in neat epigram.

> Cease, ye prudes, your envious railing,
> Lovely Burns has charms, confess.
> True it is she has one failing,
> Had a woman ever less?

Burns himself had an axe to grind in this affair. In 1787, on his first coming to Edinburgh, he had met Creech and arranged for his works to be published. On his Border tour he wrote a complimentary epitaph on Creech with the chorus, 'Willie's awa.' But Creech was so tight-fisted that he kept the hard-up poet hanging around for months in a hell of frustration, before he would pay him his dues. Burns felt very bitter, for he was too proud to 'dun' anyone for a settlement. No doubt this sustained resentment encouraged him to immortalise Miss Burns, who had been so shabbily abused by magisterial hypocrites.

> Sticks and stanes will brak ma banes
> But names they'll never hurt me.

That was the common reply chanted in my boyhood, to anyone calling insults. But a story of Scotland immediately after the obnoxious union of 1707, tells of a beautiful lady who answered an insult in a more desperate manner.

A number of unwelcome English Commissioners of Customs had established themselves in Edinburgh, as elsewhere in Scotland. Amongst them was a handsome but vain and arrogant man named Captain Cayley. One of his acquaintances was Mrs. MacPherson, aged twenty, daughter of a well-known Jacobite. Cayley's landlady deceived Mrs. MacPherson and induced her to visit her house, thinking Cayley to be absent. But Cayley was waiting for her and grossly insulted her by taking liberties with her person. He compounded the offence by spreading a rumour through the town that she was an easy piece.

A day or two later Cayley called on Mrs. MacPherson at her own home, perhaps to apologise. But she had heard the libel on her character and was in no mood for reconciliation. She produced a pair of her husband's pistols and ordered Cayley out.

He began to treat her flippantly, and jokingly asked if she was going to act a comedy. She took him up on this and told him that unless he left instantly he would be playing the principal part in a tragedy. He still delayed, and made to approach her, so she discharged the first pistol and shot him in the left wrist. He then drew his sword and looked as if he meant to run her through, so she shot him through the heart at such close range that the powder burnt his shirt-front.

His corpse lay as it fell, nobody in the house, especially her husband, mentioning the tragic business to outsiders. Mrs. MacPherson, who was several months pregnant, which perhaps explains her behaviour, was out of the town before the magistrates were told of the murder. She was never brought to trial, for a simple reason. She could not be found. But a grand-aunt of Sir Walter Scott told him that when she was a small girl at Swinton House near Duns, she had seen this beautiful young lady who was being concealed there in a secret apartment. Scott says that Mrs. MacPherson eventually returned to Edinburgh but was never charged. Perhaps because at that time (of the Porteous Riots) the sympathies of all Scots were with the woman who had pistolled an English Customs Commissioner.

It is amusing to hear of true instances of people who have not been quick to make a retort.

A taciturn man, riding with his servant mile after mile with not a word exchanged, came to a village where a number of poultry were being fed in a yard. He turned to the servant and asked, 'Do you like eggs?' 'Yes,' answered the man.

A year later they passed the same hamlet where the hens were once again in evidence. 'How?' queried the master. 'Poached,' was the reply.

A more extreme case, much more authenticated, came from the Campsie Fells, a picturesque and sequestered area not far from Glasgow. This region is believed to be the last place in Scotland where blackmail, in its original sense, was levied. In the year before the Forty-five Rising, MacGregor of Glengyle collected blackmail, or protection money, from cattle farmers in Campsie parish. But our story deals with the minister of Campsie in Covenanting times nearly a century before Gregor Glun Dubh was operating.

The Rev. Archibald Denniston was preaching one Sunday in 1655 in the Kirkton of Campsie, when the dragoons arrived to evict him for being a non-conformist and disobeying Cromwell's orders. He was just about to end the first 'head' of his sermon when he was forced immediately, with his wife and bairns, to leave the Kirk and manse.

Six years passed. Charles II was restored, and Dennistoun was allowed back to his parish. He ascended the pulpit on the first Sunday as if nothing had happened in the long interval and began,

'Dearly beloved brethren, I come now to the second 'head' of my sermon . . .'

In Orkney two brothers shared a croft. One morning Mansie walked out after breakfast without a word to Billie, went down the road, and disappeared towards Kirkwall.

He emigrated to America, where he did well in business for a few years. Bad times came and he kept back just enough for a passage home. As he came up the road to the cottage he saw his brother sitting by the cheek of the door mending a spade.

'Where on earth have you been, Mansie?' he asked.

'Oot,' replied the emigrant.

'Possession is nine points of the Law'; this is an axiom that has been universally put into practice, but rarely so bluntly as in the London train shortly before it left Aberdeen.

An English businessman had arrived in good time to make sure of a seat but had to go to the toilet before the train started. He placed his brolly on the seat to reserve it, but on his return he was very upset to find that the carriage was amply filled by half-a-dozen well-built, weather-beaten Buchan farmers, and his expensive brolly was lying among their feet.

He angrily picked it up and spluttered, 'Have you no respect for my property, and furthermore, don't you realise that a brolly laid on a seat indicates that it has been reserved?'

The farmers stopped talking and eyed him as if he were some exotic creature.

'Aye, mebbe that's the wey o't doon in Lunnon,' said one, 'but in Aiberdeen it's erses that coont.'

Let us leave the last word with a reverend gentleman. He was saying grace at an Edinburgh dinner-party of perhaps a score of church officials. He had a very soft voice. After the blessing he began his dinner.

'You didna say grace,' accused one of the grim-faced elders.

'Aye, I did,' replied the minister.

'I didna hear you,' retorted the elder.

'I wisna speaking tae you,' replied the minister quietly.

Tight Fists

Scots and Jews are singled out for ridicule on the score of tight-fistedness. No matter how generous many of them have been, both financially and culturally, the thrifty side of their nature is always emphasised and represented as meanness. But this biased view is common to all nations. The French have for centuries ridiculed the provincials of Limousin for their niggardly habits. In Scotland the Aberdonians are the targets; even in Bulgaria there is a 'mean' town which, however, like Aberdeen, makes an industry out of its avarice and encourages a joke factory. Some years ago I was asked by a Bulgarian agent to supply Aberdeen stories for export, so I suppose the Bulgarians actually believe that, in their miserly town, identical twins are never photographed together. One child only is taken and the photo duplicated. Perhaps, as in Aberdeen, they walk on tarry roads on hot days to re-sole their shoes, or take longer strides all through the year to save their shoe-leather, or remove their spectacles when not needing them to save the wear and tear on the glass.

However ridiculous such stories seem, they have been out-done in real life by dedicated misers, most of whom had not even the excuse of poverty. Some of the most infamous were Englishmen, contrary to accepted propaganda. The details of their mean acts were witnessed and recorded by a very reliable author, Dr. William King, a learned Jacobite, who moved in high circles.

John Churchill, Duke of Marlborough, victor of Blenheim and other bloody conflicts, was heaped with awards by the English Crown and Parliament. At his death he left a million and a half pounds, worth a hundred times more at present values. Yet, when he was very old and infirm, he would walk home from the Assembly Rooms in Bath to his house, on a cold wet dark night, to save sixpence for the hire of a sedan chair. His wealth was left to a grandson of one of his political enemies, who squandered it.

Sir James Lowther, who had estates in Scotland, bought a twopenny cup of coffee and pocketed the change from sixpence. Being lame and feeble he went home in his coach, but on examining his change he was enraged to find that the poor woman who kept the coffee-house had given him a counterfeit halfpenny. He immediately drove back to the coffee-house, demanding a good halfpenny. His income was £100 per day.

Sir Thomas Colby killed himself by rising in the middle of the night after taking a sweating powder. He had suddenly remembered that he had left the key of the wine cellar on a table, and he feared that a servant would rob him of one of his many thousands of bottles of port and sherry. He died intestate, and left £200,000, which was shared among half-a-dozen country labourers, whose wages were a penny an hour. How gratefully they must have toasted his avarice, which brought them such unexpected good fortune.

Another rich man of King's acquaintance bargained with an oculist for sixty guineas to cure his blindness. When the operation for cataract was perfectly successful he pretended he had difficulty in seeing, so that he could persuade the oculist to accept a third of the fee.

I myself knew a miser in Peebles sixty years ago, who borrowed an egg from a neighbour one Sunday morning on the pretext that he had a rasher of bacon, value a penny, to go with the egg. There used to be a comical saying, in imitation of an Irishism, 'If we had some ham, we could have had some ham and eggs, if we had some eggs.' Perhaps the Peebles miser got the idea there, for he crossed over to another neighbour to borrow bacon to go with the egg.

But his best exploit in stinginess was when his neighbour died. He went over to the newly-bereaved lady.

'Guid day to ye, Mistress Rae. I'll hae to assure ye o' ma sincere sympathy in your terrible loss. John has noo passed away to where there's neither pain nor sorrow, nae need to worry aboot ony material maitters. I wad like fine to gang up the morn to St. Andra's Kirkyaird, but to tell ye the truth ma auld stand o' blacks is gey sair worn and a bit green-mouldit. Dae ye think I could borrow John's for the occasion?'

I can give my word too, as to the truth of this story from Gretna. A man who had bought a joint of mutton from Carlisle market was hailed by a notorious miser and, as it was a hot day, asked if he would like a drink of 'soor dook', or buttermilk. He unwisely accepted. They began a long 'crack' on this and that, and it came on to noon. To the visitor's surprise the miser asked him to stay for dinner. As the meal proceeded he complimented his host on the nicely cooked meat, to be rudely brought back to earth with the reply, 'Aye, it's a nice bit o' meat. You should ken, for you bocht it in Carlisle this mornin'.' While the conversation was going on, the miser's wife had stolen away the parcel and cooked it.

Another story sticks in my memory from childhood. A friend of ours had a charlady, a status symbol, whom she employed one day a week. She and Mrs. Mop sat down to 'high tea' together, but all the delicacies in the form of bridies or cream-cookies were not put out on plates. The employer kept the choicest ones in a paper-bag under the table, and surreptitiously slipped them on to her own plate.

Hard drivers of bargains are quite often paid in their own coin. Irishmen, in earlier days, used to bring flocks of geese over to the West coast ports of Wigton and Cumberland to sell them in late summer to be fattened up for Christmas. One such goose-herd left his flock in a by-way and bargained with a tight-fisted farmer's wife. She offered him a few shillings a head which offended him so much that he indignantly turned away, shouting over his shoulder, 'Begod, before I would part with my geese for that miserable sum, I'll put rubber heels on the buggers and drive them to London!'

In the hungry Twenties and Thirties of this century people were driven to desperate shifts to eke out an existance, but they made jokes about it. 'Shamrock tea was not specially packed for Hibernian supporters. It was a nickname for very weak tea, hardly strong enough to run out of the pot, where you were lucky if you could find four leaves in it, hence the name.

This parsimony was surpassed by the Sunday School teacher who promised his class a picnic on the Pentland Hills, for a season's perfect attendance. They were to be rewarded with 'tea-cakes and aerated waters'. On arrival at the shore of one of the city's reservoirs he gravely handed each child a bun. Then he took out a tin of Health salts and, throwing a generous handful of salts into the reservoir, he cried out, 'Hurry up now, children, drink it while it's fizzing.'

In days when wine was not the popular drink it is now, and only a fraction of the cost, a tight-fisted old lad came into the licensed grocer's shop.
'Hoo muckle is it for a bottle o' guid port wine?'
'Here's a vintage. Ten years old. Twelve shillings.'
'Naw, naw. Far ower dear. What's yon ither beside it?'
'Very good. Rich Red Ruby. Seven and six.'
'Canna look at it. Onything cheaper?'
The grocer ran down a list and finally, fed up, he held out a bottle.
'There you are now. There's a good British style port. One shilling.'
'O aye, but is it good for the blood?'
'I canna say, but I ken this. It's bloody good for a bob.'

People who want to carry their miserliness beyond the grave can do it legally by putting stupid clauses in the will, for the law does not count avarice as lunacy, though it is incurable madness. But there is a recorded case of an ill-used legatee who managed to remove the gross injustice. It was easier in this case, for the will was oral and not written.
A countryman lay at death's door with a malignant fever. As he was past curing, he called his wife to his death-bed, to hear his last request.
'My beloved wife, you have been a great comfort to me for many years. You have laboured hard and never once complained. I would like you to carry out my last wishes exactly as I say.'
She promised faithfully, her eyes brimming with tears.
'I have a very good horse and a very faithful dog and little else, apart from this cottage of ours. I would like you to go to the market, whenever I am decently buried, and sell the horse for as much as you can get. Give the money to my father and mother and say that it is to recompense them for bringing me up. Then sell the dog, if you wish, and keep the money, or, if you love the dog, keep him as a companion for your widowhood.'
The wife's tears were not long in drying, after the death of this grateful son. She was a religious woman, however, and resolved to keep her solemn vow. She took the horse and dog to the town market where she knew an honest dealer.
'I have a good horse here, as you can see.'
'Yes, a fine young beast. What do you want for him?'
'Listen carefully. I want two pounds for the horse and sixty pounds for the dog.'
The merchant was naturally very surprised but, as the horse was such a good bargain, he took the dog with no comment. The widow gave the two pounds to her mean husband's parents and went home reasonably content that she had carried out the terms of the will.

In the Orkneys, Shetlands and Hebrides, life was often at a low ebb, especially in early spring when the salt fish and potatoes were nearly done and the pasture had not begun to appear. Many a family had to subsist on boiled whelks, or buckies. Feeding a large family at any time was a problem.

A Shetlander, for a treat, had killed a fat hen that was off the lay. It was brought on to the table, round which sat eight hungry bairns. As soon as the grace was said all the little voices were lifted up in chorus, 'I want a leg, I want a leg.'

Father hammered on the board with the handle of the carving knife.

'Bairns, wheesht dis meenit. Dost du think I'm carvin' a speeder?'

The Laird of Milnwood, in Scott's *Old Mortality*, is a very fair specimen of a Scottish miser. Scott had plenty of such skinflints to draw upon from his own acquaintances. 'Gin there's onything totally uneatable,' said one such economist, 'ye may gie it for charity to the puir.' A grim touch of humour deals with Milnwood's death-bed scene as described by his housekeeper. The dying man happened to spot a wax candle burning by his bedside, so he called for it to be snuffed and a mutton-tallow-dip brought in its stead. His last earthly remark was, 'A tallow-candle's guid eneuch to see to dee wi'.'

Another canny Scot and his wife were holidaying in a seaside lodgings. They occupied a bedroom upstairs above the dining-room. Early in the morning the husband awoke to find that his partner had passed away during the night. He gravely weighed up the situation then walked to the head of the stairs.

'Mrs. MacTavish, are ye there?'

'Aye, what is it, Mr. Morton?'

'Just one boiled egg for breakfast the day, Mrs. MacTavish.'

Two gourmands were on a guzzling holiday in France, enjoying the table delicacies of a district noted for cooking trout to perfection. Both were very particular as to details, each selfishly arguing on the merits of his own style of preparation. One evening they almost came to fisticuffs on whether trout should be fried in butter or in olive oil. Neither would give in and they retired to bed very upset.

The mental upset proved too much for the butter cook. In the early hours his friend, the olive oil protagonist, awoke to find the other in *rigor mortis*. Not so parsimonious as the bereaved husband above, but still putting greed before friendship, he shouted to the chef, 'Fry both trout in olive oil.'

There are even more morbid tales of economies practised in Scotland. A young farm servant was seen on a station platform in the Borders, in the good old days before Beeching vandalised the lines.

'Where are ye aff to, sae early in the mornin', Sandy?' asked the station master.

'I'm leavin' for guid. I've had enough o' the folk up at the Mains.'

'Man, ye've only been there hauf a term. What ails ye at them?'

'Ye've nae idea what a hungry crowd they are. D'ye ken, at the back-end, three auld yowes deed o' the braxy. The maister had them sauted doon and we fed on saut mutton till New Year. Then the auld broon coo deed, that wad ne'er see saxteen again. She was intae the brine as weel, and we had teuch beef till last Friday. Then to croon a', last nicht, bless me, but the maister's auld mither ups and dees. Sae I thocht tae mysel, Sandy, it's time ye were gettin' oot.'

A canny Scot looking to the future in no very optimistic mood, visited the cabinet-maker to order his coffin.

'Aye, Willie,' said the joiner, 'What are ye efter the day? Some shelvin' for the cupboards or a bit o' fencin'?'

'Na, man, I want shelvin' for masel, and I've drappit in to seek professional advice.'

'Ye look set for a century, Willie, but naethin' like bein' ready when the ca' comes. What kinna timmer did ye hae in mind?'

'I've aye had an ambition for a guid bit o' aik, gin it wasna ower expensive.'

'Aik, that wad come to aboot eicht pun.'

'Ower dear. What aboot pitch pine?'

'I could hap ye in that wi' a' the fittins for three pun ten.'

'Still ower muckle siller to throw awa'.'

'Weel, here's my last offer and a richt bargain. I could gie ye a white Norway deal for thirty shillins—but it wad only be fair to warn ye. Your erse wad be through the bottom o't in twa months.'

In a remote part of the Highlands a number of crofts had been supplied with electricity, when the grid was first installed. The head accountant noticed that the bills seemed to be for minimal charges, barely coming to more than a few shillings per quarter. So he sent the inspector to investigate, perhaps suspicious that the Highlanders were 'milking' the power.

'Do you not use the electricity supply very much?' an old couple were asked.

'Not very much, but we use it every day.'

'What do you use it for?'

'It's very handy in the gloaming. We put on the electric globes to help us to see to light the paraffin lamps.'

When the steam engine was at the height of its glory, the larger stations were equipped with magnificent lavatories for the general public as well as travellers. The Waverley Station had a lavatory on the French system. The Gents' apartment had forty-two lockable single-seater privies, two being free for the benefit of those who were caught short of change, an exigency which the authorities do not now visualise. This great Cloacal Chamber was known far and wide as the 'Forty-twa'.

Now this rich witticism is explained when we know that there were exactly forty-two city fathers on the Town Council. There was also a very famous regiment, officially named the Royal Highlanders, and popularly The Forty-Twa, about whom many rude ditties were sung. Citizens who wished to crack a joke, at little expense of cerebral energy, used to excuse their withdrawal from company for natural reasons, by remarking that they were off to join the Forty-Twa, or to take their seat in the Town Council.

A miserly fellow was seen climbing slowly up the Waverley Steps, ruefully rubbing the back of his head.

'What's up, John? Have you had an accident?'

'Aye, I was doon at the 'Forty-twa' havin' a wash and brush-up, when the seat cam doon on the back o' ma heid.'

A publican in the North was trying to cut costs. A customer told him that electricity was expensive and that he should switch off all unnecessary devices. Once on the road to economy he went to ridiculous lengths for he even switched off that necessary evil, the pub clock. However to kill two birds with one stone he gummed a paper over the dial, reading 'Nae Tick'.

The Forth Rail Bridge was one of the seven wonders of the modern world when it was built about ninety years ago, though some simple travellers, viewing the great cantilevers, wondered how the engine was going to climb up the steep incline and down the other side three times in a mile. But, even travelling uneventfully along the horizontal, it was supposed to bring you luck if you ever threw a penny from the carriage window, about the middle of the bridge.

An Aberdonian or a Fifer, or some say a Hielandman, was seen in the Waverley Station, coming off the North express along with a crowd of cheery folk. But he was very dismal.

'What's the matter, Mac? Are ye oot o' luck?'

'Oot o' luck. That's exactly what's wrang wi' me.'

'Hoo's that, Mac? Onybody deid?'

'Wor' than that. I threw ma penny ower the Forth Bridge to bring me luck.'

'And did it no?'

'The vera opposite. The string broke.'

A penny was once a useful sum. In ancient Britain for centuries the penny was the unit of currency. Now it is indeed reduced to penury. In my youth a 'Saturday Penny' was the carrot held before us for a whole week. Poorer kids got a 'make' or a halfpenny, but the shopkeepers did not despise 'makes', or even farthings.

'Penny Weddings' in Scotland were very popular and, even when officially abolished three centuries ago, they were still observed. All the guests had to do, was to bring at least a penny, but not more than a shilling. The collection was spent on meat and drink and the surplus money went to the plenishing of the bridal home. 'Penny Hops' were also run on the same lines, to ensure that nobody was excluded for want of cash.

In the Old Town of Edinburgh in the Twenties there were many ritual sayings familiar to me about 'wings' or pennies. Shopkeepers were tormented by small boys and girls popping their cheeky faces round the door with such chants as this, spoken with an affected lisp.

A pennyworth o' chewwies (cherries)
Nae chewwies, gie's bewwies (berries)
Nae bewwies, gie's wock (rock)
Nae wock gie's ma penny back
An' I'll go tae anither shoap.

A shorter but less intelligible request was for a 'pennyworth o' bum-bees' waistcoats,' or 'cock-sparries' elbaes.' If the request was for a pennyworth o' broken biscuits and it met the answer 'I've none', the cheeky retort was, 'Break us a few.'

It was quite common, in country towns and villages, for customers to buy a long string of provisions, tea, sugar, meal, herring, all at a penny. Greengrocers in working districts of Scottish towns supplied a pennyworth of mixed vegetables for broth, usually swede turnip, leek and carrot, with parsley thrown in *gratis*. It was indeed a world built on a penny, now gone into limbo.

In Berwickshire there was a saying, 'This is like the fiddler o' Chirnside's breakfast, a' pennyworths the-gither.' His son, sent with the order, used to recite it by heart.

A pennyworth o' tea, a pennyworth o' sugar,
Three penny loaves, a pennyworth o' butter,
A pennyworth o' he-herrin', for ma faither likes milts.'

In Reston, Berwickshire, lived a noted miser, John Home, whose only child was never granted his Saturday morning penny. His father used every trick he knew to avoid giving the boy any cash. When the lad pleaded for a bawbee, or halfpenny, to buy toffy or gundy, his father put his hands in his jacket-pockets and flapped his long coat-tails as if he were flying, chanting this rhyme, which soon became popular throughout the Merse of Berwickshire.

Willie Burd, Willie Burd,
Here's a bum-bee,
Quo' the miller o' Reston
To his little Willie.

John Home was such an outstanding example of a pathological miser that he deserves a full description.

His mill was thatched with wheat straw which, through the years, had rotted in many places. On a wet day the water poured in everywhere, despite the planks, old sacks, and flat stones covering the holes. He said he would rather drown than employ a professional 'theeker' or thatcher.

In cold weather he kept warm by running up and down in the barn with a heavy load of corn on his back. He bought neither coal, wood, nor peat, though all of these were to be had for little more than the cost of transport. He dragged branches of green alders, one of the least combustible of woods, from the riverside, and broke them for fuel, though they provided little but acrid smoke.

He starved his poor horses. When they halted through exhaustion brought on by hunger, when drawing in corn or potatoes, or ploughing, he pelted them with stones, crying 'There's hard corn for you, you lazy brutes!'

He treated his housekeeper little better, though it was commonly known that she was the mother of his only son, 'Willie Burd'. At her lying-in, before Willie's birth, he made 'parritch' for her. On carrying in this far-from-appetising mess, he addressed the poor woman in this uncouth way; 'Will ye hae them drappit (into milk) or separate, ye damned cow.'

Out of pity a kindly farmer gave 'Willie Burd' a half-crown. Home demanded it but the laddie refused to give it up, which half-pleased his father, as it showed proof of his miserly paternity.

When near his end, in 1802, he refused to make a will, saying, 'Damn it, I may live these hundred years yet.' But he perished soon after. 'Willie Burd' and his mother, Jenny Gardiner, inherited everything, including the leaky roof and the skeletal horses.

Dr. George Henderson, to describe John Home, quotes three lines from Robert Blair's poem, *The Grave*, incidentally a favourite poem of Burns,

O, cursed lust of gold. How oft for thee
The fool throws up his interest in both worlds,
First starved in this, then damned in that to come.'

Burns wrote a satirical song on an imaginary crone, the wife of a hypothetical man of Linkum-doddie, the local name of a small farm on Tweedside. He ends each verse—

Sic a wife as Willie's wife
I wadnae gie a button for her.'

Burns must have known of the common, but illegal, custom of selling wives to get rid of a thorn in the flesh, and at the same time raise a little cash, the amount depending on the merits of the article. It was only in England that the firm belief in the legality of such sales was held. In Scotland the making and breaking of a marriage was easy, so sales were not justifiable.

Burns was often in Carlisle, both privately and professionally, and may have heard of wife sales, but it was several years after his death that a notorious affair took place in Carlisle Market. On 7 April, 1832, the Town Crier announced the sale of the wife of Joseph Thomson, farmer. The couple had decided to part without the expense of a divorce. At noon the wife was placed on a large oak chair, with a straw halter round her neck, and Jo began a catalogue of her vices and virtues in that order.

According to his biased view the vices exceeded the virtues, which seems a most unbusinesslike method of auctioneering.

'She is a born serpent, a tormentor, a domestic curse, a night invasion and a daily devil. To be as much avoided as a mad dog, a roaring lion, a loaded pistol, cholera, Mount Etna.'

On the bright side, 'She can read novels and milk cows, make butter and scold the maid. Cannot make rum, whisky or gin, but has long experience in tasting them. I offer her for fifty shillings.'

Not surprisingly there were no takers at first, but about one o'clock a brave man named Thomas Mears bought her for twenty shillings and a Newfoundland dog, and all four parted quite content, and no more is known of them.

Frugality and make-do are perhaps not so much admired as they once were. It is interesting to note how William Murdoch, the father of the Gas industry, achieved the first rung in the ladder of success by what seemed ridiculous parsimony. He went from Ayrshire to seek an appointment in the English Midlands. At that time workmen of any ambition wore 'lum' hats, so when Murdoch was admitted to an interview he carried his tall hat under his arm and placed it on the table, while under interrogation. Being nervous, he did not make a favourable impression. On leaving, in his anxiety, he knocked his hat to the floor where it fell with a resounding thump. The chairman of the examining board asked what in Heaven's name it was made of.

Murdoch replied bashfully, 'I couldna afford the price o' a silk hat, sir, so I just set to and turned one for myself, oot o' wood, and varnished it.' He got the job.

It is said that life can be maintained on one olive a day, but it would need to be a very sedentary existence. But some folk have subsisted on very little, provided they had enough water. The Gaelic proverb says, 'Ye can aye get a drink oot o' the burn, when ye canna get a bite aff the brae'.

The value of water is borne out by a strange tale of a woman named Jeffrey. She was a coal-bearer, who, like all the mine-workers in the Tranent and Dalkeith coal-field, was a slave, tied from birth to work underground in the most laborious and degrading circumstances. The coal was either carried up in baskets or dragged up an incline in wooden sledges. The only light was from a candle. Jeffrey's candle went out, and, as all her friends had gone home, she had no guide, and wandered through narrow workings for hours until she fell exhausted. Her friends, missing her after a time, sent the town drummer and bagpiper through the underground workings, without result, for she had got into some disused roads underneath the kirk, and could not hear even the beating of the drum or the shrill piping. Strangely, as she lay, exhaustedly fainting away and coming to at intervals, she heard, as in a dream, the congregation singing psalms above her, for the seam where she lay was part of an 'ingaun-mooth', or horizontal shaft, and she was only twenty feet below ground.

To stay alive she devoured her leather shoes and flavoured them with blood sucked from her arm. But what saved her, for the fortnight before she was rescued, was the regular dripping of water from the roof, which she caught in the palm of her hand. Compared with this extreme case of survival, many of our modern slimming diets are sumptuous feasts. In Chaplin's film, *The Gold Rush*, Charlie is seen eating his boots, laces and all, but how many realise that this has actually been done under the Lothian coalfields.

One of the strangest misers in the South of Scotland was James Blaikie, a joiner, whose house stood by the River Leader, some distance from Earlston in Berwickshire. He was as strong as any three men put together, and never hired a man to help him, thereby saving many a penny. In sawing long planks of wood out of whole trees, he used a saw-pit. He held the top of the saw but instead of employing a man to pull it from beneath, he tied a heavy stone to the other end of the saw and allowed gravity to do the job.

Few men could even lift the stone which he kept pulling up hour after hour. He made coffins, as all village joiners did. Expecting Death to come knocking at his door any day, he had his own 'cabinet' always ready, but if a purchaser came along he sold it and immediately set to and made another.

To his great annoyance he died, aged seventy-three when he happened to be 'oot o' a coffin', so his last command above ground was to his spouse Marion Sclater to go and buy a coffin from a joiner in Earlston. If it was any consolation to this very independent miser, he was buried in a grave in his own garden. He had dug it himself twenty-five years before, to save the few shillings fee for a grave-digger, in the local churchyard.

An even stranger case of the same macabre miserliness comes from Anstruther Wester in Fife. Last century there lived a slater and plasterer named Alexander Batchelor, or, as it is pronounced in Fife, Sandy Baisler. He owned a substantial house beside the Old Kirk of St. Adrians. In his spare time he decorated the inside and outside walls with shells from the nearby shore and made ornate plaster mouldings on the ceilings. Buckies, or cockles, being the most numerous, his house was called the Buckie House. But his eccentricities were taken beyond this pleasant pastime. Obsessed with mortality to a morbid degree, like Blaikie, he made his own coffin, and decorated it with small shells, cockles, whelks, cowries and periwinkles. He stood the coffin on end beside his bed so that it was the last thing he and his wife saw at night, and first thing in the morning. Perhaps this was a form of revenge, for he was hag-ridden by Mrs. Batchelor. She would not allow him to wander off as he willed, but allotted him a piece of plasterwork to complete, before he went out to drink with his cronies at the nearby tavern. A good idea occurred to him for making drink money. He was willing to stand in his coffin, simulating a corpse, for a fee of threepence, to provide his friends and neighbours with entertainment. He died in 1863 and was buried in the churchyard across the road.

As he had no fitting epitaph I wrote one for him on the centenary of his death.

Sandy Baisler's Epitaph

Here Sandy lies, a Baisler from his birth
But tholed a woman's tyranny on earth:
When he desired to dander forth a-reeling
She cramped him to a span-lang stent of ceiling;
Yet, freed to search the shelly shores of Fife,
He picked up nothing but what pleased his wife;
Only with her indulgence he'd depart
With drams to warm the cockles of his heart:

T'enjoy a foretaste of eternal rest
He made and lined with shells his ain deid-chest,
And for a threepenny fee forenent his bed
To favour friends he feigned to be dead:
On his good slater-work the Lord looks down
And recommends his tiling through the town;
As for his weakness, it can not be seen
However Satan glower with elshin een,
For like the hermit-crab weel Sandy kenned
Safe in a shell to hide his latter end.

After the death of Prince Albert in 1861, Queen Victoria continued to spend much time at Balmoral Castle, the scene of many happy holidays before her bereavement. In 1866 the Deeside railway was extended from Aboyne up to Ballater and the Royal train frequently used it.

The driver took in water about halfway to Ballater, not far from a small Deeside farm. One autumn day when the train was halted the farmer approached the guard and asked if he could be permitted to present the Queen with a box of fine black grapes from his own hot-house. The guard called an equerry and that gentleman thanked the farmer and handed the box into the Royal coach.

On the return journey from Ballater a few days later the equerry descended from the train at the halt with a letter of thanks from Queen Victoria. The farmer opened it and read the beautifully inscribed epistle signed by her majesty.

He did not appear at all pleased and turned to the royal servant, 'Aye, that's a' vera weel, ma mannie, but far's ma wee boxie?'

An old Scots proverb says, 'A greedy ee ne'er got a guid pennyworth'. Nowadays one can only 'spend a penny' metaphorically, but not in a shop, where a pound is now small change. The humble herring, or haddock, once the mainstay of the poor, either as tatties an' herrin' or fish and chips, is a luxury, as this short tale shows.

An Auld Reekie housewife rushed into the local fish shop and plumped a large bowl on the counter.

'A pound a' fillet!'

'A pound ye don't!' retorted the fishmonger, laying a safe bet.

Quacks

'I firmly believe that if the whole *materia medica* could be sunk to the bottom of the sea, it would be all the better for mankind and all the worse for the sea.' So said Oliver Wendell Holmes to the Harvard Medical School, in which he was a professor. This looked very much like rocking the boat. He was bitterly attacked and amongst other abuse he was called a rattlesnake. But he must have had good grounds for his opinion. What annoyed the doctors was to be brought down to the level of the many quacks who moved westwards with their wagon-loads of pills and squills, imposing upon the simple souls in the new homesteads. Every Tom, Dick and Harry imagined, and still does, that he could do the job far better than a college medico.

One of the most famous quacks in Scotland was an Italian named Giovanni, or John, Damian, who came over the Border early in the reign of James IV and made straight for the court with all his phials and hocus-pocus. He persuaded James to give him large sums of money to purchase crucibles, furnaces, flasks of *aqua fortis*, metals of many kinds and, of course, apartments to hold these. He was on the well-worn path of transmutation of base metal into gold, one of the fantastic ideas that fascinated the philosophers of the Middle Ages; the other parallel delusion was to discover the elixir of life. Damian's experiments worked, but in reverse. He turned the King's gold into dross.

But such is the force of a powerful personality that his failures were plausibly explained and he was awarded a benefice. He was made Abbot of Tongland in Kirkcudbrightshire. In the end, like most quacks, he fell a victim to his own delusions, for he did what hucksters should never do. He began to convice himself.

He decided to prove that a man could fly by his own exertions, an idea that still seems to haunt us. He said that he could make a pair of wings that would carry him, not across the English Channel, but from the centre of Scotland to France. He set to work and with a party of workmen made a handsome pair of wings composed of thousands of feathers large and small. The scene of the launching was to be the west side of Stirling Castle, where there is a steep cliff and also an artificial plateau surrounded by turf benches, named King Arthur's Round Table. Here the King and the court with many curious commoners gathered to watch Damian sail off the crag and fly away south.

But the deluded aviator did not fly a yard. He fell in a crumpled heap at the foot of the hill breaking a thigh. When he had recovered from his injuries he explained that the cause of his failure was the composition of the wings. He had instructed that only eagles' feathers were to be used, which would bear him to immense heights, by their very nature. Whereas some hens' feathers had been mixed with the eagles' and, as their instinct was to make for the barnyard midden, they had brought him quickly down to earth. This line of thought was characteristic of the logic of the age and was probably accepted as a good excuse.

William Dunbar, who was jealous of Damian's appointment to the Abbotship, which he coveted, did not spare the charlatan in his verses. He accused him bluntly of cutting veins and letting his patients bleed to death; of murdering many with poisonous draughts, of prescribing laxatives so violent that they would have killed a strong horse; whosoever took one of his draughts, 'their hips went hiddy-giddy'; his purgatives, given to thieves, saved them from bothering the gallows. As an alleged, but really imagined, punishment for his blasphemy in trying to fly, Dunbar makes all the birds of the air, ravens, hoodie-craws, owls, hawks and eagles, mob him and tear him to shreds. But the fates of Damian and Dunbar are alike uncertain. Both are thought to have died about the time of Flodden, 1513, when James and the Flowers o' the Forest perished also.

But Damian had many successors in Scotland, and elsewhere, though there were always many who distrusted them, as popular tales show.

A doctor, annoyed at the constant criticism of his profession, exclaimed, with some heat, 'At least, nobody can bring any complaints about me.' 'No,' was the instant reply, 'For they're all in the kirkyard.'

The possession of a talisman was once thought to cure all ailments. A popular one was the famous Abracadabra. It was a triangular piece of parchment on which was written the enlarged name of the chief god of the Assyrians. The name had to be written in such a way that the three points of the triangle held an A while the three bases were filled by the whole name. Originally the name of the god Abraxas was carved on a stone and his followers numbered thousands; but, latterly, the talisman degenerated into a quack remedy for belly-ache, tooth-ache, bone-ache, any kind of ache. The parchment, to be effective, had to be hung round the neck on a linen thread.

Other talismans, just as ineffective, are camphor-filled lockets, hung round the neck to ward off infection; pieces of potatoes held in the hand and worked into a sticky mess to cure rheumatics; a piece of hemp string tied round the waist next to the skin to stop lumbago. The most effective cure of all was a strong hemp rope, fastened tightly round the neck of the complainant, just before he or she dropped.

It is surprising that in this age of extensive medical research there are still millions who prefer the ju-ju man and his talismans. In Scotland, a longish time ago, there was a good old cure for all ailments. It was made into a popular song.

Ay wear a flannel next your skin,
Ay wear a flannel next your skin,
Ye'll live to be auld

And ye'll never catch cauld
If ye ay wear a flannel next your skin.

There were all sorts of parodies on songs of this kind. A favourite in Glasgow was one which gave a certain remedy for bile and also for other ills that flesh is heir to.

Ile, ile, paraffin ile,
Drink it right up when you're bad wi' the bile,
Drink it right up and lie doon on the flair,
And ye'll never be bothered wi' bile ony mair.

People, for many centuries, did not bother with doctors if they were in touch with the seventh son of a seventh son, or failing him, the seventh daughter of a seventh daughter. By a mere accident of birth the above people made quite a steady income from quackery. All they had to do to turn a dishonest penny was to lay hands on the sore spot or prescribe a drug 'which had been a family secret for generations,' probably a brew of dandelions or some other hedgerow plants accessible to any first son of a first son.

Kings and queens, or indeed, any royal persons, no matter though they had waded through blood or bastardy to reach that sacred status, also had the inherited power to cure others, even though 'Physician, cure thyself' was a motto they did not live up to. In their case the disease was scrofula, an old name for tuberculosis of the bones and glands. It is small wonder that there was a queue, as lengthy as that which files by Lenin's sarcophagus, all desirous of the royal touch, for there was no cure known to medicine until this century, for tuberculosis. The whole business was Grand Quackery. It is said that the Merry Monarch, Charles II, touched over 90,000 persons during his reign of twenty-five years, an average of ten per diem, but some days were busier, we assume, for it is recorded that on one occasion several persons were trampled to death. The last person said to be touched for scrofula in Britain was Dr. Samuel Johnson, when a small child. But even later than Johnson, Prince Charlie, perhaps to strengthen his claim to the throne, touched a small girl in 1745. He is also said to have touched an older girl, Clementina Walkinshaw, about the same period, but not for the same complaint.

The list of famous quacks is relatively short, but there were multitudes of lesser-known charlatans who were drawn to fairs and markets, or practised in villages. One of these, who had no wish for fame, got more than his fair share of it before he was done. He was John Wilson, schoolmaster of Tarbolton, Ayrshire. Like many parochial dominies, he was paid a mere pittance, and depended for his livelihood on keeping a grocer's shop. By chance he got hold of some books on medicine, which he studied to such effect that he felt qualified to cure all the fleshly ailments of Tarbolton. He put an ungrammatical card in his window, 'Common disorders at shop gratis,' which should have made his shop a place to avoid.

At a masonic meeting where Burns was present, Wilson gave an address based on his little medical knowledge, which in a few days drew forth the satirical poem *Death and Dr. Hornbook*. The alias of Wilson was a direct allusion to the hornbooks used in primary schools by beginners. They were not books, but resembled in shape an oblong hand-mirror. Enclosed in a wooden frame was a sheet of strong paper protected by transparent horn. On the paper was a large cross, followed by the alphabet, capitals and small letters, then the vowels and consonants, the Lord's prayer and the Roman numerals.

The theme of Burns' poem is well-known. Burns, staggering home from the pub, meets Death on the way with his scythe. They have a crack and Death pours forth his complaint. Dr. Hornbook (Wilson) has stolen his trade and kills great numbers with his quack cures. But Death, going on his awesome errands, mutters a fearsome threat,

'I'll nail the self-conceited sot
As deid's a herrin'.'

The satire was circulated throughout the parish and Hornbook was laughed out of his school and shop. But he eventually had cause to thank Burns, for he went to Glasgow and set up a school in the parish of Gorbals, which was then a pleasant village by the banks of the Clyde, south of the town. He also took on the post of registrar of births, marriages and deaths, and as the population of Gorbals increased, so in proportion did Wilson's fees, from both occupations. He survived until 1839, outliving his satirist by forty-three years, which is a recommendation for his style of life, though we are not told if he took his own medicines. He was heard to say more than once, 'I have often wondered what set Robert Burns upon me, for we were aye on the best of terms.' It was never proved that Wilson's medicines had a lethal effect.

The poet, whom Burns perhaps too generously acknowledged as his main inspiration, was Robert Fergusson. He, when a student at St. Andrews University, acted the part of a quack doctor, for a joke. He was crossing from St. Andrews to Anstruther with his professor, William Wilkie. They passed over a lonely moor near Dunino when a cottager informed them that a young man lay ill nearby of a malarial fever, a common complaint. Fergusson, a high-spirited lad, pretended to be a doctor and went to the patient's bedside, pulled a serious face, gravely felt his pulse and prescribed a perfectly harmless brew of feverfew, a strongly scented herb that grew profusely round the cottage garden. To the surprise of the patient's family, the 'doctor' would not accept a fee for his services.

But money was the incentive of all quacks. Three such men, two of them Englishmen, and one a German, practised in Glasgow and Edinburgh and all intermediate stations, in olden times.

Parsons was the non-medical quack whose headquarters were in the Cowgate of Auld Reekie. He travelled round the countryside setting up stages to attract the many-headed. From these eminences he sold his wares, the most popular of which was the elixir of life with the fancy name Orvieton. This was universally known through Europe as an antidote to poisons and its common name was Venice Treacle, though it got its trade name from Orvieto, the native place of the inventor.

Parsons advertised it in his bills as 'an antidote against infections, distempers, and helps barrenness.' The Scots apparently preferred to risk these evils rather than spend bawbees on Orvieton, for he was last heard of offering it at reduced rates; also included in his offer was a fine cabinet organ to be auctioned. This would make a change from the kind of organ recitals his patients were so keen on.

Barrenness was not so much feared as fecundity. There was practically always a certain discovery of fornication for the female partners, but we learn from an old ballad that quacks were able by drugs to bring about abortions. The lines are:

To pluck the leaf frae aff the tree
To twine my bonnie babe and me.

The tree was probably a poisonous kind such as the yew or the laurel, and no doubt witches were well up in distilling abortive drugs, thus giving good grounds for hunting them down.

Another English quack was Dr. Green, who attracted crowds by employing a tumbler, or acrobat. But the tumbler proved a bit too agile, for he eloped with Green's takings, and his rogue of a master had the impudence to advertise in the Edinburgh press that he had been robbed, and to warn people against the robber.

Neither of these quacks came up to the magnificent standard of John Pontheus, a German of the century before. Several times he set up his stage in the middle of the High Street of Edinburgh. He called himself a professor of music and he used this accomplishment to attract great crowds. On his stage a jester pranced about, cracking jokes and performing antics. On a tightrope strung slantingly high across the street from the lofty tenements of either side an acrobat danced, and slid down on his chest like a bird, his arms and legs extended. He also performed somersaults on the rope, alighting skilfully on his feet without once coming to grief.

Pontheus was honest, compared with the normal drug dealer. His drugs were so good and cheap that country doctors and chemists flocked into Edinburgh to buy them. He certainly livened up the city.

Another honest German, Herman or Hyman Lyon, a Jew from the Baltic, was wrongly reputed in Edinburgh to be a quack. He was a very gifted and highly trained doctor, but he was unfortunate in the choice of his speciality. Had he made himself out to be a heart, liver, brain or bladder specialist, he might have been honoured. But he chose what was the very urgent and unmentionable complaint of corns. He was that most maligned of all humanity's benefactors, a corn-doctor. The old stage quip recalls their status. 'My ancestors came over with the Mormons, William the Corn-curer and all that.'

Although Lyon had spent five years studying medicine at the College in Edinburgh, he was refused a degree at the final interview, though several gentlemen who had been less than diligent at their studies, were granted degrees. Corns were *infra dig*, though none the less painful for all that.

Lyon privately published a book on corns, not of course under that ambiguous title. He gave it the Latin title *Spinae Pedum* or 'Thorns of the Foot', a very apt description, as any sufferer knows. At that time in the middle of the long French Wars, there was no transport for the P.B.I., Poor Bloody Infantry. Foot-slogging was the lot of the British warrior in the Napoleonic time, and a large proportion of the casualties were due to blisters gone septic, and corns. Lyon's book, had it been circulated, would have saved thousands from agony, for it gave tried and tested advice on foot-care. Instead of a deserved fame, he worked under a shade because of the snobbery of the age. But many a prominent lady or gentleman was glad to stump up his or her guinea, that being Lyon's normal fee for a private consultation.

'Pills and squills' was a rhyming description of an apothecary's stock-in-trade. The pills were made by an apprentice on the prescription of his master. As a fourteen year old on a holiday job I once had the privilege of making pills, ointments, tonics and syrups for a well-known old-fashioned chemist. I was astonished at the vast quantities of powdered chalk, sugar and lard that were consumed in that lucrative trade. The simplest and cheapest materials went to the making. Squills were prescribed in many cases of heart and kidney complaints. The squill is a kind of sea-onion. The Scottish bluebell, if by that patriotic term is meant the wild hyacinth, not the harebell, is the humble cousin of the squill.

For two and a half centuries Anderson's Pills were the cure-all in Scottish homes. The ingredients were a well-kept secret. Anderson was a physician in the reign of Charles I. His daughter inherited the patent and passed the secret on to a surgeon in Edinburgh. There is a curious portrait of Anderson and his daughter, the doctor holding a book and the girl a pill the size of a walnut. Obviously the pill was enlarged so that it would show in the painting. But it looks as big as a horse-pill, which recalls the old tale of the farmer who got a horse-pill from the vet. and was told how to administer it to the restless patient. The vet. gave him a tube a little larger in diameter than the pill. He was to put the tube down the horse's throat and blow.

The next day the vet. met the farmer, his neck all wrapped up.

'Did you not do as I suggested?'

'Yes, but the horse blew first.'

Anderson's Pill was simply a concoction of the juice of the leaves of a kind of aloe plant. It was a purgative. A good dish of hot stewed gooseberries or rhubarb would have been just as effective at no cost.

Many a doctor's sanity has been saved by a strong sense of humour. Few have put it to such purpose as a Doctor Campbell. Growing impatient with the theories of a school of medicine known as the 'hermetics' who claimed an infallible way of prolonging life, for a joke he wrote a 'learned' treatise on an absolutely certain way to achieve a century. He proved to apparently logical satisfaction that the breath of young women contained elements for prolonging life.

Various people took Campbell's irony at its face value. One doctor even decided to put the hint to the proof. He rented a lodging in a female boarding school so that he could be sure of a constant supply of young ladies' breath, whether from a distance or quite close we are not told.

The theory of this elixir of life was even supported in a pamphlet written by a pedant with the illuminating name of Mr. Thicknesse.

Emma Hamilton was the wife of Sir William Hamilton and the mistress of Horatio Nelson at one and the same time. The whole nation, including Sir William, knew of Nelson's adultery. But neither he nor Emma was embarrassed. In her case, not surprisingly, considering her early life.

She had been a nanny in London until her handsome figure and beautiful features took the fancy, first, of Greville, a statesman, who sent her to have lessons in singing, dancing and acting. She now became a friend of Romney, the artist, who painted her in various poses. Her fortunes now underwent a change. Greville got into debt and began to search around for goods to convert into cash, but the only realisable bit of any value was Emma. She had excited the depravity of Greville's uncle, Sir William Hamilton, who had a considerable fortune. To put it bluntly, Hamilton got Emma in exchange for paying his nephew's debts, which led to many tantrums from Emma who resented being bought and sold. She was by this time a brazen hussy.

She fell in with Dr. Graham, the most famous quack of the age, and in alliance with him proceeded to shock London, a difficult task in an age of high living and low thinking. Under the assumed name of Vestina, Goddess of Health, she took part in scandalous performances in the Temple of Health in Pall Mall, London. If her name was based on the Vestal Virgins she did not act up to it, for, not even in a vest, she bathed with the naked Dr. Graham in a mud bath before packed houses, who paid sweetly for the spectacle. Then Dr. Graham delivered his 'Hymeneal Lectures' which we would call 'Sex Lectures for the Married'. These went down well in London, but Graham braved the wrath of Presbyterian Edinburgh and gave the same naughty lectures in a chapel in Carrubber's Close in the High Street, which in my youth was a hot-gospel centre.

Graham lived a torrid existence in a sense, but he was a fanatical believer in low temperatures for good health. He slept on a bare mattress, with all the windows open, and wore no woollen underwear. He tried to get permission to build a health-house, on the summit of Arthur's Seat, but the commissioners refused permits for this sanatorium. He might have saved himself the trouble, for there are hundreds of houses in the Southern Uplands much higher than the top of Arthur's Seat. The inhabitants have always been healthy. Graham lived extravagantly, and died in poverty near Glasgow. Emma, his high-flying mudlark, also lived extravagantly, for she inherited the incomes of both Hamilton and Nelson, but she, too, died in poverty near Calais.

Edinburgh is fortunate in having Holyrood Park in its midst. For centuries the ladies of Auld Reekie went there on May morning to wash their faces in the dewy grass, to retain or regain that school-girl complexion. If that failed, they had to resort to a complexion quack, and get their lilies and roses out of a pot.

Other health-giving habits were sea-bathing from horse-drawn huts on wheels from as early as 1761, on the shore between Leith and Portobello. But that, of course, was before the days when the untreated sewage from Auld Reekie was poured by the million gallons into the Firth of Forth. When this monstrous nuisance was in full blast, for over a century, sea-bathing was wittily described by a disgusted native as 'Not so much swimming as going through the motions.'

There were indoor salt-water baths, heated by a stove, centuries ago, in Leith, where the object was to promote health and avoid scandal, certain days of the week being reserved for ladies only.

None of these precautions were able to prevent the outbreaks of plague. Very·drastic action was taken against anyone suspected of carrying plague. In 1530 a woman named Katherine Heriot was accused of the double crime of theft and of bringing contagious sickness from Leith into the city. She was ordered to be drowned in the Quarry Holes near Greyfriars. In the same year of grace a poor soul called Janet Gowane was accused of having pestilence upon her and her cure consisted of being branded on both cheeks and expelled from the city, probably to die in a ditch.

When the New Town of Edinburgh was built many of the inhabitants moved over the valley to the north, leaving the stinking wynds and closes and courts. A satirist of the times wrote this couplet on their feelings when they occupied the fresh new dwellings.

The New Town ladies as they sniffed the wind
Sighed for the joys that they had left behind.

Let us turn from the Good Old Days to a comical craze that raged like the plague for many years. It was the science of phrenology, or 'Bumps', which occupied otherwise sensible men for much of their lives. It is one of the unexplained mysteries of human mentality that a person can think sensibly on practically every subject except one, when they entertain the most extravagant delusions. A true case is on record of a lunatic who wrote eminently sensible letters to his family until he came to the PS which invariably consisted of the sixty-four dollar question, 'Will you please tell me what you did with the meat that you took out of my head?' The phrenologists were affected in much the same way.

The chief of these head-measurers, whom we should hesitate to call a quack, was George Combe. He was born in Edinburgh and took up the legal profession, whereby he became quite wealthy, and fussy in his habits. He was tall, thin and handsome. His hobby, phrenology, was to occupy much of his life and the lives of a circle of friends.

First, they studied their own heads, as they were readily accessible, and their owners were willing to have them divided up (superficially, of course) into thirty-five 'localities'. These areas of the skull were given 'lang-nebbit' names and phrases, which immediately gave some people inflated ideas of their own brain-boxes. For example, a person fond of breeding a large family had his area of philoprogenitiveness awarded perhaps nineteen marks out of twenty. The greedy-guts got high marks for acquisitiveness, the bully for combativeness, the fop for love of approbation.

When the Phrenological Society got tired of the excellence of their own craniums, they sought out other worlds of intellect to conquer. But few people were willing to wear their hearts on their sleeves or their character on a blue-printed skull, so the experimenters were forced to go to places where nobody was allowed to object. These were the lunatic asylums and the jails, where they no doubt gave the inmates of the first a low count for wit, and of the second a high mark for destructiveness and acquisitiveness, but to neither group good marks for hope.

George Combe's best experiment was without doubt conducted on the rich and handsome daughter of the famous actress Mrs. Siddons. He examined her head and, after several experiments, gave her full marks for amativeness, adhesiveness, love of approbation and form. My own faculty of wonder is full to bursting to know how one of the most desirable *pièces de résistance* in Britain formed a matrimonial alliance with a middle-aged dry old stick of a Scottish lawyer. She certainly ought to have had her head examined, inside.

The most blood-chilling episodes in this story of skull-quacks have still to come, and force one to ask the double question, Was no one scared, or was nothing sacred?

As is common knowledge, the multi-murderer William Burke was condemned to be hanged and anatomised, while Hare, for having spilt the beans, was given leg-bail. Here was a chance not to be missed by Combe and Co. Never in Scottish criminal records had any wretches shown such callous disregard for human life, with no pity for old or young, the beautiful or the simple-minded. Measurements of Burke's skull were sure to prove the depravity of his character, or perhaps the depravity of his character was sure to prove the measurements of his skull, or something.

Luckily, the scores that Burke made in different areas of his skull have been preserved for posterity, and they prove something quite different and very extraordinary, which should have made the phrenologists change their hobby for skittles.

Burke's moral organs were more highly developed than they ought to have been, as shown by his crimes. His localities of benevolence, love and conscientiousness were well-developed, his organ of destructiveness was average. Professor Munro sawed off the crown of Burke's skull to examine the brain. It was perfectly normal. In fact, neither on the outside nor inside of the cranium, was this multi-murderer, this monster, whom the Scottish mobs would like to have torn limb from limb, shown to be other than a decent church-going man who would apparently hesitate to hurt a fly.

Before he left County Tyrone he was an exemplary character, hard-working and musical, married amicably to a decent woman. In short, the law seems to have hanged the wrong man, for William Hare was the desperado who corrupted Burke. He was a man of vicious and brutal habits, who on one occasion in an inn near Balerno, kicked a companion about the head and face with iron-shod boots, to his severe injury.

Did Hare's phrenology reveal this? Far from it. His destructiveness was below average. Benevolence was well-developed. Ideality was large. Wit was full.

We now turn to an account of ghoulishness perhaps without equal in our national Museum of Horrors. It shows the length that solemn quacks will go to, in pursuit of their alleged scientific conclusions.

Jean Armour died, aged sixty-nine, on 26 March 1834, and arrangements were made to lay her beside her husband in the Burns Mausoleum in St. Michael's Churchyard, Dumfries, on 1 April. The remains of Burns and his two sons had been exhumed from the north corner of the churchyard in 1815, and deposited in the newly-erected mausoleum. On that occasion an enormous crowd had assembled and with great difficulty had been prevented from carrying off, as relics, the bones of the bard and those of his young sons. Jean Armour's death seemed a God-given, or perhaps a Devil-inspired chance, to turn the burial of 'Bonnie Jean' to good account.

On the eve of the burial, six ghouls, MacDiarmid, Rankine, Kerr, Bogie, Crombie and

Blacklock, crept in the gloaming towards the churchyard, clambered over the walls and gathered at the mausoleum. Any feelings of degradation which they may have had, they confessed, 'were overcome by the thought of the great benefit to humanity that would accrue from the exact knowledge of the assessment of Burns' skull.' They might even be able to prove to the satisfaction of all phrenologists and other owlish philosophers that the owner of the skull had had the ability to write splendid songs, poems, satires and epigrams.

The skull having been unearthed and dusted, plaster-casts were made. Three more eminent ghouls joined the party, and before returning Rab's cranium to the mould, they solemnly stood around in a nine-point circle and passed the relic from hand to hand to see how it fitted their hats. It was too large for many of them, so they concluded that as far as cubic inches went, Burns excelled them all. It is as well that they did not remember that Byron had a small skull, or they might have felt superior to that genius.

The clocks of Dumfries now tolled the ghostly hour of one. All Fool's Day was fairly begun, and perhaps Rabbie was laughing sardonically from the Elysian Fields.

What did the measurements reveal? The astounding fact that Burns got full marks for philoprogenitiveness, which he was in the habit of writing with four letters, not twenty. His wit, or mirthfulness, was not up to standard and, as for his language, it was uncertain. Later that 'Hunt the Gowk' morning, his skull was most appropriately enclosed in a leaden box where it still remains as a symbol of what happens to a rare spirit who finds himself enlisted in an awkward squad.

Phrenologists, like psychologists, can pass some odd judgements, so, with no regrets we leave them and pass on to a modern practice which is just as liable to be abused, the Kiss of Life.

A young man walking along the beach in Ayrshire came upon a couple in bathing attire by the edge of the tide. The man was frantically kissing the unresponsive girl.

'Hullo, there. It's a bit public for that kind of thing. Gie the wee lassie a chance.'

The kisser looked up.

'I've just rescued her from drowning. I'm giving her the kiss of life, can't you see?'

'Oh, I'm sorry. Is she no' comin' to?'

'I think so, but I'm still drawing a lot of water from her mouth.'

The other looked thoughtful.

'I'd like to offer you a tip,' he said. 'As a practical plumber, can I suggest that you pull her backside oot o' the watter?'

Summing up this chapter of charlatans and ignoramuses, we are left with a grave mistrust of all claims to knowledge and ability, as well as of all prophecies of what is, or is not, possible. Heavier-than-air flight was dismissed as a chimera by notable men of science, so also was atomic power, space flight and landing on the moon, and these deliberate judgements were proven wrong soon after. Reputations, for good or evil, are often proved wrong by hard facts. Medicines that were 'worth a guinea a box' two generations ago are laughed at now. Like Anderson's Pills, Orvieton, the Elixir of Life, and King's Touch, their charms are fled.

Charles II asked to be pardoned for being 'such an unconscionable time a-dying.' It must have seemed even longer to him than to his attendants, for he was fed by the Royal Physicians with a loathsome mess, the main constituents being the pulverised brains of monkeys.

George V, in his last illness, two and a half centuries later, was given a concoction of the dark dorsal flesh of herrings. Neither panacea was any more effective than the rat-droppings that Montaigne complained of, five hundred years ago, or the non-tobacco cigarettes to stop nicotine addicts, which recently cost the inventors a packet.

Appearances are deceptive and the 'bedside manner' has often hidden a stubborn practitioner of out-moded 'remedies'. Even in the heart of the Aesculapian stronghold, the Royal Infirmary, deception has occurred. A visitor, seeing, in the words of Daniel, a 'man clothed in a long white garment', asked, 'Excuse me, are you a student coming out for a doctor?'

'No, I'm a painter comin' oot for a pint.'

Walking on water calls for a very delicate method of locomotion. Water-spiders do it all the time. The greatest precaution must be taken not to break the surface tension. I have never managed to avoid doing this, and I doubt if many people have, though numbers have asserted that they could walk on water, but have been speedily disillusioned. Both the following examples come from Scotland.

A religious maniac, in Covenanting times, named Peter Mackie, set all Perth in an uproar with his prophecies and wild sermons. So great was his faith in the power of the Lord, he announced, that He had given Peter Mackie the same miraculous powers as his Redeemer.

One day hundreds of persons assembled on the banks of the Tay, nearly all possessed of the firm belief that the enthusiast would walk over the water, though there were a few cynics. Peter walked confidently down to the water's edge, then paused and said that, as the glitter of the water dazzled his eyes, quantities of sawdust should be thrown on the surface. Alas, not enough sawdust was thrown on the river and Mackie walked farther and farther in, until the water came up to his mouth and he was in danger of drowning. By this time there was no sign of Father Tay bearing up his foolish son, so Mackie cried aloud to heaven, 'O, Lord, ye'll surely no droon Peter Mackie this way, gaun on your ain errands.'

Jean Brown kept a sweetie shop in the Potterrow of Edinburgh. She began increasingly to hear voices from outer space, and to see visions of angels and of Christ. In less prosaic and down-to-earth regions than the Potterrow she might have been revered as a saint. One day when on a visit to Kirkcaldy she heard a voice calling to her to set out on a journey to pass through the Jordan. Her geographical knowledge was vague but she had an idea that, like Ramoth-Gilead, Jerusalem and Babylon, the River Jordan lay in the South Country, on the far side of Kinghorn.

She set off on her sanctified pilgrimage and very soon arrived on the shores of the Firth of Forth. No whit deterred, she started to pass through the 'Jordan' and was with great difficulty rescued, despite her determined struggles to reach the Promised Land.

She acquired fame and an increased sale of confectionery, because of her adventures, no doubt handing out accounts of them with pokes of gundy to the gaping bairns of the Potterrow.

Hypochondriacs are usually incurable, for their imagination is out of reach of the materia medica. A relation of mine had a severe attack of hypochondria. If anyone had a pain she was certain to have had it much worse, or would presently develop severe symptoms of it. One day her father was talking of the illness of one of his friends, enumerating all the symptoms, deliberately going into the gruesome details. To each one she echoed her similar traumatic experiences. At last her father turned on her in exasperation.

'Did you dee, Lizzie?'

'No.'

'Weel, then, Willie beat ye there, for he did.'

Fair Maids

The schoolboy who derived the word virgin from the Latin vir, and the English gin, a trap, was showing a cynicism beyond his years, but his derivation was wrong. Virgin can be descriptive of males or mountains, even on rare occasions of widows or meadows, of broadswords or butterflies.

Unfortunately it is an emotive word, the very mention of which brings a blush or a bluster, depending on personal feelings.

Virgin birth is an even more sensitive field of discussion. Those who are cynical about religious beliefs are not very pleased to know that virgin birth is one of the commonest things in nature. It goes by the 'lang-nebbit' name of parthenogenesis and it describes the reproduction of certain kinds of insects, by females, without fertilisation by males. If medical science proceeds as it is doing, virgin birth may soon become the norm, and the lab. bench will supplant the marriage bed. Those who stick to the old-fashioned style will perhaps adopt for a slogan 'Spare the rod and spoil the child.' We may even have two classes of citizens, testis babies and test-tube babies.

In olden days virginity was universally recommended, but rarely adopted as a life-style. The priest in one parish told one young lassie that virginity was a rich treasure which God had put in a treasure-chest to be severely guarded. The naive young lady replied that she was well aware of the treasure God had given her. 'Unluckily' she continued, 'God has also supplied most of the young men with a key which fits easily and exactly into the lock of the treasure-chest.'

97

A young man had fallen madly in love with a country wench. He found her extremely shy and even prudish. When he ventured to take a kiss she repulsed him, and any other liberties she viewed with horror. Being a decent young fellow he respected her virginal behaviour and, when the wedding-day came, he praised his betrothed for having resisted his advances.

She said, 'Now you can understand the reason for my behaviour, which must have tried your patience many a time.'

'Yes, indeed, it did,' he answered, 'But I can tell you this in confidence. Had you given in to me I should have had nothing more to do with you.'

'Don't I know that. Many a time, before I met you, I yielded to eager young men and never saw them again.'

If the church recommended virginity, the medical profession did not always support it. There was a bluff old country doctor in Duns, Berwickshire, who was experienced in the primitive life of many of the honest folk of the farm-rows and lonely hill-side cottages. Both sexes were hardy, and birth and death well within their capacity. It was not unknown for a bondager, or woman hired to help a male worker, to be suddenly delivered of a child in the middle of hoeing a field of turnips. She would wrap the infant in a shawl, leaving it lying by the hedgerow while she continued her field labour.

The doctor was not even called in. We can imagine the irritation of our medico when he was constantly visited by a robust-looking young woman, who complained always of 'being awfu' no' weel.' He decided to shock her into better behaviour.

On her next visit he told her abruptly to strip to the skin. She did this very reluctantly.

'What ails ye, woman. I'm a doctor. I'm not going to set about you.'

She was in a glowing state of good health.

'Have ye got a man?' he queried.

'Na, I've ne'er had a yin.'

'Then you're a virgin, eh, one of the few in the parish.'

'I suppose sae, doctor.'

He approached her and gave her a good slap across the belly with the back of his hand.

'D'ye ken what's the matter wi ye?

'Na, doctor.'

'What ye need is a guid wheech.'

Locally in the Merse, this expressive word had several meanings, all having the sense of a sudden rapid movement.

It was a reproach to a woman to remain a virgin for long after marriage, but the husband was usually held responsible.

An elderly medical professor in a Scots university married a fairly young woman. This caused some amusement to his students, increased by a dislike of the professor for his harsh marking of their papers. They decided to get some of their own back.

On the day following the wedding a great crowd of cheering students gathered outside the medical lecture-room. The cause of their hilarity was an official notice pinned to the door.

Bulletin

Professor Brown spent a very restless night.
Mrs. Brown's condition remains unchanged.

It seems that when a virgin in Scotland changed her condition to that of a wife she had to adopt a new style of dress. Unmarried girls, not necessarily all virgins, went bare-headed.

The old proverb says:

All is not gold that glisters
Nor maidens that wear their hair.

At one time it became very popular in Scottish towns for ladies of all conditions to wear a plaid over their bare heads and shoulders. Two Acts of the Edinburgh Town Council were passed in the time of the Civil War, forbidding women to wear plaids over their heads. The wording is very quaint:

By the wearing of plaids 'matrons were not to be discerned from hures and lowse-living women, to their own dishonour and scandal of the citie.'

The women ignored this male interference with their costume and continued to sport the tartan, even at the risk of being taken for hures. In my youth practically every woman in the Old Town of Edinburgh and in Central Leith dressed in the above style, usually wrapping their infant in a fold of the plaid. Their hair was combed straight back from the forehead and secured in a bun with an ornamental comb, after the Spanish style.

Burns' attitude to the lassies need not be examined. He was a great admirer of virgins and helped quite a number to sustain, and sometimes to drop, the burden of their virginity that Nature had loaded them with. In the Day Book of his Border Tour he noted that he fell under the spell of two lovely lasses. Here are his high-flying sentiments.

'Charming Rachel Ainslie. May thy bosum never be wrung by the evils of this life of sorrows, or by the villainy of the world's sons.'

'Sweet Isabella Lindsay. May peace dwell in thy bosum uninterrupted except by the tumultuous throbbings of rapturous love. That graceful form must grace another's arms.'

It is pretty plain that Burns would have been highly gratified to make love to both of these ladies. He seemed quite jealous of such of the world's sons as were to take these fair maids into their arms.

Clarinda was neither a virgin nor a widow. Had she been either, there is little doubt that 'Sylvander' (Robert Burns) would have been her lover in more than sentiment. She had been married when seventeen to a Mr. Maclehose, a West Indian merchant. She had borne him four children, three of whom had died in infancy. Then her husband left her, and when she met Burns in 1791, she was very disillusioned. She was thirty-two, the same age as Burns. The attractions she had for the poet were her good looks and wit, but, more than both, the fact that she was unattainable. She was virginal, despite her past.

She sent him a plain truth in verse, which was also a warning.

Speak not of love, it gives me pain
For love has been my foe.
He bound me in an iron chain
And left me deep in woe.

He might well have repeated these other lines to himself as he left her apartment, unrequited.

She kicked me downstairs with such exquisite grace
That I felt she was kicking me up.

When she was old (for despite her bad start and varying fortunes, she came of a hardy stock and lived to be over eighty) she wrote in her diary, forty years after meeting Burns, 'O, may we meet in Heaven.'

As an old Scots preacher said, probably thinking of one of Jonathan Swift's witticisms, 'It tells us in the Guid Book that in Heaven there will be nae marrying or gieing in marriage. In short, brothers and sisters, though we dinna ken what they dae up there, we ken fine what they dinna dae.' So if Sylvander and Clarinda have met in Heaven, Jean Armour will present her marriage certificate in vain to the recording angel.

In the primitive times of the Christian Church, the deacons used to prove their powers of resistance to temptation by sleeping with virgins and leaving them intact. Perhaps they got the idea from the Old Testament incident where King David, cold in bed, had a curvacious hot-water body put in beside him, and 'knew her not', a quaint Jacobean expression which adds spice to the parting remark, 'Nice to have known you.' What the deacons' *pièces de résistance* thought of the arrangement is not recorded.

A notable Christian lady named Susannah was so named after that lady in the Apocrypha whom the elders of Israel tried to get into bad reputation but who was so skilfully defended by Daniel, especially in his cross-examination of the accusers, that she was cleared of any stain. But the later Susannah was not so fortunate. She was a friend of St. Ambrose, whom he recommended to make a vow of perpetual virginity. She obeyed him, but the flesh is weak and she strayed on to the primrose path.

She had to be punished in some notable way, so her friend Ambrose sentenced her in as gentle a way as he could. She had to appear in public in white linen and recite the 50th psalm each day for a certain period. This was equivalent to writing one hundred lines, 'I must not commit adultery.'

The 50th psalm has twenty-three verses but the most pointed one is that which says, 'Thou hast been a partaker with vile adulterers,' which probably brought a blush to her cheeks.

A young nun in modern times had been taken in an unchaste act. She was summoned before the old beldame who ruled the roost. She got a scorching lecture on the evils of fornication, to which she listened with fitting meekness, probably not entirely convinced.

'I'm truly repentant, Mother,' she muttered, 'What penance do you give me?'

Mother Angela replied, 'I want you immediately to eat these two raw lemons.'

'This is a very lenient sentence for my dire sin,' muttered the penitent.

'Yes, but it is only a preliminary, and it will take that smug, self-satisfied smirk off your silly face.'

A particular young man, a virgin himself, wished to ensure purity in his prospective bride, so he got in touch with the man in charge of the novitiates in a local convent, and became acquainted with a young lady of demure appearance who did not wish to take vows. So struck was he with her eminent suitability that, on the wedding-day he loaded her with presents of all sorts. On the second day of the honeymoon she passed this remark, 'You know, Cyril, I can't understand why you've been so good to me, just for what we do in bed. Father O'Neill only gave me an orange.'

When renovations were being made at Coldingham Priory, the workers came across a cavity in the wall in which was the upright skeleton of a young woman. She had been immured alive centuries before. This was the unspeakably evil way of punishing vow-breakers. Little wonder some of them made up all sorts of miraculous and incredible tales to avoid the accusation of incontinence, such as the following.

In the Middle Ages two pious virgins went out into the fields at the Feast of the Nativity, 8 September. They lay down on pillows of straw, meditating on the birth of the Saviour. They knew no more, according to their story, until the Feast of St. John, 27 December. The four months had passed in a flash, during which they had had a vision of the infant Jesus.

When they came back to consciousness a beautiful male infant lay between them in the straw. The child was accepted with reverence by a nearby religious house. To the agnostics a more simple explanation suggest itself.

The town wits in my youth used to bandy about a series of battered jokes about virgins, which was perhaps to get their revenge against jilts.

There was one about the new clerkess who joined the office staff. Her name was Virginia. They called her Virgin for short, but not for long.

A mass meeting of the local Virgins Association was held last week – in a telephone booth.

The schoolboy of classical ambitions was asked by the Latin teacher to give the degrees of *rara avis*, a rare bird. His answer was a good effort.

'*Rara avis*, a rare bird; *rariora avis*, a rarer bird; *rarissima avis*, a most rare bird; *virgo intacta*, the rarest bird of all.'

The arms of the former City of Edinburgh were a castle propped up by a maiden and a deer. Both represented traditions connected with the old city. The stag was prevented from turning on David I by a miracle, a cross sent from heaven at a critical moment. The maiden referred to the legend that the British tribe who occupied Edinburgh used to keep their virgins free from danger in the castle whose ancient name was Castle Agned, or the Castle of the Maidens.

East of Edinburgh, a mile from the Castle, was a well, dedicated to a Pictish princess named Triduana. She, in her turn, was pursued by a would-be ravisher, who had fallen in love with her beautiful eyes, among other features. To spite him, she sharpened a forked stick and blinded herself. On this account the well was resorted to by all those afflicted with sore eyes. The water was reckoned a cure for this trouble alone. The stones from this well were rebuilt last century into St. Margaret's Well in Holyrood Park, and St. Triduana's Well now flows in a pipe under Meadowbank Stadium, no longer 'a sicht for sair een.'

The mother of Glasgow's saint, Mungo or Kentigern, was Thenaw daughter of Loth, the King of Lothian. She had an illicit affair with the British King of Cumbria. When her illegitimate son, Kentigern, was born, her father Loth put the pair of them into a coracle in the strong waters of the Forth, thinking to see the last of them. But the east wind, for which Edinburgh is still famous, blew the coracle up the estuary on to the shore at Culross, or Cu'ross, in West Fife. Who should be there to welcome Thenaw and her babe but St. Serf?

After many trials Kentigern founded the religious see of Glasgow and proved the truth of another Scots proverb that 'a bastard may be as guid as a bowstock,' meaning in horticultural terms, that a cabbage not of legitimate seed may be as good as one from known seed.

Thenaw was canonised, an honour which she did not expect when she was in the Cumbrian Monarch's embraces.

St. Catherine had a chapel at Glencorse in the Pentland Hills, a few miles from Edinburgh which, at first sight, had a curious name. It was the Church of St. Catherine the Virgin, or St. Catherine of the Hopes. This does not mean that, like any other virgin, she had expectations; hopes is a south-country word for valleys.

Joan of Arc was known to her countrymen as La Pucelle, or The Virgin. History says that she was burned at the stake by the English in 1431 and died a virgin. But French archivists, seeking through documents in Rouen, found certificates of her marriage to a wealthy citizen of that town. On 1 August 1439, eight years after her incineration, she was awarded 210 French pounds by the city of Rouen for services rendered by her at the siege by the English.

A Scottish Maid of Orleans was Maid Lilliard who led and inspired a party of the Scots army at the battle of Ancrum Moor in the Borders in the sixteenth century. A stone with the following rhyme in memory of the heroine was erected by the roadside. I remember getting off my pushbike to read it sixty years ago, when the road was solitary and white with dust.

Fair maiden Lilliard lies under this stane
Little was her stature but muckle was her fame
Upon the English louns she laid many thumps
And when her legs were cuttit aff she fought upon her stumps.

Lilliard, like many Scottish women, joined the menfolk in battle, to be avenged of the atrocities which Henry VIII perpetrated upon the Scots people of all ages and conditions. She followed her lover into the battle on Ancrum Moor and, on seeing him slain, took up his sword and contributed to a complete Scottish victory by slaying several enemies before being brought down.

A well known Border family, the Tweedies, are said to owe their name and origin to a very unusual, if not unique experience. A young woman, recently married, and all but a maiden, had been left by her bridegroom at brief notice because he was called upon to follow his landlord on a Crusade.

On returning to Tweedside seven years later the squire of the cross was greeted by his wife, accompanied by a handsome boy of about five. A little mental arithmetic convinced him that, unless she had had an elephantine pregnancy, the boy must have been conceived more than a year after his departure.

Indignantly he sought an explanation. She told him that one summer evening as she walked by the Tweed a water-kelpie had jumped out and forced her. Whether the crusader believed her or not he was gentleman enough to accept the situation. After all, it was an age of miracles.

He replied laughingly, 'I jaloose we'll hae to ca' the wee chiel, Tweedie.'

Perhaps the fairest judgement that can be passed, if one is needed, on the behaviour of maidens is in another proverb, 'Licht lassies mak willing lads.'

The word virgin can be applied in irony. In the Stockbridge area of Edinburgh a worthy old baker named Veitch, having some cash to spare, built a square of one-storied cottages enclosing a grassy green. The cottages were rented cheaply to laundry women, who, after washing their linen in the neighbouring Water of Leith, spread them out to bleach on the green, where, being always overlooked, they were not likely to be pilfered.

The neighbours decided that as all the laundresses were single women they would change the name Veitch's Square to Virgins' Square, though they knew full well that, for some of the inhabitants of this pleasant quadrangle, the title was purely honorary.

In olden times the Scots had a proverb, 'When petticoats woo, breeks come speed.' This had its parallel south of the Border, in the English saying, 'It's time to marry when the maid woos the man.'

In the uplands of Galloway the maids had a rough and ready way of attracting the attentions of the lads, though it did not always lead to the altar. A local preacher condemned this old custom in the following exhortation to his congregation.

'The time o the cutting o the peat-mosses is at hand, my friens, when the lasses will fling bits o clods at the lads, my friens, and then they'll seem to run away, ye see, and the lads'll follow them. Then the lasses will gang tapselteerie and seem to fa' heids-ower-goudie, as if something had trippet them up, my friens. Then the lads will fa' ower the tap o them, my friens, and sae begins skulldudderie and houghmagundie, my friens, which is the beginning o a' the evil and which sends mony a worthy chiel to everlasting hell-fire where on a bed o the blue burnin brimstane, my friens, they may lie for ever mair, my friens. Amen, my friens, and dinna say when ye gang to the peat-cuttin that ye didna ken. For I've warned ye. Amen, my friens, We will now pronounce the benediction.'

St. Abb's Head is the highest promontary between Leith and London. It is a wild awe-inspiring place, where in storms the North Sea dashes against the fearsome cliffs. In olden times it was the site of a nunnery founded by Abba, a daughter of Ethelfrith, heathen king of the Angles whose kingdom extended into what is now Scotland.

At first sight it seems strange that a princess should have given up her life of prosperity for one of deprivation. But she did not do this without compulsion. Penda the heathen king of Mercia, the neighbouring English state, went to war with Ethelfrith, and Abba did not wait to be ravished by this royal ruffian. Being genuinely alarmed for her virtue she fled in a frail boat up the rocky coast and was spotted by a hermit as she was being carried by a storm past the headland.

The tradition is that a second mysterious person, supposed to be a guardian angel, was also in the boat. At any rate she was rescued and in gratitude she set up the nunnery which attracted virgins to a life of dedication for several centuries.

A lighthouse was built on the headland in 1861, the beam being visible for over thirty miles, as great a boon to shipping as the nunnery had been to distressed maidens.

Rab and Cathie, two unemotional Scots, were courting, or so the rumour went in the Border village. They had been walking out for a year or so, but not even holding hands, and hardly exchanging a word. At last, perhaps overcome by the peace and beauty of the moonlit scene, Rab stopped and looked meaningfully into Cathie's eyes.

'Will ye marry me, Cathie?'

'Aye.'

They resumed their silent walk for perhaps a mile.

This time Cathie stopped and broke the silence.

'Hae ye naething else to say, Rab?'

Rab hung his head for a moment.

'Na, I doot I've said ower muckle a'ready.'

In a Strathclyde school the Occupations officer, in the good old days when there were jobs, was questioning some sixteen-year olds.

To a bright young lass he put the question, 'What would you like to be, Rita, my dear?'

'Yin o thae lasses in the airyplanes that gangs frae the kitchen tae ser the lads wi their denners.'

'O, an air-hostess, Rita?'

'Aye.'

'But why?'

'Ye meet some nice chaps.'

'But being an air-hostess requires long special training. Besides you can meet nice young men in works and offices.'

'Maybe ye can, sir, but they're no strapped doon.'

A young dairymaid in a large isolated farm in the Southern Uplands complained to the farmer's wife that she had been raped in the dark by one of the farm-workers.

'Are ye sure it was yin o the men aboot the place, Nan?'

'Whae else could it be? There's been naebody up at the Cleuch for weeks, for the roads are blockit wi snaw. I've no been oot o the place, either.'

The farmer lined up his workers, the four ploomen, the twa herds, the orra-man, the lads and the auld gairdner Tam. Nan was told to point to the guilty man. She pointed to several in turn, who all denied it. In desperation she came to old Tam, over eighty, and accused him. He was silent and this was interpreted as guilt, so he was severely rebuked by the farmer and docked of a month's wages to repay the offended maid.

A long time after, the true culprit, when in drink, boasted of his conquest. Tam was asked why he had taken the blame.

'I was ower prood tae deny it,' he admitted.

On a golf-links in Fife, two holiday golfers, a man and a maid, strangers to one another, decided to play a round together.

Both were nervous and had a slight stammer, on account of it. At the second hole the young man said, 'I th-think we sh-should introduce each other. My name's P-P-Peter, but I'm no a s-saint.'

The girl smiled. 'G-glad to m-meet you, P-Peter. My name's M-Mary but I'm no a v-v-very good player.'

In my boyhood we had a somewhat similar stuttering joke. We would go up to some cheeky young hoyden and ask, with a leer, 'Would you please oblige me wi' a f-f-few matches?'

When her indignation had given place to confusion we continued, 'I ken why ye were blushing; ye thocht I was gaun to ask ye for a f-f-full box.'

Aggro

The history of all races of man is rich in aggravation. Scotland has more than its fair share of it, despite the reputation of the Scots to be guided by the Bible, where Solomon advises against retaliation, though he was on a sticky wicket himself, as he slew his brother Adonijah and his cousin Joab. One of the first texts I was compelled to memorise, as a tender infant, was, 'A soft answer turneth away wrath, but grievous words stir up anger.' A text I liked better, because it was comical, was this, on the same lines, 'Surely the churning of milk bringeth forth the butter, and the wringing of the noose bringeth forth blood; so the forcing of wrath bringeth forth strife.' I knew about both these operations as a boy during the 1914-18 war, for we used to shake the top of the milk in a bottle to make tiny quantities of butter, otherwise unobtainable. And at school it was not uncommon to be threatened with a 'couple o' black horses and a bloody driver,' that is, two black eyes and a bleeding nose. I gave and got a few myself.

Still, it saddens me now to reflect that the human race has never taken Solomon's advice and is just as ready to pour oil on a fire as it was three thousand years ago.

Regrettable though aggravation, violence, and all such elemental forces are, they provide the very stuff of literature. Crime pays, whether printed within garish covers, or splashed on TV. I make no excuse, therefore, for these interesting tales of deeds of aggression, nearly all with a Scottish setting.

First, however, to dismiss the suggestion that all Scotland is a stage for violence, I would like to describe a few parts that can claim to be havens of peace, free from crime. They deserve prominence as little nooks in the Scottish landscape, miniature Edens. By the way, there are two Edens by that name in Scotland; they are both beautiful smooth-flowing streams. The longer is in Fife, entering the sea at St. Andrews; the shorter is in the Borders, a tributary of the Tweed. There is also a district in the North-West of Aberdeenshire named Paradise.

The island of St. Kilda knew little of the wicked world far beyond the horizon of the surrounding Atlantic. Crime was unknown, though human tragedy was far too common, when bird-catchers fell to certain death from the stupendous cliffs of Hirta when the heather ropes parted. A large proportion of the infants died from tetanus or suffocation. But there was no constable or representative of the law on the island. The people lived in a primeval state of anarchy, which is wrongly used as a term of abuse. They neither knew of the bloody continental or civil wars, nor sent a single recruit to meet a violent death, or fire shots in anger.

The Island of Gigha, off Kintyre, is not without reason named God's Isle. For ages they have had no need for the forces of law and order, though violence was not unknown, in which case the people executed justice without interference from 'Scotland', as the mainland is called, that alien land across three miles of salt water. At the North End of Gigha by the roadside is a forked standing stone. Originally it was used in drawing up the long-boats from the Western shore in winter, but latterly, anyone condemned of a serious crime, such as witchcraft, had his or her head wedged in the fork, while the executioners pulled the legs. The grave of an old witch is still pointed out nearby. That was centuries ago, but it tells us that even in Paradise there is a Satanic presence.

About twenty years ago a special constable, or 'bobby's labourer', was the law's representative. I asked him what he considered to be his duties. 'They don't need the law at all in Gigha,' he said, 'I think it is my duty, when I hear that the police are coming from the mainland to pay us a visit, to go round the island and warn everybody that they are coming, so that they can get all the unlicensed vehicles off the road and hide the unlicensed guns and generally become respectable, law-abiding people.' If this principle were universally adopted the crime rate might not decrease, but the number of arrests would drop spectacularly.

I think something of the same atmosphere must have prevailed in the Midlothian parish of Heriot, near the source of Gala Water. When the Hawick branch of the old North British Railway was being engineered about 1847, hundreds of navigators, or navvies, were employed. Frequent bloody battles occurred between the Scots, Irish and English, so bodies of hefty 'polis' had often to be brought up the line from Edinburgh and farther afield, to put the riots down. But once the railway was established, peace reigned. Not a single arrest was made by the constable of Heriot for seventy-five years, a world record, though it was generally known that trout and salmon-poaching, as in all the Borders, was universally enjoyed. I have heard that a fresh-run fish was often stranded on the door-step of the police-office.

The only comparable instance of extreme lawfulness was in Inverness in the eighteenth century, where the vault between the first and second arches of the bridge over the Ness was used, first as a jail, then, when the town had run out of criminals, as a madhouse, there being no scarcity of lunatics. The cell was only six feet square and so horrible that it was reported that the prisoner was permitted to spend the night in lodgings in the town on condition that he returned in the morning.

This 'open prison' idea is not new. When the new jail was built it was completely different and a grim fore-shadow of the conscriptive age that we now live in. It was a magnificent edifice in 'Carpenters' Gothic.' The ornate steeple, 130ft. high, was a replica of the St. Andrew's Church in Edinburgh and it cost as much as the prison. But the Almighty was not deceived by this pseudo-holy headpiece, and registered his contempt of it by sending along an earthquake in 1816 which twisted it, or in the vernacular, 'thrawed its thrapple'. It had to be taken down. During the seismic season the jail-birds were all set free, to wing their way wheresoever fancy took them, but a promise was extracted from each to return to 'durance vile' when the jail was made secure.

Some time before this free-and-easy arrangement there was an equally compromising situation. An English army officer wrote, at the time of the Jacobite risings of 1715 and 1745, that it was impossible to hold any clansman in Inverness because his relatives made it a point of honour either to break down the door of the jail, or to get themselves appointed turnkey. It is well known that Rob Roy could never be kept for long in prison, because he made sure that his own caterans were appointed to all the jails in Scotland.

But there were prisons in Scotland from which it was almost impossible to escape, though desperate men and women sometimes managed to do so. Edinburgh Castle had dungeons deep down in the living rock, where many a hundred found release only in death. The Bass Rock prison, surrounded by a treacherous sea beating round its horrible cliffs, drove many inmates mad with its depressing surroundings and the hopelessness of confinement. These grim places may now have attractions for the romantics but they were for long the home of Giant Despair.

We now turn to the men of blood who frequently were above the law in a land where, as was said, the legislature was like a spider's web; the little flies were caught, but the big ones burst through.

Bluebeard's story used to fascinate little children, though when they grew up they perhaps laughed at their fears as imaginary. Yet Bluebeard really existed, both in France and Scotland. The French Bluebeard, who concerns us least, was Jean de Laval, one of Joan of Arc's captains. He helped at the coronation of Charles V in Rheims Cathedral and was, to all intents, a religious man. He became very rich and powerful, acquiring many castles and estates. Finding time hanging heavy, he turned to alchemy and experimented in transmitting base metals to gold. Failing in this, he dealt in black magic, which was not a confection then, for very noxious and devilish ceremonies accompanied it. He induced children from eight to eighteen, under various pretexts, to enter his chateaux. They were never seen again, being subjected to horrible ritualistic tortures ending eventually in death. So many children disappeared that suspicion attached itself eventually to de Laval and his associates in cruelty. They were arrested and put to the various tortures in which mediaevals specialised, the rack, the thumbikins, the cords, the wedge, used in all Christendom at that time. They confessed under duress to the murders of over a hundred young people. In the subsequent story of Bluebeard, published two centuries later, the children were transmuted and a sexual element was introduced by making them young wives who were butchered and thrown into the locked room of horror, which the last victim-to-be entered, curious to find its secret.

The Scottish Bluebeard had his castle in Ayrshire on a wild headland between Girvan and Ballantrae. Carleton Castle, long a ruin and still to be seen, was the den of a wicked baron, Sir John Carleton, known in the traditional ballad as 'the fause Sir John'. In the legend he successively married a large number of young ladies, and after appropriating their dowries, he made away with them by pushing them over the cliffs into the sea at a headland called the Gamesloup.

But he was to meet a different kind of match in the person of a heroine named May Collean. However naive she appeared to him, she had her wits about her. No doubt she had heard of his nasty habits and was always ready for his tricks. On the day following the wedding and bedding, he led her out to the usual jumping-off place.

He commanded her first to take off her richly ornamented bridal garments, which doubtless he wanted, to allure the next victim. She remonstrated and said it was not

107

respectable for her to strip in broad daylight even before her bridegroom. She asked him to do the gentlemanly thing and turn his back while she did a strip-tease. This is when he slipped up, or rather down. She charged him and pushed him over the edge. He ended as crab-food a hundred feet below. The young widow skipped cheerfully back to Carleton Castle, where she lived happily and prosperously ever after, on the wealth of her short-term hubby.

This story bears far closer resemblance to the nursery tale of Bluebeard than that of the sadisitic Jean de Laval, where the marriage element is quite absent.

Some distance north of Bluebeard's castle we come into Burns' country where almost every mile has memories of the bard. But here also we contact two of the most evil and heartless villains in all Scots history, both members of the infamous Kennedy family, Earls of Cassilis. Although gifted and energetic scholars, statesmen and soldiers, like all the Campbell earls, they were also quite without pity in carrying out their purposes. Christianity might never have been introduced, as far as the Kennedys were concerned.

Gilbert, the fourth Earl, took after the character of his father, also Gilbert, who had plotted, as a traitor, with Henry VIII, to assassinate Cardinal Beaton, but died before he could do more harm to his country. His son, however, in his short life, earned a bad reputation for cruelty by capturing a local abbot who had a title to the church lands which Kennedy had stolen. He stripped the holy man and roasted him before a slow fire in one of the dungeons of Cassilis Castle, until he was forced to renounce his claims to the estate. George Buchanan, the famous historian, hearing of this barbarism, and having himself a small pension from the income of the estate, became alarmed. To protect himself from torture by fire, he put his person under the protection of King James VI, otherwise he might have been spitted like a mutton carcase.

John Kennedy, sixth Earl, was very much worse than his barbecuing grandfather. On the surface, like most of the Lords of the Congregation, he was a most godly man, a leader of the Covenanters and an ambassador to both Charles I and II. He was a member of Cromwell's House of Lords. He had married, for political purposes, not for love, Jean, the daughter of the Earl of Haddington, very much against that lady's wishes. She was already the sweetheart of the handsome dashing Sir John Faa of Dunbar, one of a famous Border gipsy family.

After Jean had been married several years and had given Cassilis three children, word came to John Faa, that Cassilis had been summoned to attend the Assembly of Divines at Westminster. With a band of his gipsy clan, Faa crossed the Galloway hills and descended on Cassilis Castle. He carried off his former sweetheart and had put several miles between him and the Castle when the Earl returned unexpectedly. With a strong escort he chased and captured Faa and the lady and all Faa's clansmen, fifteen young men. With a refinement of cruelty this Covenanting saint forced his countess to witness the hanging of her lover and his followers. Jean was imprisoned in the Castle for the rest of her life and occupied the weary bleak days of remorse making tapestry. Cassilis meantime took another wife and, for extra measure, disinherited Jean's three children. To further aggravate his cruelty, he employed a sculptor to make carvings of Johnny Faa and his clan victims on the balustrades of the staircase.

The well-known ballad, *The Raggle-Taggle Gipsies, O,* is founded on this true tale of hypocritical aggravation. The Kennedy line died out a century later. In accounts of the family in the *Encyclopaedia Britannica* there is no reference to the above unsavoury incident.

'Hell holds no fury like a woman scorned.' The story of Fenella's revenge certainly shows the hellish cunning of a Scottish, or rather Pictish lady of mediaeval days. The tale is no mere legend. It is historically true and an account may be read in Latin in the *Annals of the Scots*.

The great grandson of Kenneth McAlpine was Kenneth McCalum, or Kenneth III. Like his ancestor he put down Pictish revolts with much bloodshed. In one such rebellion the leader was a young Pictish noble, the only son of Fenella, the daughter of Cunechat, Earl of Angus. Kenneth beheaded the young man near Dunfinnan, with many of his followers. Fenella naturally swore to be avenged, but she pretended to have forgiven Kenneth.

Some years passed and at last it seemed that the land enjoyed peace. Kenneth lived in a great castle near Kincardine, the ruins of which are still to be seen. Fenella invited him, with a large retinue, to pay her a visit in her castle in Fettercairn, among the thickly wooded hills to the west of Kincardine. She provided a great banquet with various meats, sweets and wines. Then she requested Kenneth to make a tour of the many apartments, to admire the furniture, tapestries and paintings. When he had expressed his delight at these luxurious furnishings, she said that she was holding her choicest piece of ornament in reserve. It was not only a masterpiece of craftsmanship, it also held a magnificent personal gift for his majesty. It was not, however, for the common herd to see. He was asked to go alone into this splendid chamber.

Unsuspectingly, and drawn by curiosity and greed, he entered the room, and Fenella locked the door behind them and stood in a recess while Kenneth walked in amazement towards an assemblage of curiously carved Pictish mythological animals resembling hell-hounds, dragons, elephants and griffons of all sizes, with tapestry showing hunting and battle scenes. In the midst of these stood a life-size statue of a god holding a golden apple.

Fenella told Kenneth that this was the gift she had reserved for him and requested him to take it from the hand of the image. But the apple concealed the catch of a powerful spring. As he lifted it the twanging of several crossbow strings filled the chamber and a shower of steel-headed bolts flew from crevices in the walls towards the statue. One of these bolts transfixed the king's jugular vein, and he fell to the floor.

Fenella made her escape through a secret door and, long before the king's retinue began to sound the alarm, she was a mile away, up in the branches of the thick primeval forest.

Kenneth's men, in the words of the old Scots historian, 'brak doon the dure and fand him bullerin in his blude,' or, as we say, weltering in his blood.

The hue and cry was on to catch Fenella, but the tradition has persisted in Kincardine for a thousand years that, so dense was the forest all the way to the sea, Fenella clambered along the intertwined branches, unseen by her pursuers, and found safety in her seaside castle of Den-Fenella, or Fenella's Fort.

I was a tree-climber in my youth and I occasionally clambered from one tree to another, but it was hazardous and slow. I do not believe that Fenella, a middle-aged woman, covered the eight miles from Fettercairn to the coast by 'swinging herself along from one branch to another,' unless she was a sorceress and changed herself into a squirrel.

Our sympathy goes out to Fenella, for she took a just revenge. But we have no moral justification for sympathising with an aristocratic female assassin of the eighteenth century, named Katherine Nairn, unless on the rather false grounds of her youth and beauty. At the age of nineteen she was married by her parents to an elderly man of property named Ogilvy of Eastmilne. It became just another case of 'What can a young lassie dae wi' an auld man?' She had had no say in the matter and after putting up with him, and perhaps muttering many a time 'O, dreary's the nicht wi' a crazy auld man,' she met his very much younger brother Patrick, a lieutenant in the Gay Gordons, and soon Katherine and he were like fire and tow. The Laird of Eastmilne may have had suspicions, or he may have caught them *in flagrante delicto*, but quite clearly he soon after died of poisoning, and Katherine was arrested on suspicion and brought to Edinburgh for trial on two counts, murder and adultery.

She arrived in an open boat at the Shore of Leith to be welcomed by a vast throng always ready for a free show. If they expected to gloat over a poor dejected cringing creature, they were in for a shock. She came ashore laughing and chaffing with the seamen. The crowd were not to be deprived of their amusement. They turned nasty and tried to lynch her, or at least give her a good drubbing. But the City Guard got her safe and sound into the Tolbooth of Edinburgh, thinking that the Leith Tolbooth was not impregnable.

She was tried and found guilty on both charges, but the death sentence was delayed on the only valid grounds for such mercy. She was seven months pregnant. To whom, we can make a fair guess. A midwife or howdie, Mrs. Shields, was engaged to attend Katherine in prison and to help in the delivery. But Mrs. Shields put her own construction on 'delivery' and entered into a scheme to deliver the mother and child together—from the Tolbooth.

She pretended to have raging toothache and wrapped her head in a thick gravat, or scarf. She went in and out of the Tolbooth moaning and moping as if life was past bearing. After a few days of this, when the warders had grown accustomed to her entrances and exits, Mrs. Shields wrapped her scarf round the condemned woman's head and shoulders.

Katherine acted the part perfectly and so loudly did she howl in mock agony that the turnkey slapped her for a 'howling auld Jezebel', expressing the fervent wish that he might never see her again.

His wish was granted, but only just, for Katherine made what might have been a fatal mistake. She intended to go to the house of her father's lawyer, but knocked instead on the door of one of the law lords whose footman at once recognised her and raised the alarm.

She fled and hid in a cellar down some old backstairs near her uncle's house. She was then taken secretly in a coach driven by one of her uncle's clerks, posting with fresh horses, all the way to Dover. Even this perilous adventure failed to damp her high spirits, whose outbursts nearly betrayed her at several posting inns on the road south. Her conductor was relieved to part with his mettlesome passenger when they eventually set foot on French soil, where British law did not run. She had crossed the Channel in the uniform of a junior military officer. As she was far advanced in pregnancy, her corpulence must have aroused suspicion, when belonging to a mere lieutenant.

She eventually emigrated to America where she married and had a large family. Did she ever reveal to her grandchildren the lurid episodes of her early life? Did she ever have remorse for having poisoned her first husband and having been the prime cause of the death on the gallows of her lover, her accomplice in crime? Or did she just laugh it all off lightly as the diversions of a romping teenager?

Few murders aroused more horror than that committed by the Rev. John Kelloe, minister of Spott, a secluded Haddingtonshire parish, nestling under a wooded hill named the Doon. A beautiful little burn, embroidered by primroses and wild violets in early summer, flows through Spott and enters the sea near Dunbar. In short, a more peaceful part of God's earth could not be imagined.

Despite this natural charm, Spott has seen more aggravation, more open cruelty, more slaughter and huddling away of innocent victims than even the most bloodstained acres of European or Asiatic cockpits. It is little wonder that John Kelloe, a man of God, was induced to follow the example of the evil-doers in his parish. Their malevolent spirits must have influenced him.

The first battle of Dunbar was fought near Spott. Bruce fought on the side of Edward I against Wallace and the Scots who were defeated with much slaughter. The second battle of Dunbar, on practically the same ground, ended in Cromwell's Ironsides slaughtering thousands of Covenanting Scots. But these were the fortunes of war and all the actors knew the risks.

Violence in peacetime was contrary to justice, yet Spott seemed to be put on the spot at all times. A rector of Spott, Galbraith, a senator and King's councillor, was assassinated in Edinburgh by a burgess named Carketle in 1544. Another prominent native, George Home, was tried for the murder of Darnley, and was assassinated by Douglas of Spott, who made sure that justice, even personally administered, would be done. But a far worse crime was committed by the roadside just a short distance to the west of Spott in 1704. A number of deranged old women were burnt alive as witches in one of the last 'incremations' in Scotland. There is an iron memorial post still marking the atrocity. These acts of violence on the person took place both before and after John Kelloe's crime, which occurred in 1570.

The Rev. John Kelloe's wife was a poor, but very handsome and attractive girl, witty and affectionate, small but well-shaped; in fact Kelloe was a man to be much envied. He had met and married this lady some time before being given the living of Spott, and this eminently desirable promotion seems to have started the rot, for this parish both before and after the Reformation, was one of the plums of the Church.

Kelloe began to harbour ambitions. He was no longer content to live humbly and enjoy the charms of his 'bonnie wee thing'. He became possessed of a roving eye, which alighted upon the well-endowed daughter of a local laird, whom her influential father managed to keep anonymous when things came to a crisis.

With murder in his heart Kelloe began to deceive his wife with a show of affection. She was in the seventh heaven of delight, but she was soon to be translated to another world.

One Sabbath morning in August 1570 when the fields were ready for harvest, Kelloe decided that the time was ripe for his crime. As she was on her knees, saying her prayers of thanks for God's blessings, he crept up behind her. He drew from his pocket a rope which he had fondled for days, wound it round her slender neck and strangled her. He then tied her up to an iron hook which he had fixed on a beam in the loft, by the same rope arranged in a noose. He next bolted the gate into the manse from the inside and stole out by the parlour window, stepping delicately down to the kirk where he soon had his congregation drooling in the pews over a splendidly emotional sermon. The afternoon service was even more inspired.

After the double service he invited two or three parishioners to have supper with him. When the party arrived at the manse they found the gate locked. On knocking furiously and persistently, Kelloe expressed anxiety at getting no answer. He said that he hoped nothing had happened to his lady, as she had been melancholy for some days.

They broke down the lock and began to search the manse. At last they discovered the body, still warm, but lifeless. Presuming suicide, the parishioners did their utmost to restrain Kelloe from attempting his own life. He went into paroxysms of grief, struggled to grasp a knife to cut his own throat, blamed himself for leaving his wife alone, and all the time floods of crocodile tears coursed over his broadcloth.

The poor little corpse was buried in the kirkyard amidst every sign of sorrow, and the minister made a visible effort to keep his courage up in the face of the sympathetic congregation.

He might have got away with it, but he began to feel what the ancient Angles of his parish called the 'Agenbite of Inwit,' or the pangs of remorse. After six weeks of self-torture, reinforced by his Calvinistic belief in the reality of hell-fire, he went down to Dunbar and confessed all to a colleague there, who already suspected Kelloe, because he had described a nightmare too circumstantial to be a mere dream.

He was taken immediately to Edinburgh and convicted on his own evidence. His punishment was made to fit the crime. With real tears of penitence now, he was strangled on the Gallow Lee, that gruesome spot amongst the hedges and green fields, between Edinburgh and Leith, close at hand to a road once named Lovers' Lane. His corpse was burnt to ashes and scattered to the four winds of heaven.

Kelloe's fate was much more horrifying to the religious of the age than appears to us, for the belief in a literal resurrection was widely held. Here is how a poet saw the General Assembly of Bones.

> Scattered limbs and all the various bones advance,
> the neck perhaps to meet
> The distant head, the distant legs the feet . . .
> See through the dusky sky
> Fragments of bodies in confusion fly.

But the scattering of ashes was preferable to what happened to Norman Ross on the same execution ground in 1752. He had been footman to Lady Baillie, a Berwickshire lady, who had succeeded her two childless brothers to the title of Wedderburn. The crime was brought on by Ross's love of money. He knew that the old widow always kept a well-lined purse on her person, never leaving it lying about, so he hid himself in her bedroom and waited until she fell asleep. She undressed and before going to bed she put the purse in a desk and locked it up. She had fallen into her first light sleep so Ross thought himself safe to open the desk, but he made a slight noise with the lid. The lady awoke and began to shout for help. By chance, a knife used for cutting fruit was lying by the bed. Ross attacked her with it and mangled her throat so frightfully that she died the next morning.

After the attack Ross leapt from the window which was two storeys up. He broke a leg and, not being able to escape, crawled into a cornfield where he hid himself, creeping out at night to feed on pease, beans and turnips. His hide-out was at last discovered and the wretch was driven by the constables, first to Greenlaw and then to Edinburgh. Here he was summarily tried for murder and hurried to the Gallow Lee where he was hanged.

That was not the end of this tale of horror by any means. A local butcher, Nichol Brown, one of the large mob that such entertainment always attracted, whether to show his distaste of Ross's crime, or for mere bravado, made a bet that he would cut a large slice of flesh from the dead man's thigh. By night he carried the criminal carrion to his house nearby, fried it and ate it for dinner before an admiring audience of drunken friends. His wife naturally objected to this anthropophagy in the kitchen and began to scold him. As a suitable conclusion to his day of barbarity he murdered her with a butcher's cleaver. Being apprehended 'red in tooth and claw', he was dealt with as expeditiously as the man who had furnished his hot gigot, and was soon hanging alongside Ross, whose corpse, minus the steak, had been tarred and gibbetted at the Gallow Lee. It hung there for many years, an object of disgust and dismay to all those who took a dander along Leith Walk. On wild moonlight nights, as it swung and creaked overhead, it must have acted as a deterrent to all would-be cut-throats.

These atrocities were of course the subject of ballads. We give a couple of verses about Norman Ross, who, being a native of Inverness, got little sympathy in the South country.

> The Lady's gaen and Norman taen
> Norman wi' the bloody hand
> Now he will hae to pay the kain
> For being at the Deil's command.

Norman Ross wi' pykit pow
Three corbies at his een
Girnin in the gallows tow
Sic a sicht was never seen.

I mentioned earlier that the thirteenth child and first son of the Duke of Eglinton had been so unlucky as to be shot by Mungo Campbell, in a poaching affray on the Duke's estates. Campbell had been an excise officer at Saltcoats but had fallen in with some disreputable companions, who, rather than face the severe punishment visited on night-poachers, had resisted the Duke and his gamekeepers. Such poaching affrays, involving manslaughter, were quite common in the Lowlands; in the Highlands the natives took what they wanted without question.

Mungo Campbell was tried and found guilty. He was sentenced to death by hanging, but he 'cheated the widdie', or gallows, by doing away with himself the day following his condemnation. The judge, too eager to satisfy the popular hatred of Campbell for his murder of the beloved young heir, directed wrongly that the criminal's body should be handed over to the professor of anatomy. Campbell's counsel objected and pointed out that a *felo de se* could not be legally anatomised, though he could be forbidden Christian burial. Mungo's body was accordingly buried in unconsecrated ground near the foot of the Salisbury Crags.

But the Edinburgh mob, the same independent body who had defied Queen Caroline and the Westminster Parliament and executed Captain Porteous in the riots a generation before, again took the law into their own hands. They dug up Campbell's corpse and amused themselves by tossing it about for some time. Tiring of this they carried it up to the highest point of the crags, several hundred feet above the plain, where there is a 'chimney' called the Cat's Nick, known to all Edinburgh boys to this day. From this eminence they tossed the body, to fall a sheer hundred feet, and yelled as it bounced down the steep screes towards the city.

After the mob had retreated, Campbell's friends rescued the outraged body and to save further indecencies, weighted it in a canvas and sank it from a boat into the deep channel between Leith and the island of Inchkeith.

I could recite many more gruesome tales of aggravation, for the legends are manifold. The violent men, the hard men, the viragos, the assassins, the poisoners, are well represented. But I would like to mention one or two less grim instances of confrontations before the chapter ends.

Students of the American War of Independence have been perhaps puzzled by the opposing versions of the Battle of Bunker or Bunker's Hill, where the Americans were defeated, but which they regarded as a moral victory. There was another Battle of Bunker's Hill in the same year, 1776, but in the Old World. It was a comical affair, however.

Where St. James Centre now stands, at the east end of Princes Street, there was once a mound separated from the Calton Hill by a deep gully. A colony of Picardy weavers, optimistic about the Scottish climate, planted that hill above their village with mulberry trees. But the site retained the name Mulberry Tree Hill, shortened in time to Multree's Hill. When the New Town was built, a handsome square of tall tenements was planned for this site and named St. James Square. Robert Burns lodged here in 1786 when he first came to Edinburgh. The rent was eighteen pence per week.

But some years before, on the laying of the foundation stones of the new scheme, when a huge crowd had collected, two rival builders began a heated argument which, of course, was encouraged by the mob, always ready for a free show. Words failed to satisfy the builders, so off came the jackets, and a fisticuff comedy began, egged on by boys big and small.

Just at that moment word came through from the London coach that a battle had been won, though with considerable casualties for the British at Bunker's Hill in Boston. The crowd took up the news and of course applied the name to the boxing-match in progress. St. James Square was ever afterwards named Bunker's Hill, and time has had its revenge on this locality, for the present imponderable mass resembles nothing so much.

Aggravation is often comic. The old Scottish divines were apt to exaggerate the sins of their congregations and to threaten them with hell-fire. As time wore on and the weekly fulminations from the pulpit were repeated, the effect was to lessen the dread of after-life retribution.

One of the most aggressive preachers was Black John Russell, whose stentorian tones and brimstone message are so scathingly described in Burns' *Holy Fair*. He had been a schoolmaster in the North of Scotland before taking up the ministry. He was a tall, strong, black-bearded man of very serious countenance. He denounced all forms of sin and consigned the sinners to everlasting blazes. His descriptions of Hell were very vivid and he got great joy from describing the torments hereafter.

At the Sacrament, or Holy Fair, at Kilmarnock, which Burns witnessed, the ale-tent was not far from the pulpit, and the noise of revelry from the boozers drowned the gospel message of a young preacher. Black John then took the pulpit and thundered his sulphurous message so fiercely that the refreshment tent emptied and the sinners stood trembling before the denunciations of the dominie.

But noo the Lord's ain trumpet touts
Till a' the hills are roarin
And echoes back return the shouts
Black Russell is na spairin.
His piercin words like Hielan swords
Divide the joints and marrow
His talk o' hell where devils dwell
Our vera sauls does harrow
Wi fricht that day.

A vast unbottomed boundless pit
Fill'd fu o' lowin brunstane
Whase ragin flame and scorchin heat
Wad melt the hardest whunstane.
The half-asleep start up in fear
An think they hear it roarin
When presently it does appear
Twas but some neebor snorin
Asleep that day.

Examples of aggravation, trivial and serious, are very numerous. A few illustrations of totally different types will perhaps suffice.

When Burke, the mass murderer, was sentenced for doom, the Edinburgh mob went on the rampage. They broke the windows of Dr.Knox, the anatomist, who had bought one of the corpses, though to tell the truth, he had little need to buy such suspect goods, as he already had a hundred 'subjects' in storage. For her own safety, Mrs. Burke had been

114

lodged in the Calton Jail. On a snowy morning, the streets appearing deserted, the jailer thought it was a good chance to let her out, with the infant she was nursing, wrapped about her in a shawl.

But as she crossed the North Bridge on her way to the Cowgate, she was recognised, and before she was half over the bridge, a hostile crowd had gathered. The presence of the innocent babe saved her life, for the crowd contented itself with snowballing the wretched woman, until a posse of constables took her under protection. As snow normally lies on the Edinburgh streets for only about ten days in any year the odds against Mrs. Burke and her child escaping severe injury were about thirty-six and a half to one.

Muggers there have always been. The law used to make them pay the extreme penalty, which was the more readily exacted if mayhem, or maiming, was the purpose of the attacker. In Edinburgh there dwelt a notoriously violent bully named John Boyd, suspected of robberies with violence and other crimes against the lieges.

In the 'wee sma'oors', between one a.m. and four, he used to lie in wait for gentlemen coming down the Candlemaker Row from the taverns to their quarters in the Castle, or Lawnmarket. As the chances were in favour of the revellers being under the weather, Boyd looked for easy pigeons to pluck.

One early morning, as he lay in waiting in a doorway, two of these gentlemen approached, obviously in a merry humour. They were Dr. Symons of the Edinburgh Regiment of Militia and Lieutenant Ronaldson of the same regiment. They had been at a dinner-party close by.

Boyd sprang out, with an accomplice, and attacked them. The ruffian struck Dr. Symons a severe blow on the nape of the neck, tried to wrest his sword away from him, knocked him down and rained kicks on his ribs with steel-shod boots. The doctor staggered to his feet, in severe pain, but burning with rage. He pursued Boyd down the steep street, sword in hand. Near the foot of the Row he overtook Boyd, where the struggle was renewed with violence, until in desperation the doctor ran Boyd through the thick of the body with his sword.

Boyd was left bleeding in the gutter while Dr. Symons, thinking he was only slightly wounded, staggered up the hill to his lodgings. But the following dawn the police picked up Boyd *in rigor mortis*, just where he had fallen. Dr. Symons was arrested on a charge of manslaughter, but allowed bail. At the trial by jury the verdict of 'Not Guilty' was recorded, the plea of self-defence being accepted. Everyone agreed that the mugger got what he asked for.

James VI was the author of a book vehemently condemning the smoking of tobacco. He could do little to put down this universal habit in England but he went into action in Scotland when he heard that the minister of Gullane in East Lothian had been caught smoking his churchwarden pipe. Like an aggrieved schoolmaster catching a prefect having a fly puff in the jakes, James used all his powers of sanction and expelled the poor incumbent from his United Kingdom, probably to Holland where all three sexes, men, women and clergymen smoke, when, where and what they like.

The General Assembly of the Churches, once called the 'Annual Wembley of the Lord', after the great exhibition of 1924, fills the streets, coffee-rooms, restaurants of Edinburgh with dog-collars and summer frocks and hats.

One sunny forenoon the pavements of Princes Street were so congested, with knots of overspills from Kirk committees, that a testy old native overflowed with bile and, in an un-Christian spirit, apostrophised the nearest visitors.

'Meenisters! Meenisters! They're just like muck! Spread aboot ower the land they bring mony benefits, naebody can deny. But gaithered thegither in a muckle bourach, they're nocht but a bloody offence to the senses.'

In conclusion, aggravation seems to be a built-in constituent of human nature, whether it be on a grand scale or on a trifling level. It is scarcely comical when it involves humanity in vast conflict as has happened over the centuries, even prior to the super-atomic set-up of today.

The Royal Families of Europe were proud of their gentle taint of debauchery, homicide, parricide, fratricide, genocide and a hell-of-a-lot-more-beside. Wherein did they differ, except in degree from the two Irish washerwomen having a ding-dong on a stairheid in the Sautmarket or the Coogate?

Kathleen: 'That's no lodger ye have, Miss Bridget.'
Bridget : 'And do ye know the father o your brat?'
Kathleen: (shaking her fist) 'Sure, there's no daicent woman knows ye. Ah, but I do.'

It may be deplorable, but it certainly supplies spice to existence, and gives point to the story of the young man-about-town who confessed to the father that he had had a fearful dream of going to heaven and also to hell.
'And what was your verdict, my son?'
'Sure, father, give me Heaven for comfort, but Hell for company.'

Even in the closest relationship, as we have shown, there can be the bitterest aggression. Indeed it is a historical truth that some Highland clans, blood-related, fought long and bitter feuds with each other despite their common ancestry. The Clan Chattan and Clan Kay, who fought to the death on the Inch at Perth in 1490 were of the same blood.

But a tale just as true comes to us from the annals of Old Edinburgh. In the Tron Parish, not far from the High Street, the assistant minister made regular visitations to the older parishioners who had missed a few Kirk services, to find out if they were needing help.

At the top of a twelve-storey tenement, right under the slates, lived two old sisters in a miserable garret. They had not been seen at Kirk for some time. The minister knocked and waited. He knocked again but got no response so after a third and louder knock he turned the door-handle and peeped in.

A curious sight met his eyes. A broad white chalk line ran across the small room from the middle of the doorway to the middle of the tiny hearth. On either side of the fireplace, where a little coal-fire burned, sat an old lady in a chair, knitting and paying no attention to the other. The chalk-line, leaving the floor-level, also ran across the middle of a plain deal table on which, at either end was a cup, saucer, plate, knife, fork and spoon.

The two sisters had fallen out, but could not separate as this was their only shelter, so they had decided to share everything, but to have no communication across the border. The man of God had to address each separately as if they were a mile apart and to bid them each a separate 'Good-night' as he left. No doubt, as he descended to earth from that tiny hell, he drew comparisons with the Christian sects who had created similar divisions.

Caught Napping

Everybody gets caught out at some time, either by chance or by design. This provides amusement for the onlookers, especially if the victims have been very sure of themselves. As the cynical French philosopher Rochefoucald said, 'In the misfortune of our best friends we find something which is not displeasing to us.'

Probably the most embarrassing moment in any woman's life is to be waiting at the altar for a bridegroom who does not turn up. This actually happened to Mauritia, a young Dutch lady, a grand-daughter of the Prince of Orange. She was betrothed to Colin, Earl of Balcarres, one of the foremost noble families in Scotland. The Prince of Orange himself, afterwards to be William III of Great Britain, presented his fair kinswoman with a pair of magnificent emerald ear-rings.

The wedding-day arrived and the church was filled by a party of rich and noble guests. The bride stood at the altar, the clergyman and choir were ready. But, as the minutes dragged on, there was no sign of the bridegroom.

Messengers were sent to his home in haste. They burst in to find him calmly eating his breakfast, in his nightgown and slippers. He had quite forgotten that this was his wedding-day.

The story is comical so far, and everyone was prepared to laugh the whole incident away in the merriment of the wedding-feast. But now a tragic storm breaks on the affair.

Colin rode in haste to the church but, as was excusable, forgot the wedding-ring, safely locked up in his writing-case. A friend happened to have a ring and gave it to Colin for the ceremony. Without looking at it closely, he slipped it on the bride's finger, not knowing that it was a mourning-ring, fashionable at that time, and carrying on the seal a death's head and

117

cross-bones.

The bride did not glance at it until the end of the ceremony when, to everyone's horror, she fainted away. The bridegroom explained how this had arisen and promised to bring the proper wedding-ring immediately. But Mauritia was so superstitious that she could not drive the horrible symbols out of her mind. She declared that she was certain she would die within the year, and her presentiment was alas, too truly fulfilled.

Punctuality is the politeness of princes but royalty should not jump the gun. This happened when Victoria and Albert paid a visit to Edinburgh shortly after their marriage. They did not want a fuss but the magistrates felt that they would be failing in their loyalty if they were too unceremonious.

The royal yacht was anchored in the Firth of Forth off Newhaven, and it was arranged that the entire route leading to Holyrood Palace would be hung with bunting and signs of welcome. Windows were rented to spectators. Triumphal arches, decked with nosegays, were erected, and military bands were alerted to welcome the young couple.

But man proposes and Royalty disposes, On the morning of 1 September the young couple decided to take time by the forelock and rise early. They came ashore when most of the citizens were at breakfast, and the magistrates, thinking that they had an hour or two to wait, before getting into their carriages, were seated in the City Chambers arrayed in their regalia, robed and chained and nervous. As a contemporary reporter said, 'They sat silent as Roman senators awaiting the irruption of barbarians.'

Word of the disembarkment had come to the Castle. They had probably spotted the landing, by field glasses. Boom! Boom! went the beginning of the Royal Salute. Dismayed and panic-stricken, the bailies jumped to their feet and rushed for the coaches. It was 'Devil take the hindmost.' Some drove like furious Jehus to eastward, some north, some south. The crowds followed, puffing and blowing in the attempt to keep up with the horses.

Hosts encountered hosts at every cross-roads, until Edinburgh was filled with a routed army of dishevelled, flushed and angry folk.

By this time the Queen and Consort had passed Holyrood and were well on their way to Dalkeith Palace, where they were to dine with the Duke and Duchess of Buccleuch before proceeding by road to Taymouth Castle. Dalkeith was seven miles off. Some of the magistrates had hopes of reaching the royal route before the Queen, but alas, when they had lashed their poor horses to a foam they arrived only to see the dissolving dust of the Royal progress in the distance.

Acts of God, in the shape of storms, earthquakes, eclipses and floods, can catch people napping despite meteorological forecasts and predictions of astronomy. Eclipses of the sun, moon and planets have been predictable for ages by a method based on cycles. The Chinese knew this method long before the Greeks. But people who were ignorant of this calculation were scared stiff by eclipses. It was said to be an eclipse of 1263 which discountenanced the Norsemen and caused them to lose the Battle of Largs.

An early king of the Picts and Scots was deposed and killed by his subjects because of his name, Ciricius or Gregory. As it happened there was a total eclipse of the sun visible in the Scottish Highlands on the feast day of St. Ciricius, 16 June 885. This was represented as a sign from God that Gregory was to be eclipsed also; his enemies carried out God's will.

I vividly remember the total eclipse of the sun on 29 June 1927. With hundreds of others I climbed Arthur's Seat to witness the shadow of totality rushing across the Lothian landscape towards us at supersonic speed. It covered us for forty seconds only, but made an impression of doom even on sophisticated people. What a total eclipse did to naive mediaevals, steeped in religious superstition, it is hard to imagine. There will be another total solar eclipse visible in Britain on 11 August 1999 unless something dramatic happens to prevent it.

Earthquakes are catastrophes that happen to other people far away, we think, never to the British. But we do have our little earthquakes here also. There was one recently near Gretna which brought down many chimney pots in Carlisle and made the wally-dugs dance in several towns in Central Scotland. But they have been more serious. Four people were killed in Colchester, Essex, in 1884 and, in the winter of 1839-40, Comrie had 140 earthquakes, or one per day on average.

Thunderstorms are more common. They can cause quite as much embarrassment as any other Acts of God, if we except the Edinburgh winds gusting to storm force as they strike the face of the North British Hotel and funnel up the Waverley Steps. The police used to station two hefty bobbies at the head of the steps on windy days to assist storm-tossed ladies across the pavement. A regular crowd of spectators attended this entertainment, as many of the ladies' skirts were blown around their shoulders.

Electric storms, although rare in Edinburgh and Glasgow, seem to be controlled by gremlins, for they strike at the most awkward moments. I shall prove this by quoting circumstantial evidence from four widely separated occasions, which caught everyone napping.

The earliest was on 13 September 1744. The remarkable thing about this thunderstorm is that it presaged an event of shattering importance which took place in the very same spot exactly a year later, almost to the day. As far as I know, nobody took this prophetic sign at that time, nor has anyone since noticed the connection of these two unexpected events.

On the morning of that day a most awesome blackness began to gather over Midlothian. It increased towards the afternoon and concentrated over the Old Town. Flashes of sheet and forked lightning were followed by the father of cannonades. Hailstones five inches across fell, shattering slates and windows. Then a unique phenomenon appeared in the shape of a tremendous waterspout, writhing like a dancing dervish over the steeples and the chimney-stacks. Luckily the demon was attracted towards the precipices of Arthur's Seat, leaving the town intact. The volcanic cone seemed to split the spout in two. The western cascade fell with avalanche force upon the hillside above Hunter's Bog, and ripped out a chasm sending hundreds of tons of turf, soil and rock into the valley. This chasm, which is still a prominent feature, was wedge-shaped and, because of this, is named the 'Gutted Haddie.' (The Gutted Haddock).

The eastern spout swept down the hillside towards the village of Duddingston several hundred feet below and carried away the gable-end of a cottage, before pouring into the loch and flooding all the nearest meadows.

Nobody heeded this far-from-gentle hint of coming political events; these were the descent upon Britain of a small army of ragged ill-equipped mountaineers who put the establishment into such a panic that it did not recover its equilibrium until it had indulged in frenetic butchery and genocide for several years. I refer to the 1745 Rising.

In mid-September 1745, a year exactly after the waterspout, Prince Charles' army drew near to Edinburgh. The city was taken by Lochiel's Camerons on the 17th, and the main force, to avoid the guns of the Castle, in Hanoverian hands, put Arthur's Seat between them and danger, and camped on the hill-slopes above Duddingston, exactly where the eastern branch of the waterspout had swept down.

They remained for a day or two to recruit men and provisions. Hearing of the approach of Sir John Cope with a strong force they left Duddingston at dawn on the 21st and three hours later won a sweeping victory, sending Cope off with a countenance to match his uniform, to bear the news of his own defeat to the astounded English.

Had such a prophet as Thomas the Rhymer, the Brahan Seer, or any old Highlander with the second sight been available, keeping a weather-eye open, this embarrassing rebellion, which caught the British powers napping, would have been anticipated, but a glorious field for romantic song-writers and novelists would have been rendered sterile.

Forty years on, almost to the week, only a mile away from the above natural disaster, a Scottish genius, James Tytler was preparing an artificial disaster for himself in the shape of a Montgolfier balloon. This hot-air balloon is very popular nowadays, but much safer than in 1784, because the heating equipment now is lighter and more controllable. Tytler needed a cast-iron stove and coal or charcoal, which added considerably both to the weight of the gondola and the volume of the balloon. He had made his balloon and basket out of readily available material. The balloon was barrel-shaped for ease of construction.

On the early morning of 27 August after several abortive attempts, the cause of the failure being the clumsy iron stove, Tytler heated the balloon, pitched out the stove and immediately flew up to a height of 300ft., which he measured by a line hanging overboard on a weight. The spectators had tried to prevent his apparently suicidal flight but he had pushed them off. The air now began to cool as the stove was gone. Tytler descended nearly as quickly as he had risen. Within half-a-mile of his point of departure, he came down in a marshy meadow, shaken but unhurt.

He decided to try another flight and advertised it so fully that a large crowd gathered to be amused. As it chanced the weather was sultry and 'hingy'. That is to say, plumps of rain were to be expected. He rose some way off the ground again, ignoring the ominous sky. Perhaps the prominent mass of hot air attracted the electric currrent; the report is that the balloon was struck by a lightning flash and ruined. Tytler came off again uninjured. He was lucky. Had his balloon been hydrogen-filled, as some were, he could have been roasted. On the other hand, thunderstorms are rare over Edinburgh, even if highly selective, so he was unlucky in this respect.

The third electric storm which seemed to catch everybody napping was in the summer of 1852 at the unveiling of the statue of the Duke of Wellington at the East End of Princes Street. The Duke himself was nearing his end, dying in September of that year, but his bronze statue, mounted on his favourite horse, Copenhagen, had pleased him so much that he had two, replicas made.

A vast crowd gathered for the unveiling in Edinburgh. Amongst them were many veterans of Waterloo, who in some cases had not seen one another since that bloody Sunday thirty-seven years before. They were now old men, many crippled and bearing crutches as well as medals.

As the hour of unveiling approached, what should gather over the city but the opportunist thunder-cloud, ever on the look-out for a big occasion. In the midst of the impressive ceremony the lightning struck, the thunder filled the heavens and the deluge descended. As they say in the Borders, it rained 'auld wives and Jeddart staves.' The poor old veterans, many in their only suits, were drenched, and no doubt, as in the famous 'Wet Review' of 1881, in the Queen's Park, numbers of them would perish of pneumonia and other ills.

A wit of the time remarked that it was small wonder that such a combination of lightning conductors such as the Iron Duke, by the sculptor Steell, cast in bronze, should have attracted an electric storm. The wonder was that the Duke and Copenhagen were not melted into a shapeless mass. But they are still there to this day, the Duke bare-headed, pointing the way to the bus-stop for Portobello.

The fourth and last of this series of storms took place in 1893, a summer which, in the opening words of Alexander Smith's *Summer in Skye*, 'leaped upon Edinburgh like a tiger'. A polar bear would often be a better simile.

The months of June, July and August had been torrid and rainless. There was an epidemic of fever and diphtheria amongst children, due to the lack of water to flush the drains. At last, when the reservoirs which supplied the city were reduced to muddy pools (for the great Tweed reservoir at Talla was many years in the future), the Town Council held an emergency session.

Glasgow was in better shape for many years before this. It had acquired Loch Katrine as a supply and had even raised the level to ensure a solution to some of the city's drink problems.

The emergency meeting in Edinburgh began in stifling heat, with arguments and recriminations raising the temperature even higher. The sky grew black as the pit, the gloom intensified. Then came the most appalling flash and heaven's artillery opened up right overhead. The rain and hail lashed the roof of the council chambers. The streets ran from gutter to gutter like rivers. All traffic stopped and still the torrent continued hour after hour. So did the debate on the water shortage until at last it dawned on the speakers that the problem no longer existed, but had been replaced by another more pressing. How to get home in the downpour with not a horse-drawn vehicle on hand.

In this generous fashion did the Almighty answer the prayers of the Water Engineers, and remind the Council to put more trust in their own motto *Nisi Dominus Frustra*; In vain unless the Lord help.

We move now to Glasgow to show how a generous downpour in the gathering ground of the Clyde, away up on Daer Water and on Crawford Muir, came to the aid of the city and helped them to turn the tables on their enemies.

During the Covenanting times the Privy Council did everything in its power by persecution to force the West Country into open rebellion. They ultimately succeeded in this cruel design and put down the uprising with heartless cruelty. One of the goads they used to incite rebellion was to let loose the 'Highland Host' upon Glasgow and Ayrshire. 5000 wild clansmen, led by their chiefs, were turned out in the Whig country to rob and destroy. Their only fault in the eyes of the Council who employed them was that they committed no cruelty or outrage upon any person, and in this respect they were much to be preferred to the Scottish Dragoons wearing the King's colours.

Several thousand Highlanders returned to their bens and glens laden with booty and driving their stolen horses packed to exhaustion with everything under the sun plundered from the Covenanting country. But a large body of 'redshanks' (as they were called by the Lowlanders) were still occupied in the ruination of the Ayrshire countryside. Finally, on the completion of the destruction, this contingent, about two thousand strong, set off homewards laden with spoil. There was only one barrier to their progress to the North, the River Clyde. As it was well known that the summer drought reduced the flow to a depth of two feet, so that only small rowing-boats could navigate where now great ocean-going vessels can pass safely, the Highlanders anticipated no difficulty in fording the river.

But for once, Jupiter Pluvius, the capricious rain-god, was on the side of St. Mungo's bairns. There had been days of heavy rain away up in the Lowther and Lead Hills. Every burn from Little Clyde to Gonnar Water sent its contribution. Bonnington Falls and Cora Linn presented an awesome scene as whole trees, carcases of cattle and broken water-gates were hurled further to destruction into the abyss.

When the caterans came to the village of Gorbals they were dismayed to see the Clyde running red from bank to bank and rising every minute. At that time there was only a single narrow bridge, built in the fourteenth century, named the Stockwell Bridge. A large number of students, considerably supported by irate citizens, who had been robbed recently by the larger body of Highlandmen, gathered at the North end of the bridge with weapons of all sorts, to oppose the crossing. The Highlanders saw that they could make no progress, as passengers could only cross in double file, so they entered into negotiations with the Glaswegians and finally agreed to terms, which were these; they would be allowed to cross in parties not exceeding forty at a time.

But, as each party was escorted up into the town and put on the road for Dumbarton and Loch Lomond, its members were relieved of their loads of pillaged goods and with many curses in Gaelic, not loud but deep, they took their way back to their bens and glens as unencumbered as they had arrived.

However much they may be in keeping with the scene, the present requisites at Burns' Suppers of kilts, brogues, dirks, sporrans and ornamental jackets were for long looked upon in Ayrshire with contempt and hatred. The traditional Ayrshire dress for the men was the blue woollen broad bonnet, the short jacket, knee-breeches, ribbed stockings and leather shoes. The women wore the dress common to most country women in Scotland, shawl, bodice, petticoats, with bare legs and feet most of the year. It might be a better idea to adopt the Ayrshire dress for the annual celebration.

An episode of confusion on an extended scheme which abounds in comical situations took place when 'Nappy' meant something less soothing to small children than it does now. It was short for Napoleon Bonaparte, who was used as a bogy-man to frighten 'waukrife' bairns.

An ancient method of raising the alarm was resorted to. In the event of an invasion by sea, or by air (for there was fear of balloons being used), a wide-spread pattern of beacons was set up from Land's End to John o'Groats. In theory, a French landing anywhere in the British Isles would arouse the nation within hours. But the 'False Alarm' which was confined only to the South of Scotland, shows the weakness of the system. Had a flotilla landed French horse and foot on Solway shore, the island might well have been in Nap's hands at a vulnerable point.

On 31 January 1804, a glare was seen by a watcher on Hume Castle in Berwickshire. This had once been a real castle in the days of Border warfare but had fallen into complete ruin after the Union of 1603. About 1790 the Earl of Marchmont had rebuilt it as a 'folly', using the stones of the ancient fortalice. As it stood on a hill of about 900ft. it was visible from most parts of the Border. Consequently, when its beacon went up as a result of a lack of judgement on the watchers' part, corresponding flares appeared within minutes from the basin of the whole vale of the Tweed.

Some of the mounted militia, or Fencibles, had long distances to travel over miry roads and open country to reach their rallying points at Kelso, Dalkeith and other towns. Walter Scott, himself a fervent patriot, rode all the way from Liddesdale to the alarm call. By noonday on 1 February, all had gathered to face the fierce mustachios of the hated Gauls, only to find it had been much ado about nothing.

But a most amusing sidelight is reflected from this glaring indiscretion. A band of volunteers were boozing in a licensed toll-house near the village of St. Boswells. About midnight, when they were paralytic, someone, less tight than his fellows, noticed that the nearby Eildon Hills had stopped being extinct volcanoes and were belching fire and smoke. Gradually it percolated their whisky-sodden skulls that the demon Nap was upon them. Off they rode to their distant rendezvous forgetting to pay the bill.

A year passed after the 'False Alarm' before the party re-assembled to celebrate the glorious event of their nebulous war over the Corsican tyrant. But the landlord had flitted, so they searched all round St. Boswells until they traced him to another boozing-den. For generations, each last day of January, the descendents of these intrepid foes of the French met in the Buccleuch Arms to toast the 'False Alarm', providing themselves with a good excuse to follow up the Burns Suppers of the previous week.

But a sobering footnote must be added, which by chance I am able to supply.

Many French prisoners-of-war were held in Scotland during the latter years of the long war. they were ill-treated in places like Glencorse and Edinburgh Castle, as any reader of Stevenson's romance *St. Ives* will know, but luckily for the honour of Scotland, many hundreds, mostly officers, were placed on parole in country towns and allowed a lot of freedom. Many of them were skilled in arts and sciences and left evidence of this in the articles they made for sale to the Scots.

Over 200 were located in Kelso, in the heart of the False Alarm country. Here these gay Froggies brought an exotic sparkle into the bucolic lives of the natives, especially the ladies, who were generally delighted to entertain the gallantries of Old Gaul. The motto of the Border lassies was, 'Even if you can beat them, join them.' But the sour old wet-blanket of a gazetteering minister of the parish did not agree. In his statistical account he concluded; 'The French prisoners on parole, to a very noticeable degree, inoculated the place with their follies.' I hope that this was not an innuendo against the manhood of the French, by the use of the word 'follies' in the same sense as it described Hume Castle, 'a massive but useless erection.'

The next tale is of a Scot who was caught napping in a compromising position. He was William Lithgow, probably the traveller who holds the world's pedestrian record, for he walked 36,000 miles, equal to one and a half journeys round the earth, in his nineteen years of travel through Europe, North Africa and the Near East.

What was the force that compelled him to start on this great journey? It was the merest mischance which befell him in his native town of Lanark. He was a notorious flirter whose motto was, 'He who loves and runs away may live to love another day.' But Lithgow very nearly didn't, for, as he was canoodling with a lusty lass, her brothers came along and caught the amorous pair in the act. They debated how they would end Lithgow's courting career once and for all, short of homicide, and decided to cut off his ears, a well-established penalty for deer-poaching.

Thereafter he was known all round Lanark as 'Lugless Willie Lithgow', so he decided to take his shame out of his native land.

He has achieved fame, though at considerable risk to his life, as he records in the journal of his peregrinations. He was arrested by the Inquisition and imprisoned as a heretic, by powers who needed no encouragement to hand heretics over to be burnt at the stake. He was lucky to be at last set free, for had the secret of his cropped ears come before his captors he would probably have been executed for fornication.

We should now for a change study another but cannier Scot who refused to be caught napping in the very long period of his life as the minister of Ruthwell in Dumfriesshire. In the fifty-four years of his ministry from 1617-71 there were many changes in the government of Scotland, each one attended by drastic upsets in religion. The Wars of the Covenant, the Civil Wars, the Commonwealth of Cromwell and the beginning of the 'Killing Times' under Charles II were all calculated to force decent men to renounce their beliefs several times. But Gavin Young was like the famous Vicar of Bray, the clerical turncoat of Berkshire, whose chorus was,

And this is law I will maintain
Until my dying day, sir,
That whatsoever king shall reign
I'll still be Vicar of Bray, sir.

He remained minister of Ruthwell for even longer than the Vicar of Bray had done under the persecutions of Bloody Mary and Elizabeth. Through all Young's period when fanatical hatred reigned he 'keepit a calm sough,' attended to the parish needs and did not neglect his domestic duties either. His wife Jean Stewart lived up to the philo-progenitiveness of that royal clan by bearing him 'thirty-one dear bairns' in his incumbency of Ruthwell.

Only one piece of holy vandalism blotted his long ministry, not due to him, however. In the Kirk there had stood the thousand-year-old Ruthwell Cross on which were carvings and fragments of an ancient Christian poem in Northumbrian dialect. The General Assembly of 1644, in blind fanaticism, ordered the cross to be broken down and thrown into a corner of the churchyard. Only in modern times was it recognised as one of the treasures of early Christianity, from a district converted by St. Cuthbert. It was then re-assembled and installed once more in Ruthwell Kirk.

When the Day of Judgement arrives nobody will be able to excuse his or her unpreparedness, for it has been so long forecast that surely we shall not be caught napping. The year 1000 was generally thought to be 'now dat de Kingdom's come and de year ob Jubilo.' The wealthy gave away their goods to the poor, but no doubt regretted their charity in time.

1866 was prophesied in *Brown's Bible Dictionary* as the Second Coming, and this was generally believed in Scotland. My grandfather was fond of a quiet joke. In 1865 he was a Kirk elder in Dumfries and was called to a meeting to discuss the building of a new church to replace the old. He solemnly proposed that the new building should be of wood rather than of stone. This proposal was indignantly repudiated by the minister and the session, and Mr. David Macgregor was asked to explain his ludicrously inadequate suggestion. He quietly explained that, as a practical engineer, he did not support the expenditure which a stone church would incur when all that was needed was a temporary tabernacle.

'But this is not to be temporary. It is intended to be permanent,' he was told.

'I would refer you gentlemen to the Rev. John Brown's statement that the millennium is to arrive next year, in 1866, after which we shall all have a permanent abode in the heavens.'

His explanation was received very drily.

The most splendid event ever planned in Scotland was the Eglinton Tournament. The Earl of Eglinton, of rich possessions and high descent, had the splendid idea of ushering in the Victorian Era with a mediaeval tournament in the grounds of his castle near Kilwinning in Ayrshire. Preparation started shortly after Queen Victoria's Coronation in 1837 and lasted for two years.

Galleries, fences, marquees, jousting arenas and pavilions were erected at enormous expense. Many of the costly decorations had come from the Royal Coronation.

Crowds from all over Britain arrived on the day of the opening, 28 August 1839. The Ardrossan Railway, recently opened, brought thousands. Gigs and coaches plied from Glasgow at extravagant fares.

Knights and viscounts, Queens of Beauty, noble maidens, men-at-arms, all in mediaeval costume, set off from the Castle. Alas, they had not reckoned on the weather. A plumping shower baptised everyone. Up went thousands of black umbrellas, eclipsing the glory of the Middle Ages.

Bravely the knights charged one another, soaked with pitiless rain and soiled by mud. When all were ready for the Grand Banquet the dining pavilions were found to be ankle-deep in water.

Next day the weather was no better despite the presence of Prince Louis Napoleon, later to be Emperor Napoleon III. The third was at least fair and some tourneys were held, but the final day was worst of all, wind supplementing the torrential rain, routing the gallants and ladies and driving them from the field. It took many years to erase the miserable memory of the Eglinton Tournament, which deserved better treatment.

Social climbers are fond of name-dropping and we often have to take their word for their high-shelf acquaintances. Now and then one of them is caught out with a loose ball.

One such bore was in a carriage full of Border farmers returning in a jovial mood from a lamb sale. The well-connected gentleman had been telling of his relationship with the Earl of This and the Honourable So-and-So. The train drew nearer Melrose and the triple heights of the Eildon Hills appeared. A pawky farmer thought it was time to prick the bubble.

'Excuse me, sir. Ye seem to be vera weel conneckit wi mony o' the best Border faimilies. Ane o' the auldest and best respeckit hereaboots is the Eildons o' Melrose. Nae doot ye'll be some kin to them.'

'Yes, indeed, I cannot at the moment recall the exact relationship but I have heard my mother speak of them as second cousins on her side of the family.'

Modern plumbing has puzzled many an innocent soul. When water-closets were first introduced in Scotland a number of country people took some time to get used to the idea. An old lady visiting a modernised house for the first time was heard to pull the plug several times in the toilet. She was so long in the place that her friend knocked on the door and asked if she was feeling all right.

Back came the perturbed answer.

'O, no, I dinna ken what's come ower me a' o' a sudden. I was a'richt afore I cam in, but every time I rax up my airm to pu' mysel aff the seat wi the haunle, the water fair gushes oot o' me.'

During the North American campaign in the Seven Years War both French and British employed Red Indians to wage a merciless conflict on the opposing palefaces. Sentries were posted by day and night around the British stockade camps, for the wiles of the redskins were many. In a certain camp near Ticonderoga, encompassed by primeval forest, were a mixed company of British troops, of whom many were Highlanders.

The officers were worried because for some weeks past, night sentries on outpost had been found scalped in the morning. Every precaution was taken to warn the sentries not to doze off for a second and to shoot at every suspicious object. But sentries who shoot for little reason are not popular when they alarm the whole camp in the depths of the night, so the scalping continued.

It came the turn of a clansman of Lochaber to do sentry-go. He had been an experienced stalker for years before enlisting. He was very intelligent and he argued the case out as he mounted guard. The sentries who had died had been keen soldiers, observant of danger, not likely to be caught napping. Therefore they must have been deceived by some apparently harmless object. What could it have been? He determined to be suspicious of every movement.

After an hour or two he heard a snuffling some hundred paces off in the dead leaves and brushwood. There was a faint moonlight and at last he saw a porcupine searching hither and thither for food. Many of these animals lived thereabouts in the forest. They were stout and heavily built, covered with hair and long quills and quite harmless.

The sentry amused himself by watching it moving backwards and forwards. Then he had a sudden thought. His unfortunate comrades perhaps had also seen porcupines acting in this harmless manner. He became more suspicious of it. Then he noticed that such movement as it made brought it just a little nearer to his post. He decided to take no chances, raised his musket slowly and fired at the middle of the procupine's bulky body. It gave a peculiar groan and lay still. By this time the camp was aroused and men carrying lanterns and torches were running to find the cause of the shot. An officer began to accuse the Highlander of firing unnecessarily, but, in reply, he led them over to the body. It was, as he guessed, a redskin covered by a porcupine skin, scalping knife at the ready.

That is, I confess, a very simple tale, but it has an application of universal interest, for it gives us a means of detecting smooth operators. Each move they make brings them nearer to their goal, so don't be caught napping.

Even at most unexpected times when everything seems to be jogging along peacefully with no danger lurking, up pops a nasty situation.

A family tea-party of friends and neighbours was going merrily. The tea-cakes were disappearing and the capacious teapot had been filled and re-filled. The husband and wife were entertaining the three old neighbour wives whom the cup that cheers was making more and more talkative.

In a kindly-meant remark the husband, looking at the three old ladies, said, 'Now, are ye no going to have another three cups o' tea?'

This was taken as a reproof by each of them and the party broke up pretty soon afterwards.

Smuggling had always appealed to the Scots who had no love for taxes imposed without their consent. After the Union of Parliaments in 1707 many English commissioners were sent to enforce the Excise Acts. Either by guile or by sheer force the smugglers carried on a long war, with casualties on both sides. Here is a tale from the Solway Firth of how a Galloway man, Johnny Girr of Auchencairn, played the daft laddie with the excise.

He was sailing merrily from the Isle of Man before a fresh breeze with his cargo of contraband, tubs of spirits and tobacco, when he was spotted by a revenue cutter, which gave chase from two miles away. When Johnnie saw them he sank his barrels, tied together with a stout rope. Then he took his seat at the helm and told his young assistant to lie in the scuppers.

The cutter came driving on before the half-gale, firing shots to make Johnnie haul down his sail. But he sat calmly smoking his pipe paying no attention. At last the angry revenue men drew alongside in their rowing-boat and cursed him heartily, asking him why he had not lowered his sail.

Johnnie, looking simple, replied, 'God guide us, I didna ken ye were firing at me. If I'd thocht that I wad hae been fair terrified.' The King's men saw only a stupid old man, incapable of any deception or illegal business, so they sailed off leaving Johnnie to pick up his goods at his leisure.

A sailor friend of mine came into Leith in the thirties with a few pounds of undeclared tobacco in his locker, not expecting a visit from the revenue officers. They must have been on the lookout, for one of them suddenly entered his cabin and asked to search. He could not be refused, so he soon discovered the tobacco.

'Ha, ha, what have we here, eh?' he chortled, kneeling on the bed and throwing the packets one by one on to the coverlet, counting them triumphantly. But he did not notice that the porthole was open. As fast as the packets landed on the bed my friend popped them out into the briny and when the chagrined exciseman clambered off the bed the evidence had vanished into thin air.

Kicking the Bucket

The snag about living a long time is that you tend to grow old. Whatever has been said in favour of old age, it is making a virtue of necessity to say that it is the best period of one's life. Perhaps the most honest remark about old age was made by a Roman philosopher who spoke from experience. 'Old age is not unpleasant in itself but it does take away most of one's freshness.'

There are very few animals (and that includes birds, reptiles, fish and all other species) which reach maturity, let alone old age. The great majority do not survive infancy, and most do not emerge from the egg stage. Think, for example, of the haddock, which lays 30,000 eggs or so, each season. If they all reached full haddockhood there would not be enough potatoes to make chips for them.

Man has come to assume a life expectancy, in this country, of approaching three score years and ten. He uses much of his ingenuity trying to increase this period; and quite a lot of research in inventing devices to destroy his species at all ages. Any lunatic asylum would be far more logically run by its patients than earth is by man. When I was a child seventy years ago we all realised, sooner rather than later, that we were mortal; but mortality for us was never an urgent issue, as it has become for the past forty years. The repercussions of atomic power are only beginning to affect our actions. But it is the only world we have that is at all hospitable, compared with the bleak reception we should expect on another satellite, so we cling to it as long as we can. Even with one foot in the grave, we hop along the edge quite hopefully on the other foot. It has been said that if we wish to achieve anything worth while, we should behave as if we were immortal.

Some philosophers have argued that despite what the Scriptures say, people were intended to reach a hundred. The rather strange thing is that very few of those who believed in this theory managed to practise it. I remember a case of the fanatic in England many years ago who thought that humans were herbivorous animals, as Nebuchadnezzar was during his lunacy. He persuaded the local bowling-green keeper to save the fine grass mowings for his nourishment. He died very suddenly and unexpectedly, at an early age, after a feed of grass.

Some people, who have no fads whatever, become centenarians. The reaching of a century is very common nowadays, and the Queen must have quite a job every morning in life sending out these telegrams to those who have defied Old Father Time's body-line bowling. Many of the centenarians of old were probably cheating, for there was no compulsory registration before 1855, and old men got reputations for longevity by the length and colour of their beards, and women by wrinkles and scolding power.

What merit is there, anyway, in being very old? A tale is told of Julius Caesar, that he was approached by one of his veterans and asked for a small sum of money.

'Why do you want money? Have you not a soldier's pension?' said Caesar.

'My pension is very small. I want more to help me to live better.'

'So you think you are still alive?' was the cynical comment.

Jonathan Swift tells of Gulliver's visit to the Struldbruggs. In that far-off land of Luggnagg, there was a small Minority who never joined the Great Majority. At birth they were known by a red spot on their faces which showed they were to be immortal. Gulliver, when asked how he would have conducted his life if he had been one of these Struldbruggs, told his enquirers of his splendid plans to acquire, in that order, wealth, knowledge and power, so that after a few centuries, he would be the ruler of the land. To his chagrin they laughed him to scorn and told him that immortality was the greatest punishment that anyone could suffer. He was shown some of the Struldbruggs, deaf, blind, imbecilic, apathetic, subject to all the ills that flesh is heir to, and yet unable to throw off the burden of life. After that, Gulliver had no fatuous ideas of immortality, and decided that Death henceforth had no sting. The pathetic tail-piece to this story is in the fate of the narrator, Dr. Swift himself, who passed the last seven years of his life like one of the poor creatures that his genius had invented.

There are immortal creatures on earth, however. They are these very humble forms of protoplasm which keep dividing every few hours and so perpetuate themselves at the cost of suffering a split personality. But the pleasures of these schizophrenics are few, I am told, so I should not choose to be either an amoeba or a Struldbrugg.

Scots have a reputation for possessing some strange, almost inhuman attributes. The strangest of all is their general attitude to Death, by many other nations called the last enemy. Some nations honour Death, some abhor him, some ignore him, but the Scots joke about him.

Perhaps the most typical of these droll tales is about the old man who, although dying by inches, still retained some appetite for the good things of life.

'Jeannie, woman,' he whispered from the box-bed at the wall.

'Aye, Tam, what is it ye want noo?'

'Yon's a grand ham hingin ower the windae. Dae ye think I could hae a slice o't fried for ma tea the nicht? I've been lickin' ma lips at it a' efternin.'

'Ye ken fine, Tam I wadna refuse ye onything in reason, but ye canna hae a slice o' yon.'

'What fer no, Jeannie?'

'Yon's specially reserved for your funeral, Tam.'

A couple, not nearly so amiable as the above, had proved their incompatability by not speaking to one another for twenty years. At last Willie's health began to decline and he retired to his bedroom up in the attic. His wife Aggie took up his meals, rapped on the door and left them on the mat.

One morning he began to moan. It seemed that he was nearing the last extremity. Aggie thought regretfully of their far-off courting days when they were so fond. She decided to break the long silence.

She went to the foot of the stairs and shouted 'Willie!'

To her satisfaction the feeble answer came back, 'Aye, Aggie?'

'Whaur would ye like to be buried, Willie?' she yelled.

Something in the situation seemed to annoy Willie. He summoned up all his lung-power and bellowed back,

'On the tap o' you, ye auld bitch!'

On the South bank of the Clyde, not a stone's throw from Eglinton Street, an old wifie was fast nearing her end.

'Sandy,' she sighed, 'D'ye mind when we gaed hand in hand to the Sacrament in the auld Covenantin' Kirk o' Durisdeer?'

'O, aye, Aillie. Yon were braw days when we were young. I mind them fine.'

'Weel, Sandy, there's just the ae request I'd like to mak. When I sough awa, as I'll dae ony oor noo, will ye hae me cairried awa up and buried in Durisdeer amang the Lord's anointed? For I'll ne'er lie quiet here amang the roar and the reek o' Glesca. Promise me, Sandy.'

Sandy looked thoughtful for a few minutes.

'Weel, Aillie. I'll promise ye this. We'll try ye first in the Gorbals and if ye dinna bide quiet there, as shair as daith, I'll flit ye to Durisdeer.'

A newly bereaved widower was being consoled by the minister. Gradually they came round to the business of the burial.

'I suppose you've already made arrangements with the undertaker?'

'Aye, meenister, I've done that. I wonder, if you'll be kind enough, sir, to conduct the service. We've ay been raither regular at the Kirk.'

'Of course. I'll be only too glad, for she was a pillar o' our wee kirk.'

'I've arranged for the burial to take place a fortnicht the day.'

The minister gasped audibly.

'But this is most unusual. It is unprecedented, John.'

'Maybe so, sir, but it's the corpse's will.'

'How does that come about?'

'It really goes back to oor weddin-day, sir. She said to me then, what her idea o' Heeven was; just her and me the-gether for a fortnicht in a quiet place a' by oorsels and no a single word spoken. It's gradually penetrated my mind, sir, over the last thirty years, that the next fortnicht maun hae been what she was thinkin o'.'

Sometimes the day of doom, when it dawned at last, was treated very pragmatically, and, if any deep feelings were aroused, they rarely found utterance. Possibly it was to cloak their emotions that the purely business part of death was allowed to take over the conversation.

Auld Willie Broon lay at death's door. It was plain to all that he had a short time to stay. His wife hirpled up to the bedside.

'Willie, as long as ye can speak,' she whispered, 'Will ye tell me this? Are ye for your burial baps roond or square?' (The burial baps were rolls specially baked for the funeral, but of little interest to the principal actor).

An equally particular wife was attending her dying man.

'Tam, I'm awa tae ma bed, for I've been trauchlin aboot on ma feet a' day and I'm fair done.'

'Guid nicht, Leeby,' he muttered.

She paused at the door.

'Tam, when ye feel ye're soughin awa, will ye mind to snuff oot the cannle?'

Not many people have had the doubtful distinction of being 'kisted' twice. But this happened to a farmer's wife in the Borders. To all appearances she had given up the ghost and had been coffined. The baked meats and the raw drams were all laid out, and the funeral party was ready to enjoy the occasion, when an untoward accident ruined the party.

As the bearers were bringing the coffin down the narrow, dog-legged stair, they struck it sharply on the corner-post of the bannister. To everyone's horror, a hollow moan came from the box. The lady had been in a trance, and far from being a fit subject for burial, she lived on for a further fifteen years, and by all accounts gave her husband the rough edge of her tongue for most of that time.

Once again the season came about for her to take her leave, and most people, especially her husband and the family doctor, made sure that she meant it. However, the canny Scots farmer was taking no chances. When the bearers were again negotiating the narrows at the bend of the stairs, he gave them a hoarse earnest whisper.

'For God's sake, lads, mind that bannister rail.'

Famous last words have been passed on through the ages, the presumption being that the last words a person utters are likely to be the epitome of all their thoughts and actions. The truth is the very opposite. Most dying words, if intelligible, are usually trivial and banal; only on rare occasions is some memorable phrase uttered. Sometimes, indeed, the last words bring small comfort to the doom-watchers, as in this spooky tale.

A heavy drinker suffered the consequences of his convivial habits. He began to be increasingly visited by horrible apparitions. His particular visitant was a horned figure with flaming eyeballs, dressed in a black suit. He described this horror so accurately to his friends that they decided to help him to recover his sanity by dressing up one of their number in exactly the same way, even to the horns, and with luminous eyeballs, using phosphorescent paint.

The apparition always appeared on the first stroke of midnight. Late the next evening his friends met in the afflicted man's lobby, and as midnight tolled from the neighbouring church tower, the fake spectre entered the bedroom. The delirious man was to be spoken to in reassuring tones by the made-up bogey, to convince him that his fears were imaginary. But to the dismay and horror of all who peeped round the door, the afflicted man sat bolt upright in bed, his hair on end, and shrieked, 'Good God, there are two of them tonight. They've come to carry me to hell,' and fell back dead, leaving his well-intentioned friends to form their own conclusions, as they made a rush for the open air.

Nelson left us with a puzzle. At Trafalgar did he whisper to his captain, 'Kiss me, Hardy,' or did he make the philosophical remark, 'Kismet, Hardy?' The first is almost certainly what he said, for the word, Kismet, or fate, was not in the English language until forty years later. When the schoolboy was asked 'Who said "Kiss me, Hardy",' the answer varied between Stan and Laurel.

Perhaps the most succinct of dying requests was from Robert Burns.

'Don't let the awkward squad fire over my grave.' He seemed to be referring to the Dumfries Volunteers, but a figurative meaning was probably on his mind. His fears have been more than justified in the gauche performances of many haggis-bashers.

A native of Paisley, Alexander Wilson, poet and bird-lover, was forced to leave Scotland because of his political views. In America he helped to compose a famous volume of American ornithology. He uttered this pathetic wish, when dying prematurely of dysentery, 'Bury me where the birds will sing over my grave.'

The general solemnity of authentic 'last words' makes me rather sceptical about the stories that follow, for they are humorous, even comic in some extreme cases.

A Highland cattle-thief had been cornered at last, in his own cottage, by the laird of the territory, who could legally imprison or hang on his own authority at that time. Donald was very unwilling to leave his 'black house' to go to his execution. He could see the noose hanging from the limb of a nearby tree, so he refused to budge, even at the command of his own clan chief.

At last his wife, more loyal to the clan than to her own man, pleaded with him. 'Come away, now, Donald. You could not be so discourteous as to keep the laird waiting and him such a busy man. Come out and be hanged like a true MacNab.'

And the simple savage went like a lamb to the slaughter. If a' tales were true, then that's nae lee.

Criminals on the way to execution are often said to be quite unaffected by their imminent departure. As the saying was, 'They got used to hanging, as herrings get used to being fried.' A hardened criminal is said to have requested the headsman, 'Don't take me to the gallows by the Castlegate. There's a wine-merchant there to whom I owe quite a sum of money for my last party. He might arrest me for debt.'

Another, on mounting the ladder and having the noose placed round his neck, pleaded, 'Don't touch my neck. I'm so ticklish it's sure to make me die laughing.'

When the priest, to console a condemned man, assured him that he would sup with the Lord, the poor fellow remarked, 'I don't really have much appetite tonight. Go in my place and make my apologies.'

It was the custom, in past ages in Scotland and elsewhere, to pardon the condemned man at the gallows' foot, if any woman would come forward and offer to marry him. One of the ancestors of Sir Walter Scott saved his life in this way, as I told in *Macgregor's Mixture*. A more fussy criminal was asked to marry a whore to save his neck, and also make an honest woman of her. He took one look at her and exclaimed, 'She has a limp. Tie me up.'

The parish grave-man, or grave-digger, lay dying. The minister called to console him but could make nothing of it.

'Come awa, noo, John. Ye've had a guid lang innings. Ye're lang past the allotted span. The Lord has ca'd ye to be wi your ain folk. Can ye no be content to dee?'

'Ye dinna understand, meenister. I've happit up, first and last, ower forty years, nae less than fower hunner and ninety-seeven folk, a' o' this pairish, and I was in hopes, gin the Lord had spared me till the spring, to hae made the roond five hunner.'

Two Border worthies were deep in conversation on the serious subject of funerals. 'I canna abide burials,' said the first. 'Ye gang awa up the hill yonner tae the kirkyaird maybe on a cauld drowy day in December. Ye staun roon the graveside soakit to the skin while the meenister drools on for hauf-an-oor about dust and ashes, wi the sleety draps dribblin frae his purple neb. Your feet are cauld. Ye shiver to the vera marra. Then ye gang hame and tak to your bed wi the browncaties or the pewmoany and that's your number up. Na, na, nae burials for me.'

'That's a' vera weel, Tam, but there's just yin thing ye've forgotten.'

'And what micht that be?'

'If ye dinna gang to their funerals, hoo d'ye expect them to come to yours?'

An elderly couple had been for a fortnight's holiday to Troon where the weather was exceptionally sunny. But on the day following the return to Glasgow, the husband expired. A few hours after his passing, one of his cronies called, out of shock and sympathy, so the widow ushered him into the 'Deid-room.'

He gazed in awe at the corpse for several minutes without speaking, and wiped away a stray tear from his grey moustache.

'Mind ye, Mrs. McCrone, I'll say this,' looking at the corpse's sunburnt features, 'His holiday's done him a pooer o' guid.'

The gravedigger in a city 'yaird' was a born grumbler, and he never failed to unload his grievances on any visitors who came seeking information. One day a gentleman called to ask where the Campbell burial ground was. This seemed to annoy him.

'The Cawmell grun? It's ower thonder forenent thon auld holly-buss. Ye'll no be a friend o' the Cawmells yoursel?' By friend he meant a relative.

'O, no, just making enquiries.'

Thus reassured, he felt free to air his feelings.

'D'ye ken, thon faimily, the Cawmells, hae done gey ill by me. There's na been a single daith in that faimily for ower thretty years. They've no broken grun for a' that time. Hoo dae they expect me to mak a livin'? Na, na, live and let live, says I. Thae Cawmells are no human at a'. They're monuments, no men and weemen.'

He paused in his tirade and pointed his spade at a nearby headstone of large expanse covered by long lists of names and dates.

'Noo, that's the Frasers' grun. The Frasers are a grand canny faimily for the pairish. No a year passes but I pit a Fraser doon. See here.'

He turned to a newly excavated grave and affectionately patted a large bone with his spade.

'That's Janet Fraser's thigh-bane. I mind her weel. O, aye, a fine big-baned faimily the Frasers. They've done weel by me.'

On a cold February day a dejected company of old men in their green-moulded 'stands o' blacks' were braving the sleety gale to pay their last respects to an old companion. During the service, which was 'an unconscionable time a-doing,' a deep-seated hacking cough was heard at short intervals. When it was over, the gravedigger put on his bonnet and turned to the nearest group with a business-like look in his eye.

He asked, 'Wha gied thon howe hoast?'

An old soul admitted the deed.

The grim functionary strode over and tapped the cougher on the shoulder.

'Davie, my man, it's hardly worth your while gaun hame.'

Soon after, the graveman himself developed a bad cough. The minister noticed it and sympathetically remarked one day in the graveyard, 'That's a bad cough ye have, Sandy.'

'Indeed it is, meenister, but,' waving his hand about him, 'there's a hantle o' folk hereaboots that would be gey gled o't.'

Predestination is one of the main beliefs in some religions, particularly among the Presbyterian Scots. There is more than one proverb about it. For example it is said that the man born to be hanged need never fear drowning; but only the event proves the saying. Nevertheless, many a man who has been at death's door has failed to enter it, and conversely, many who have done everything to escape the grisly spectre have been suddenly whipped away by it.

Perhaps the most remarkable case in history was of a man named John Hatfield who died in 1770 at the age of 102. When he was a young soldier, in the reign of William of Orange, he had been put on night sentry duty at Windsor Castle. A Dutch officer who had taken an ill-will at Hatfield, because of some personal spite, was looking for an opportunity to accuse him of a dereliction of military duty. On making a round of inspection he returned to the commander and reported that he had found Hatfield asleep at his post at midnight. As Windsor was a royal residence and the times were politically disturbed, the severe discipline of the army imposed the death penalty for sleeping on duty.

Hatfield was tried by court martial. He denied the charge. 'On the contrary,' he asserted, 'far from being asleep at any time near midnight, or any other hour, I was very alert and heard all the bells of London strike the hours. For example, I heard a most extraordinary sound at midnight. The night was very still and the wind being from the city I distinctly heard Old Tom of Westminster strike thirteen.'

Shouts of laughter greeted this statement, and he was sternly told that if any proof of his guilt was needed, he had supplied it, by describing what he could only have heard in a ridiculous dream. He was sentenced to be shot.

However, when the trial was reported, a number of reliable witnesses came forward and testified on oath that they had heard midnight rung with an extra stroke on the night in question.

Clockmakers explained that the striking mechanism of these large tower-clocks had a controlling pawl which very occasionally slipped, to allow twelve and one to be struck together. The chances of this happening were infinitesimal. But the chances of a man facing certain death, and escaping that fate to live for a further term of eighty years, are positively unique. The moral of this story seems to be, 'Never say die.'

Aeshylus, a famous Greek poet who fought at Marathon, is supposed in later life to have become so psychologically apprehensive of death, that he left his house on hearing that it was reputed to be about to collapse. But, as he walked away from this danger under a cloudless sky, he was instantly killed by a tortoise, of all creatures, falling with terrific force upon his skull. That was before the compulsory wearing of safety helmets on site. Had he kept on his old army helmet, it might have helped, when an eagle, a mile up, dropped the tortoise to crack it on the street.

The very opposite of this extraordinary fate was an actual incident which took place without witnesses, not so many years ago, in the West End of Edinburgh. The magnificent Dean Bridge, which spans the deep glen of the Water of Leith, at a height of over a hundred feet, used to be considered a good place for an effective suicide. The authorities sought to discourage this by putting a continuous line of sharp curved spikes on top of the parapet. but a sailor, probably a bit tight, negotiated the parapet and fell the full distance. He should have been killed instantly but, by the sheerest chance, he landed feet first into a deep pool of the river, and struck a shelving bank of gravel under the surface. He was practically unhurt and certainly verified the old proverb that 'there's a special providence that looks after drunk men and bairns.'

The final phrases 'Dust to dust and ashes to ashes' are too conclusive to give rise to any scandal or suspicion, but they have been known to cast reflections back on the deceased persons's life.

I know of a case many years ago when a mother-in-law of rather an imperious character was being buried with what seemed an unnecessarily long and unctuous address by the preacher. After what seemed an eternity, the son-in-law, who had suffered under this indomitable dame, walked rapidly out by the cemetery gates to his car, remarking rather indecorously, 'Dust to dust and ashes to ashes. Let's get the hell out of this.'

A cousin of mine, a decent-living man, by accident of timing got mixed up with the wrong cortege. He had intended paying his respects to an unfortunate young man but half-way through the service it began to dawn on him that the chief actor was a married lady of his own age who lived in the same quarter of the town. During the rest of the service he was subjected to indignant glances from several of the mourners, including the widower, who wondered on what grounds of relationship he was attending the service.

The fable of the shepherd-boy who cried 'Wolf!' too often is well known. Something of the same nature happened to a 'stranger to the truth.' He was certified dead by the doctor and 'kisted' by the undertaker. However, as he was being lifted from the hearse at the kirkyard the horrified mourners heard muffled cries from the coffin. 'I'm no deid. I'm no deid. Let me oot for Goad's sake.' They were proceeding to look for a screw-driver when the departed's widow interposed,

'Dinna listen to him. He was a damned leear when he was livin.'

A mourner at a coal-merchant's cremation service was overheard to make this caustic remark when she discovered that his ashes were to be scattered over the Garden of Rest.

'Gin there's as muckle ash frae him as there was frae his coal it'll tak a week and twa shovels to spread it.'

In the cab taking the mourners to the kirkyard was a little man sitting silently in the corner. One of the relatives asked if he was an old friend of the deceased.

'Weel, no exactly.'

'A business acquaintance, maybe?'

'Na, to tell ye the truth I've just come for the hurl.'

A fall of snow had covered the countryside when a burial was to take place. There was a thaw, then a renewal of frost, which made the ground very treacherous. The cemetery was on a steep hill at the head of the village street. As the hearse tried to mount the slippery path, the wheels skidded and the coffin of Auld Sandy slid down to the ground. It did not rest there but, gathering speed, went tumbling through the kirkyard gates on to the village main street and went sliding down the brae followed by the more active of the undertakers and relatives. The commotion drew the residents to their front-doors. Shopkeepers also dashed into the street, amongst them the local chemist to whom the leading mourner shouted, very appropriately,

'Hey, Maister Brown, hae ye got something to stop ma coaffin?'

Spooks

I may say at the start of this chapter that I have never actually seen a ghost, or even had a delusion of seeing an apparition. But I have had a number of strange experiences, not to be easily argued away.

On New Year's Day 1927, I had the nearest approach to meeting a ghost or an evil spirit.

The gale blew steadily with never a break all the seven miles from Dalkeith by Camphill. As we passed down the wood the gaunt walls of Crichton Castle towered against the flying sky. In a few moments we dropped quietly through a window into the calm, hollow-sounding grass-grown courtyard.

All was in absolute rank ruin, with the wind howling through the gaping windows of the south-west wall, shrieking up and down the circular staircase and thundering into the tall square western tower.

We carried our rucksacks and billycans into one of the dark vaults that served as kitchens in the sixteenth century. It was not yet half-past three and growing rapidly dark.

Soon we had a grand fire blazing in the enormous chimney of our bed-chamber, probably the first fire for three centuries and we the first guests. After supper we lay before the embers and yarned, the pauses marked by the whine of the gale in the great square tower, separated from us only by an open doorway. That tower, which once held bedrooms before the beams rotted away, was reputed to be haunted by the ghosts of guests done away with in the violent ages.

From outside came the confused babble of buffetted trees, broken by the sudden shriek of the larger eddies over the gaping walls of the haunted tower. I rolled up in my tartan plaid and fell asleep.

Suddenly I awoke with all senses alert, and looked at my English lever watch in the inky darkness. The plain gold hands were just visible and stood at three minutes to midnight. The evil-smelling chamber seemed to whisper insistently, 'It is the appointed time.'

Everything became inconsequential. The only thing that existed was a horror which oozed, a rank miasma, from the substance of the walls, from the air and from the deep dust on the floor. I felt no other emotion than a penetrating horror. Yet there was no active agent of terror. I saw nothing, heard nothing, none of my five senses was in action. The whole dark night seemed to be sodden by a vagueness of despair, of remorse, of unavenged suffering.

Then I looked at my watch. It was two minutes past midnight. All faded again into the void.

We woke to a cold fresh day, the wind somewhat abated. Peeping over the ridge were the blue familiar tops of the Pentlands, a splash of early sunshine upon the sugar-loaf of Carnethy. I vowed there and then to keep to the woods in stormy weather, like the roe-deer, and sleep peacefully untroubled by evil spirits.

I shall give only one more instance of a feeling of the presence of an evil spirit. There is a long stretch of bleak upland between the Moorfoot Hills and the low country of the Lothians. It has for ages been named the Hie Flat. There are several limestone deposits on it, amongst the peat bogs. Last century some of these were worked on the lonely border of Peeblesshire and then abandoned, leaving ruined cottages and derelict kilns.

One midsummer evening more than fifty years ago, I was camping alone in a scanty wood of half-dead trees on the limestone summit of the moor, about a hundred yards from a little-used ancient road. After a camp-fire supper I lay down about midnight to take a nap. The twilight persisted all night and the sunlight lingered on the high clouds well past midnight. It was difficult to fall asleep so I lay and listened to the calls of birds and animals. I heard the high-up drumming of a snipe circling the wood, the sharp *keevit* of a long-eared owl and the continuous far-off whistling of whaups, a melancholy chorus. But far from being lulled, I felt very disturbed. I would have felt much more at ease in pitch darkness.

I seemed to be watched by a malignant presence which resented my intrusion. I had slept out in the wilds hundreds of times at all seasons and had always felt at home. But not a wink did I enjoy all that long June twilight at Hillhead. When dawn came I kindled a fire, made a can of tea and left the cursed place to whatever wanted it.

It was only years later that I read of a ghostly legend connected with that place, or rather the lonely moor that skirted the wood, cut down many years ago.

A ne'er-do-weel young fellow was employed in a farm in the parish of Lasswade, some few miles from Hillhead. He was second ploughman and was noted for his abuse of horses. The farmer, though dissatisfied, could find no definite excuse for dismissing him before the term day. He could not understand why his horses appeared overworked for no apparent reason.

As it later turned out the suspect had fallen in with a young woman over the county border in the Tweed-dale area of Eddleston. He was in the habit, when all were a-bed, of borrowing one of his horses and galloping along the moor road by Mount Lothian and Hillhead to the lonely Cockmuir to tryst with his mistress.

One June evening, as he rode by Hillhead, he came upon an up-turned peat-cart which had pinned the driver to the road. The poor old carter was badly crushed and called out for help to the passing horseman. But his desperate calls for help went unheeded, for the rider did not wish to be seen on his clandestine ride. He galloped, hoping uncharitably that, when he repassed early in the morning, the carter would have died of his injuries.

But, as he returned several hours later, the man was still conscious and cried out piteously for help. But once again the ploughman rode on for the same reason as before, hoping that death would soon silence the accusing tongue. But the old man held doggedly on to consciousness and was able to give a full description of the dastard who had twice turned a deaf ear.

The whole countryside got word of the affair, the villain was sacked, nobody would employ him or associate with him. Spurned by the community he committed suicide and was buried at an upland crossroads, his grave a mark of revulsion for the rare passer-by. The legend says that his ghost, and presumably the ghost of the ill-used horse, is doomed to ride past the scene of his cruelty on midsummer nights forever, to hear again the shrieks of the injured man and to avert his eyes from the accusing victim.

It will be seen from these true accounts that I am not a disbeliever in the supernatural, though a trifle agnostic.

The ghosts of murdered persons are supposed to appear, demanding justice, to any who are disposed to listen to them. Such a peculiar event took place in the Braemar area after the Forty-Five Rising. All the circumstances are authenticated, for the case was heard in the Court of Session in Edinburgh in June 1754, witnesses being cited who claimed to have had dealings with the ghost of the murdered man.

The background of the story is Deeside some years after the battle of Culloden. Hanoverian troops occupied the Highlands after committing dreadful atrocities on the inhabitants, who had every reason to hate the invaders. Guise's Regiment was stationed at Braemar. In September 1749 a sergeant of that regiment, named Arthur Davis, disappeared. As he was a man of good character, with several years of service, desertion was ruled out and murder was suspected at first, and later presumed.

Three or four years after Davis' disappearance, when the business was almost forgotten, the story began to get about that the sergeant's ghost had been visiting a farm servant named Alasdair Macpherson. Macpherson himself repeated the story that he had been disturbed during the hours of darkness in his bothy near Braemar. He was in bed when a ghost came to the bedside and ordered him to rise and follow him out on to the mountainside. Not thinking that his midnight visitor was an apparition but that he was a neighbour named Farquharson, he rose and followed. But when, in the open, the apparition told Macpherson that he was the spirit of Sergeant Davis, and that he wished him to bury his mortal remains, which were lying exposed in a desolate place called the Hill of Christie, the ghost requested him to take Farquharson to assist him in the burial.

Next day Macpherson went to the Hill of Christie and found the skeleton, but he was so overcome by the sight that he had not the courage to handle it, let alone bury it, so he went home hoping to forget his promise. But that night the ghost re-appeared and scolded him for breaking his vow. Macpherson now promised faithfully that he would carry out the burial and he was bold enough to ask the spirit who had murdered him. The reply came without hesitation. The murderers were Alasdair MacDonald and Duncan Terig, both of whom were known to Macpherson, but not among his friends.

Next day Macpherson and Farquharson went to the Hill of Christie and buried the skeleton in a deep hole in the peat.

The secret could no longer be kept, especially as a young woman names Isabel MacHardie was now a party to it. She was a young farm-worker who slept in the same bothy as Macpherson. She had seen a naked man enter the house in the dark and go to Macpherson's bed. Her words were, 'I saw something naked come in at the door. I was so frightened that I pulled the quilt over my head. The thing walked stooping to the ground. I

137

could not tell what manner of thing it was.'

The accused men would probably never have been arrested and taken to Edinburgh except for the damning fact that Davis' fowling-piece, money and rings were seen in their possession, which, though not absolute proof, weighed pretty strongly against them.

In the prosaic atmosphere of the Law Courts, the very mention of ghosts drew loud derisive laughter from all. The counsel for the prisoners took full advantage of the simplicity of the Gaelic-speaking Macpherson. He asked him, through an interpreter, 'What language did the ghost speak in?' Macpherson answered, 'As good Gaelic as I ever heard in Lochaber.'

'Pretty well done for the ghost of an English sergeant,' commented the counsel. The ridiculous aspect of this convinced the jury. They found Duncan Terig and MacDonald not guilty, though most of the court, including the defending counsel himself, and his solicitors, afterwards swore they were convinced of their guilt.

Now, as it is not known what languages are spoken in the other world, why should not ghosts speak as good Gaelic as anyone else, if they can, by doing so, communicate their message to the person they visit?

One of the most famous ghost stories from the Highlands, which is so well established that even the most sceptical cannot confound it, is the story of Duncan Campbell of Inverawe who was killed at the abortive and bloody attempt by the British on the fort of Ticonderoga, north of New York, in the Seven Years War. I shall give only a brief outline of this.

Duncan's cousin disappeared and was presumed dead, probably by accident, possibly at the hands of an enemy. Some time later his ghost appeared to Duncan at Inverawe in a dream and promised that they should meet some day at . . . . When Duncan awoke he could never recall the strange name of the rendezvous. He had this dream often but the strange name was of a place he had never heard of in Argyll or other parts of the Highlands.

As the years went by, Duncan enlisted in the Black Watch and rose in the ranks to be commander. The regiment was drafted to North America to face the French, and marched north by the valley of the Hudson. Only when they encamped in the forest preparatory to the attack on the French fort did Campbell hear the name Ticonderoga. It was the place where he was to meet his cousin's ghost in the dream long ago. He knew he was to fall in battle and in the onslaught the next morning he died with most of his regiment.

Ghosts are said to have various reasons for appearing, apart from seeking their murderers. If someone has robbed the poor of their land or possessions, a visit from a ghost is very effective in persuading the swindler to restore the property, or, failing that, to exact a severe penalty.

I heard of a true incident which may have involved a ghostly visitor, as far as one can tell. Justice was certainly visited very abruptly on the guilty party.

A lawyer in Edinburgh had charge of the affairs of a country client in the Midlothian parish of Heriot, among the Moorfoot Hills. By a malpractice he persuaded his client that the title-deeds of his property were not valid, and, that by the law he was no longer in possession of a property he had been left by his parents. It so worried the poor client that it affected his mind and he died literally of worry.

Some time after his death, which had rather mystified the parishioners, the legal man travelled up by train to inspect and take over the vacant property in his own name. The few passengers who alighted at Heriot station were subject to scrutiny as they passed through the small village. No one knew the man from the city in the ultra-stylish suit, but sooner than a telephone message, everyone knew where he had gone and, putting two and two

138

together, made a fair guess that he was at the back of the mystery.

Two days went by and no one saw him open the door or the window storm-shutters. At last on the third day the nearest neighbours overcame their native good manners and rapped at the door. On getting no response they forced their way in and found the stranger hanging from a joist in the loft. It was regarded as suicide but quite a few old inhabitants suspected that the ghost of the injured tenant had a lot to do with it. No one would occupy the house. Eventually the slates slid off, the roof-boards rotted and the roof fell in. The gable-ends being dangerous, were demolished and the place became a heap of stones with an evil reputation.

Some ghosts haunt houses just for the pleasure of kicking up a shindy, knocking dishes off shelves, moving heavy furniture, alarming the cats and dogs and pulling the inmates out of bed. These are the vandals of the ghost world, whose only reason for haunting is to make mischief. But an interesting and authentic tale shows that some apparitions have a religious motive.

A devil-may-care officer, Colonel Gardiner, a proper rake-hell, had spent the Sabbath evening in the company of friends, drinking, gambling and telling coarse tales. He was in a very merry mood for he had made a date for midnight with a married woman of loose habits, not his wife, of course.

The drunken party broke up at eleven, and Gardiner, having an hour to idle away before proceeding to the last pleasure of the day, sat down to read an amusing book. But instead of picking up a novel, a burlesque book of verse or such-like, he inadvertently opened a religious book which his good mother, or aunt had slipped secretly and hopefully into his portmanteau. Its title was *The Christian Soldier or Heaven Taken by Storm*. As soldiering was his trade he began to pass his eye over it, intending to scoff rather than to pray.

Then he saw an unusual blaze of light over the pages. The vision of the crucifix appeared before him and a voice said, 'O, sinner, did I suffer for thee?'

He sank back in the armchair and remained insensible for an indefinite period, completely forgetting his assignation with the married lady.

Well, it is certainly an original and unusual excuse for breaking a date. We are not told how the lady took it. Perhaps with a pinch of smelling-salts.

In Scottish history apparitions have played a prominent part. In Jedburgh Castle at the second marriage of Alexander III, in the midst of all the festivities, a spectre, dressed to represent the skeletal figure of Death, glided into the banqueting-hall amidst the dancers who were entertaining the guests. The Royal bride and her maids fled in horror to their rooms to escape the apparition. But it was no ghost, just a bit of robust tomfoolery, often indulged in by mediaevals. Nevertheless, when disaster struck Scotland only a few years later in the form of the King's childlessness and early sudden death on Kinghorn crags, the fake apparition at Jedburgh got the blame.

John Knox was down on superstition, so it seems strange that two years before his death he was supposed to have been expelled from St. Andrews for raising an apparition in the shape of Auld Nick out of the earth in a kailyard. The sight of this spirit so terrified Knox's man-servant that he dropped dead with shock. I question this tale. It seems to me to have no motive and to be out of character. It may have been invented by some of Knox's religious enemies.

It may indeed have been fathered on Knox from another source. In the Canongate of Edinburgh at that time a reputed wizard named Richard Graham was encouraged by Lord Bellenden to raise the devil out of the earth in Bellenden's back garden. Graham's spells were rather too successful, and an apparition, complete with horns, scales and forked tail came up. This story seems to have more truth in it, because it is known for certain that Bellenden's widow married the Earl of Orkney and died of poverty in her old age. There may well have been a conspiracy to do away with Bellenden and acquire his estate by marriage. It looks as if this spectre was also a fake.

Horses and dogs are said to be sensitive to appearances and also to spiritual forces that humans cannot contact. When a ghost was about the house, it was said that the candles burnt blue and the dogs slunk about with their tails between their legs as if they saw something.

In the Highlands and Islands the favourite spirit was the Brownie, who, as we all know, was keen on doing a job without begging a bob. All the Brownie needed was a warm bed and a bowl of cream, and he would work his boneless fingers to the ghostly marrow, threshing, grinding or churning. But, as Sir Norman MacLeod found, to his great monetary benefit, a Brownie did not stop at manual work. His IQ was superhuman also.

We are assured, by eye-witnesses, that the Brownie was present, unnoticed, in the company of Sir Norman and other gentlemen when they were keenly engaged in play at a table game called Falmermore. This was a dicing-game, with draughtsmen to be moved. Like chess it entailed a good deal of foresight to place the pieces where they were not likely to be captured.

A difficult decision had to be taken by Sir Norman, equivalent to checkmate in chess. The stakes, which were high, hung in the balance. MacLeod hesitated for some time. Then the butler, who stood behind him, advised him where to place his piece. He took the advice and won the game.

One of the players asked Sir Norman who had taught him to play so skilfully. He answered that it was the butler. But nobody credited this, for the butler was quite ignorant of the game of Falmermore, or so he said. 'Then, that being so,' he was asked, 'how did you know how to advise Sir Norman?' 'I saw the Brownie standing behind Sir Norman and pointing with his forefinger to the place where the piece was to be put,' he answered. He it seems, had the second sight, for the Brownie was invisible to the others. It would be very useful to have such an apparition at hand when filling up the pools.

Back to more modern times, we must relate the story of Pearlin Jean, which seems to be one of the most authenticated of Scottish hauntings.

Stuart of Allanbank near Duns, when a young man, stayed in Paris for a few years, and seduced a lovely young Parisienne named Jeanne. He grew tired of her and forsook her soon after his return to his Berwickshire estates, leaving the young woman in a land of strangers and unable to pay her passage home.

She used all her entreaties to persuade him to take her back, but he rebuffed her advances coldly and even insultingly. One night, as he was driven in his coach through the gateway of his estate, she ran forward from the wood to his coach-door to greet him. He pushed her rudely away. She fell, and the iron rim of the coach-wheel passed over her head, killing her on the spot.

From that instant Allanbank and its neighbourhood were haunted by that lovely frail, dressed in her garments of silk and lace, ornamented, in her attempts to please her cruel lover, with pearls and ribbons of gay colours. As in many hauntings, the ghost still retained the clothes worn at the moment of death.

The local country people, as had always been the custom in that district of the Merse, recited a rhyme, composed by an anonymous bard.

O, Pearlin Jean, O, Pearlin Jean,
She haunts the hoose, she haunts the green,
And glowers on us a' wi her wull-cat een.

At any time she was liable to materialise and scare people with her wild-cat eyes. Several visitors to Allanbank House, even after it had changed hands following Stuart's death, met her on the stairs, or passing through the doors or walls.

Things got so bad that it was decided at all costs to lay the ghost. In Roman Catholic areas this would have been done by sprinkling holy water and performing the rites of exorcism. During the evacuation of children to country areas at the outbreak of the last war I was drafted to a house in the Highland parish of Kilmanivaig where, next to my bedroom, there was a room which had, shortly before, been rid of an evil spirit by Father MacIntosh, the local priest. But the parish of Edrom, and in especial, the House of Allanbank, was a stamping ground of Presbyterianism. In 1674 a great Covenanters' Conventicle was held at Allanbank. If any exorcising had to be done, a Presbyterian ritual was to be gone through.

Whether in the belief that God is on the side of the big battalions, or because of a belief in the holy property of the number seven, they decided to do a thorough job on Pearlin Jean. The ministers of the seven contiguous parishes were assembled for the dispersing of the intangible modiste. They rode in from Buncle, Chirnside, Hutton, Swinton, Fogo, Langton and the home stretch of Edrom. They prayed, threatened, pronounced sentences of doom and called down the fulminations of an offended god upon Jean. But this painful deluge was all in vain. She carried on with her hauntings, possibly because as far as she was concerned, they were heretics.

The ancient family of Blackadder, who had in mediaeval times held all this area, and taken their name from the river of the district, had been cheated and bullied bloodily out of their estates by the Humes. This disinherited noble family was represented at that time by Thomas Blackadder, a sturdy young bachelor. He made a date with a local lass for a courtship, down by the riverside, in a grove of alder trees. He awaited his sweetheart impatiently. At last he saw a lovely lass gliding towards him over the dewy meadow. Something about her means of locomotion aroused his suspicions. As she drew close in the dusk he found himself face to face with Pearlin Jean. He turned and ran in terror from this blind date.

A gentleman, travelling alone in a wild part of Ross-shire, was forced to seek shelter for the night in a small lonely cottage. The landlady informed him that she had a small room to let. Being an enthusiast for fresh air he asked if he could be allowed to open the window. The landlady told him that this was impossible as the wall on one side of the small window had been broken down recently and re-built, jamming the window-sash, but, as some of the small panes had been broken, plenty fresh air would come in. He naturally was curious as to the reason for this alteration, as the rest of the building seemed solidly built.

Reluctantly the landlady admitted that a travelling pedlar, only a few days before, had committed suicide by hanging himself behind the door of the room. The superstition of the country was that the body of a suicide should not be taken out by the door of the house, but by the window. As the window had been too small, a part of the adjoining wall had been broken down to remove the body. She hinted that the room had been haunted since the tragedy, by the poor fellow's ghost.

The gentleman prepared for bed in a very disturbed frame of mind. He primed his pocket pistol and laid it on the chair where he hung his clothes, though he wondered if a lead bullet would deter a ghost.

In his dreams he was attacked by a horrible apparition, and awoke in an agonised sweat, to find himself sitting up in bed grasping the pistol. As he looked fearfully round the room, which was lit by moonlight, he saw a corpse dressed in a shroud standing erect against the wall close by the window. He could see all the details of the shroud and the pale features of the dead man, his eyes sunken, his teeth set in a ghastly grin.

With a terrific effort of will he got out of bed and walked straight towards the ghost. He passed his hands over it but felt nothing. The horrible figure remained as before. He staggered back to bed and lay arguing with himself, doubting his sanity. At long last he realised that the apparition was caused by the moonbeams passing at a slant through the broken windowpanes and falling upon the newly-cemented wall. His imagination, working on the landlady's account, had filled in the ghostly details.

In a book dealing with Scotland it would be a conspicuous omission not to give at least one authenticated instance, strongly supported, of the second-sight.

Early in the eighteenth century, an officer in the army, a friend of Dr. Ferriar who vouches for the veracity of the account, was quartered near the castle of a clan chief in the north of Scotland who was credited with the second-sight.

It was believed in the neighbourhood that he had spoken to an apparition which ran along the battlements of his castle and had never been cheerful afterwards.

One day he was reading a play to his wife and daughters in the large drawingroom of the castle. Suddenly, he stopped with a strained look fixed on the door. He rang a bell and ordered a groom to saddle a horse and ride to two nearby castles to inquire of the health of the ladies there. He closed his book and refused to read any more until he had word from his messenger. He explained his strange abrupt action by saying that the drawingroom door had seemed to open and a small woman without a head had entered the room.

This apparition meant the death of someone of his acquaintance and the figure resembled one of these two neighbouring ladies.

His second-sight was vindicated, for the messenger returned a few hours later to say that one of these ladies had died in an apoplectic fit at the time of his vision.

On another occasion the chief was ill in bed and the officer friend of Dr. Ferriar was reading to him on a stormy winter night when a fishing-boat belonging to the castle was at sea.

Suddenly the chief exclaimed, 'My boat is lost.' 'How do you know?' asked the officer.

'I see two of the boatmen bringing in a third drowned, all dripping wet and laying him down close beside your chair.'

The officer jumped off the chair in alarm. In the course of the night the fishermen returned with the corpse of their companion.

One can easily appreciate why nobody wanted the 'gift' of the second sight.

Glossary

BABES AND SUCKERS
airts—compass points
bairned—made pregnant
ben bed—bedroom bed
blaw—blow
canna—cannot
crying—naming
cuddy—horse
dreep—drop down
fause—false
flair—floor
flees—flies
forrit—forward
gamey—gamekeeper
gweed—good
mooth-organ—mouth-organ
muckle—great
pee-the-beds—dandelions
sic—such
sook—suck
tip—ram
wheecht—whipped off
yin—one
yowe—ewe

TICKLING THE FANCY
baccy—tobacco
chust—just
daunder—saunter
deen—done
dizzen—dozen
doon—down
hirsel—sheep-run
hure—whore
lang-nebbit—long-nosed
leear—liar
loons—boys
lum—chimney
quaens—girls
quey—heifer
smittrie—small number

HUMAN FORM
gey job—difficult task
budgell, rumpkin—small casks

clootie dumplin—pudding in cloth
gomerils—stupid persons
loanin—country lane
pooer—power
rumgumption—common-sense
smiddy—smithy
spang—leap
steikit neive—clenched fist

STRONG WATERS
Auld Kirk—whisky
Black Marias—police vans
bitchify'd—drunk
but and ben—two-roomed cottage
dowp—backside
Ferintosh—whisky
gin—if
kailtime—dinnertime
kist—chest, box
pooch—pocket
pystle—epistle
sark—chemise
stoiter—stagger
stot—bullock
stottin—bouncing
the cratur—whisky
waucht—drink
whaup-nebbit—long-nosed
whiles—sometimes

BEDFELLOWS
claes—clothes
coft—bought
gleg—nimble
tae and tither—one and another
wean—child

EARTH-BORN COMPANIONS
aip—ape
feint a—not one
griddle—girdle for baking
heigh—high, tall
keiched—excreted
reek—smoke

143

sadill—saddle
saitt—seat
tipper-taipers—dances daintily
tod—fox
treid—mount

TIT FOR TAT
birkie—lively person
fauts—faults
higglety-pigglety—equal payment

TIGHT FISTS
aik—oak
braxy—unbled mutton
dander—saunter
deid-chest—coffin
een—eyes
elshin—awl
far's—where is
forenent—opposite
glower—glare intently
siller—money
kinna—kind of
speeder—spider
stent—allocation
teuch—tough
tholed—endured
timmer—timber
wheesht—silenced

FAIR MAIDS
chiel—fellow
tapsalteerie, heads-ower-gowdie
        —head over heels
skullduddèrie, houghmagundie
        —fornication

AGGRO.
bourach—confused heap
brunstane—brimstone
corbies—crows
girnin—grinning
pay the kain—pay the penalty
pykit pow—picked skull
whunstane—whinstone

KICKING THE BUCKET
baps—small loaves
browncaties—bronchitis
drools—slavers
drowy—soaked with mist
hantle—indefinite number
happit up—interred
howe hoast—hollow cough
hurl—coach-drive
neb—nose
pewmoany—pneumonia
sough awa—die quietly
trauchlin aboot—shuffling about